Roots, Heart, Soul

Roots, Heart, Soul

The Story, Celebration, and Recipes of Afro Cuisine in America

Todd Richards

with Amy Paige Condon

Foreword by Adrian Miller

Photography by Clay Williams

HARVEST

An Imprint of WILLIAM MORROW

HarperCollins books may be purchased for educational, business,
or sales promotional use. For information, please email the Special
Markets Department at SPsales@harpercollins.com.

FIRST EDITION

Designed by Tai Blanche

Photography © by Clay Williams
Photograph on page 159 courtesy of Adrian Miller
Rough-edge boxes © Anastasiia Veretennikova/Shutterstock
Hand-drawn lines © Olha Kozachenko/Shutterstock

Library of Congress Cataloging-in-Publication Data has been
applied for.

ISBN 978-0-358-61267-4

24 25 26 27 28   IMG   10 9 8 7 6 5 4 3 2 1

This book is dedicated to Afro Culture and all its many blessed variations—African, Afro-Caribbean, Afro-Latin, and African American. The recipes written herein represent not only an interpretation of our food, but more so an invitation to sit at the table and converse about our common heritage through food. It matters not whether we call it barbecue or barbacoa, sofrito or the Holy Trinity, whether we put buttermilk or sugar in our cornbread, or sip hibiscus tea or drink red Kool-Aid. The divisions we've been taught and absorbed, whether they be steeped in classism, colorism, or sexism, do not honor our kinfolk and have no place at this table because all are welcome to join this celebration. I found a piece of myself, a piece of my family, in the writing of this book. I have a common bond with people I don't even know because of these food traditions.

Contents

Foreword by Adrian Miller......................................xi
Introduction xiii

About This Book xix
A Soundtrack for *Roots, Heart, Soul* xx

Part I
The Middle Passage (1500–1865)   1

West Africa......................................3
Peanut and Mustard Greens Soup with
   Ginger and Tomato......................................4
Root Vegetable Stock 6
West African Fish Stew with
   Smoked Trout and Snapper......................................7

Chicken Yassa with Crispy Rice and
   Dandelion Salad 9
Chicken Stock......................................14
Sazón 15
Jollof Rice......................................18
Coconut Puff-Puff with Rum-Coconut Syrup..19

The Caribbean   22

Haiti......................................24
Soup Joumou (Peppered Beef and
   Pumpkin Soup)......................................24
Beef Stock......................................26
Chef Stephan's Epis......................................28
Mayi Moulen (Cornmeal Porridge with
   Stewed Black Trumpet Mushrooms
   and Pickled Okra) 29
Haitian Oxtail in Beef Broth with Pikliz..........30

Dominican Republic......................................33
Chayote and Codfish Frittata with
   Plátanos al Caldero (Caramelized
   Plantains) and Avena Caliente
   (Hot Spiced Oat Milk) 33
Espaguetis with Salami
   (Beach Spaghetti) 38

Puerto Rico......................................42
Tostones with Yam, Red Chili Salsa, and
   Smashed Avocado 42

Ham Hock Mofongo with Fried Eggs,
   Pork Broth, and Pickled Red Onion..............45
Bistec Encebollado (Puerto Rican Steak,
   Onions, and Salsa) 48
Sofrito 51
Coconut Pudding with Chicharron and
   Coconut Cracklins......................................53

Cuba......................................54
The Cubano (Cuban Sandwich) with
   Yuca Fries......................................54
Ham Hock Jelly......................................55
Cubano Sauce 58
Ham Steak with Red-Eye Gravy, Mango de
   Bizcochuelo and Pepper Relish, and
   Tostada Cubana......................................60
Grilled Shrimp Mojo with Black Bean
   Purée and Toasted Rice with
   Cumin Seeds and Mint......................................63
Stewed Chicken with Cuban Okra and
   Sweet Plantains and Pickled Baby Corn........67

Jamaica 69

Jerk Chicken Wings with
Lime Dipping Sauce 69

Coconut-Fried Spiny Lobster Tail with
Rum-Soy Dipping Sauce.......................70

Pepper Crawfish Cocktail with
Hibiscus Punch 74

Grilled Whole Snapper with Mango Slaw........77

Saltfish Cakes with Chilled Ackee Soup
and Mango Salsa 82

Collard Greens with Boiler Potatoes
Braised in Coconut Milk and Curry 87

North America   88

Mexico 88

Mogo-Mogo: Smashed Plantain Porridge with
Black Pepper and Sesame Seed Bacon 89

Peanut, Pumpkin, and Chile Salsa 91

Sweet and Spicy Grilled Chicken
Tenderloin with Chipotle and Tamarind
Glaze and Crushed Peanuts 92

Grilled Quail Tacos on Flour Tortillas with
Mole Poblano, Pickled Red Onions, and
Red Rice 94

Horchata with Cinnamon Cookies and
Ancho Chili–Sugar Rim 99

American South and
Appalachia 102

Hoppin' John with Turnip Greens and
Yellow Rice 103

Scallion and Smoked Cheddar Cornbread
Fritters with Red Pepper Honey 106

Grilled Catfish with Grilled Spring Onions
and Creamed Potato Hash with
Mustard Greens 109

Cola-Braised Ham and Onion-and-Smoked-
Cheddar Buttermilk Biscuits with
Arugula and Mustard Seed Dressing...........112

Four-Cheese Baked Mac 'n' Cheese with
Lobster Variation...........................115

Roasted Chicken and Dumplings with
Buttered Green Peas and Roasted
Heirloom Carrots 118

Peach Cobbler with Butter Pecan
Ice Cream 121

Watermelon Agua Fresca with Spiced and
Salted Rim 124

Hibiscus Sweet Tea with Watermelon
Pickles 126

Stuffed Cornish Hens with Rice and
Field Peas and Buttered Cabbage.................128

Sweet Potato and Squash Casserole with
Pickled Green Beans 130

Pan-Fried Chicken Livers Glazed in
Sorghum and Shaved Bulb Onions 133

Sweet Potato Pie with
Sorghum Ice Cream 135

Classic Banana Pudding 139

Banana Pudding with Meringue and
Rum Sauce 140

Part II
South to West and the Roads in Between
(1865–1918)   143

Black Cowboys and Buffalo
Soldiers 144

BBQ Shrimp with Garlicky French Bread
and Parsley Butter 146

Stewed Pinto Beans with Corn Cakes and
Jalapeño and Red Pepper Marmalade 148

Beignets with Espresso Powdered
Sugar 150

Cemita Poblana: Fried Pork Cutlet with
   Avocado Vinaigrette 152
Coffee, Black Pepper, and Cocoa-Rubbed
   Smoked Beef Brisket with
   German Potato Salad 156
BBQ Short Ribs with Crawfish and Pecan
   Rice–Stuffed Chayote Squash 162
Churros with Cinnamon-Vanilla
   Sugar 164

The Roads in Between 165
Hot and Cold Southwest-Style Country-Fried
   Rabbit with Tomatillo Hot Sauce 165
Venison Osso Buco with Stewed
   White Beans and Corn 167
Buffalo-Pumpkin Chili with Pickled Cactus
   Salsa and Crispy Blue Corn Tortilla 170

Part III
The Great Migration (1910–1970)   173

The Great Migration's First Wave (1910–1930) 174

New York 179
Stewed Chicken in Tomato Sauce with
   Crowder Pea and Arugula Salad................... 179
Buffalo-Style Frog Legs with
   French Onion Ranch Dressing 183
Berbere Chargrilled Oysters with
   Parmesan Cheese and Garlic Butter 187
She-Crab Soup with Smoked Paprika Oil
   and Cornmeal-Crusted Okra........................ 188
Hot and Spicy Crawfish Boil with
   Collard Green Spring Rolls and
   NY Cherry-Ginger Spritz............................. 193
Fried Apple Hand Pies with Cinnamon
   Sugar and Jamaican Rum Crème................. 197

Chicago 200
Grilled Skirt Steak with
   Chimichurri Sauce 206

Smoked Baby Back Ribs with
   Dad's Chicago Red BBQ Sauce 207
Grilled Corn with Ancho Chile Butter............. 211
Pulled Pork Tamales with Charred Corn,
   Alabama White Sauce, and
   Homemade Cola.. 212
Loaded Sweet Potato with Creamed
   Mustard Greens, Crispy Bacon, and
   Smoked Cheddar Breadcrumbs 218
Chicago-Style Beach Spaghetti,
   aka Fish and Spaghetti 220
Dad's Meat Spaghetti Sauce 221
Fried Lake Perch with Pimento Cheese
   and Collard Green Hushpuppies and
   Celery Root and Jicama Slaw...................... 223
Whiskey and Vanilla Salted Caramel
   Cake 227
7Up Cake 229

Afterword... 232
Acknowledgments............................. 234
Resources 235
Universal Conversion Chart 237
Index.. 238

Foreword

That's the advice that celebrated author and filmmaker Lolis Eric Elie gave me early in my food writing career. With all the books, paper-stuffed folders, and digital files on African American foodways that sat before me, I desperately needed a few words to focus me. Still, I was a little surprised by that tidbit of wisdom. Much of what I had heard and learned about food and drink seemed rooted in place with an emphasis on words like larder, terroir, and tradition. With *Roots, Heart, Soul: The Story and Celebration of Afro Cuisine in the Americas*, Chef Todd Richards reminds me that "movement" remains a relevant departure point for culinary conversation. Get ready for a front row seat to Todd's intriguing personal journey as well as the collective and fascinating food journey of African heritage people in the Americas.

When I first met Todd in 2007, he was already about movement, specifically "making moves." We attended a multiday Southern Foodways Alliance (SFA) event in Charleston, South Carolina, where he received a Glory Foods Chef Scholar Award for emerging Black chefs.

We hit it off and stayed in touch. Each time Todd and I spoke, his ambition and creativity energized me. He was the first chef I've known who simultaneously managed multiple and different culinary concepts in a variety of situations: soul food, barbecue, Southern food, Asian Southern fusion. His Chicken + Beer and One Flew South restaurants in the Hartsfield-Jackson Atlanta International Airport have gratefully and forever changed what comes to mind when I think "airport food." I'm still salivating at the thought of his Southern cuisine take on phò and the deconstructed banana pudding that I've had in his other restaurants.

On top of that, he wrote *Soul: A Chef's Culinary Evolution in 150 Recipes.* This highly acclaimed cookbook expanded our notions of what soul food is and could be. Even with all the accolades and accomplishment, I could tell that Todd was hungry for more.

Yes, Todd's a busy man with a plan, but I'm grateful that he's also generous with his time. Through our conversations over the years—often while grubbing on some delicious food—he's taught me much about African American foodways, the restaurant industry, and a chef's approach to food. What he shares has always informed my work and given it a practical, real-world dimension. I know that I'm not the only one who has benefited from his wisdom. Todd has planted seeds, and many have flourished in important and meaningful ways.

Todd—as a chef, entrepreneur, mentor, and teacher—makes moves again with *Roots, Heart, Soul*. This beautiful and informative cookbook arrives at a time when people are intensely curious about food. More and more diners want to know from where their food is sourced, to which culinary tradition it belongs, the ethics of its journey to the plate, and why the chef is an effective curator of that experience. Todd meets this cultural moment with verve. *Roots, Heart, Soul* invites us to rethink the culinary ties that connect us all.

Roots, Heart, Soul palpably explores a hunger felt by generations of Black people in the Americas. The forced removal of our ancestors from their native lands in West Africa and the sustained efforts to deny our individual and collective humanity has left a hole in our souls. Despite the horrific circumstances, enslaved and free West Africans re-created home as best they could by using familiar ingredients, such as okra, and applying their traditional culinary techniques. With that inherited knowledge, African heritage cooks dramatically shaped the food systems of the communities where they lived and the palates of the people they fed. Todd uses "Afro cuisine" to aptly describe the diverse, centuries-long, and ongoing work of these cooks. In these pages, Todd tells a story born of tragedy that ultimately becomes a narrative marked by ingenuity, resiliency, and triumph. West African cuisines still have an aftertaste that lingers in the Americas.

Todd's genius with *Roots, Heart, Soul* is that he makes you feel as if you're sitting by his side during a spiritual journey of self-discovery or on his sojourns from the South Side of Chicago to other parts of the world. To truly understand the culinary journey of African heritage cooks, Chef Todd Richards is the tour guide we want and need. Motion. Connection. Reunion. You'll love the way that this journey unfolds.

—**Adrian Miller**
James Beard Award–winning food writer

Introduction

My friend Stephan Berrouet Durand, president and cofounder of the Haitian Culinary Alliance, knew I had come to New York to eat. He was taking over the kitchen at Rebèl Restaurant and Bar, an eatery on Manhattan's Lower East Side, and one evening during my research trip, he invited me, my cowriter, and photographer to join in a celebration of Creole cuisine. There, at a long table against the back wall of the restaurant amid vivid island-inspired paintings and a pulsing Latin hip-hop soundtrack, I was reminded once again how food allows you to welcome people with open arms.

It was a reunion, of sorts, among some of the city's young chefs, many who had come to know Stephan through the Creole Food Festival. The pandemic restrictions on inside dining had only recently been lifted, and this was the first time several of them had seen one another for more than a year. There were hugs, salsa dancing, and toast after toast with small-batch rum. And, as each dish was set before us, good-natured conversations revolved around how tostones or mofongo or pikliz might be served with slight variations in the Dominican Republic or Puerto Rico. Instantly, I felt as if I were at one of my family's backyard barbecues or church potlucks, where aunties discussed the merits of this potato salad over that one.

Everyone spoke different languages, but I had just enough of my broken kitchen Spanish and broken kitchen French to know exactly what they were saying. That's when I first learned about "beach spaghetti," the Dominican tradition of bringing pots of spaghetti to the beach for big family gatherings. I shared my own family's tradition of catfish and spaghetti, where we would haul big aluminum pans of my mom's fried catfish and baked spaghetti to the beaches around Lake Michigan during the summers of my Chicago childhood. Then, as only chefs can do, we dug into the details: Did you put meat in the sauce? What kinds of cheeses? Did you leave the spaghetti noodles whole or break them in thirds?

It was as if I were meeting cousins I had never known.

It may seem trite or cliché to say that we are all connected. But the more I explore the foundations of the food I grew up with—that I serve in my restaurants, make at home, and share at friends' tables—I find that all roads intersect in places where my ancestors walked, toiled, and endured, from the African continent and the Caribbean to Mexico and the American South. I am only now fully realizing their impact on an ever-evolving American culture. When we consider their contributions, we find marginalized people most often excluded because, early on, they were denied their languages and histories as well as the opportunity to learn to read and write down their own stories. Food, then, became the shepherd of memory and history.

Were we to trace the DNA of American cuisine, as I did my own ancestry, we would find it inextricably linked to West Africa. For this reason, I have written *Roots, Heart, Soul: The Story and Celebration of Afro Cuisine in the Americas,* to go back to the ancestors to ask questions of what flavors, customs, techniques, and rituals I—and my country—carry in our DNA. The visceral and spiritual connections to the foods and dishes we call our own run bone deep. And, I believe, they course through our blood. The intricate and international connections among the various foodways of the Americas call us to explore their backstory.

To truly grasp the influences of the African diaspora in American foodways, my coauthor Amy Paige Condon, photographer Clay Williams, and I immersed ourselves in the West African, Caribbean, and Latin American immigrant enclaves of New York, Chicago, and Miami. We ate our way through street vendors, at mom-and-pop restaurants, and in people's homes. We talked with historians, writers, anthropologists, and chefs—both self-taught and trained—to explore authentic ingredients and wares and to observe and learn with the goal of connecting the gastronomical dots from Nigeria to Haiti to Mexico and across the United States—the very same journey my own family took during the past four hundred years.

The recipes that follow, most of them organized as full meals, offer reverence to the origin of dishes by acknowledging their time, place, and spirit without freezing them in the amber of history. I do not claim that these recipes—from a piquant Senegalese peanut stew and street-style fried dough bathed in rum sauce to Dominican "beach spaghetti" and coffee-and-cocoa-rubbed smoked brisket—comprise the definitive guide to the food of the African diaspora. Rather, the recipes are drawn from my travels, perspective, experience, and interrogation. They pay homage. They reflect the crucibles of endurance, necessity, and imagination that forged entirely new foodways, and in those foodways, the flavors evoked are both timeless and timely, distant and familiar.

Food is an article of faith within the Black community, yet food has become a religion of its own. I think this as I listen to folks insist with evangelical zeal that the *only* way to serve a banana pudding is with a meringue and that cornbread must be made without sugar. Or, that the brisket I served at my former restaurant, Lake & Oak BBQ in Atlanta, is not "the one true barbecue," which usually means "from Texas." They are right; it is not. Still, my brisket is most definitely barbecue, born of the backyard of my Chicago youth where my father hummed the mantra of low and slow. It is born even further back to the Taíno, who covered meat in spices and cooked them over earthen pits and fire. I believe dogma stymies evolution.

For what is our food but an evolution resulting from the collision of place and culture? When the Portuguese and Spanish colonists brought Africans against their will through the ports of Rio de Janeiro and Buenos Aires in the 1500s to work alongside enslaved

Indigenous peoples on coffee, tobacco, and sugar plantations, the Bahian seafood stew vatapá evolved from the meeting of the Yoruban and Tupí peoples. As the Dutch, English, and French joined the slave trade to support colonization of the Caribbean and the American South, the ships that held humans as cargo also ferried benne (sesame) seeds, cowpeas, yams, and watermelons. And when the enslaved were emancipated, their brothers and sisters, aunts and uncles, cousins and friends willingly and with anticipation and faith moved on from the Reconstructed and Jim Crow South to the Northeastern Rust Belt, the Midwestern factories, and the Atomic West in the first and second waves of the Great Migration. The influences of West Africa grew during the great exodus of Black people out of the American South to New York and Philadelphia, to Chicago and Detroit, and to Los Angeles and Oakland. As those who went before built the fires that others followed, food and faith traditions traveled parallel to one another.

I bear witness to this evolution in my own life. My mother's people came up out of Kentucky, my father's out of Louisiana. My Swedish, Irish, and German strands of ancestry are prominent enough to suggest that my Nigerian, Beninese, Ghanaian, and Ivorian forebears bore children by their enslavers. My Indigenous American bloodline points to the assimilation of the Igbo and the Bakongo people, who were brought through the port in Veracruz, Mexico, by the Spanish to work in the silver mines alongside native communities. Their spices and techniques melded with the Spanish and native cultures to birth mole poblano, the mother sauce to all moles. These same influences are apparent in the dishes of the Caribbean and the American South.

Where I grew up in Chicago—a city that drew resourceful immigrants from Scandinavia, Eastern Europe, Latin America, and the American South during the late-nineteenth and early- to mid-twentieth centuries—I could leave the Southeast Side and go one neighborhood over to taste slow-cooked barbacoa that whispered the familiarity of my own family's dry-rubbed spareribs. I dove into steaming pots of the Polish cabbage-and-pork stew known as *bigos* and savored the subtle hints that recalled my grandma's stewed collard greens and ham hocks. I witnessed parishioners of all walks perform the same ritual of gathering at their places of worship for Friday fish fries and potlucks, breaking bread together with common purpose. And every place I have traveled, I have seen how faith and food are inextricably tied together, and how people joyfully argue the nuances of a musky jollof rice or a velveteen mayi moulen porridge like true believers.

One of the most significant ways we create common memory and community is through food. When we gather around the table, we bear witness to all the seen and unseen hands that have touched the food—from the seed saver to the grower to the cook to the server. Whole economies, histories, and cultures are dished up for our pleasure, sustenance, consumption, and contemplation. Food engages all our senses—sight, smell, taste, touch, and sound—but it goes further and deeper when it reaches the soul, that ephemeral part of us tied to remembrance, place, and connection. That's the essence of deliciousness, where the flavors meld to express something beyond words, something spiritual. For this very reason, Sunday suppers are as important as sermons. And, when we meet someone unfamiliar yet discover similarity and share communion at the table, we reveal a significant part of our humanity. A meal shared is spiritual justice.

Creating this common memory is at the heart of *Roots, Heart, Soul: The Story and Celebration of Afro Cuisine in the Americas.* Within these pages, I explore a different manifest destiny, one rooted not in oppression and annihilation, but one propelled by culture, cuisine, and faith—and the symbiotic relationship among all three. Food and faith share the same experience. Both begin with hunger and end with body and soul sated and nourished. When we plant a seed, we have faith that it will break open and shoot green tendrils through the dark and the dirt. We believe there will be enough to sustain us all. And we pray that at our common table we will see how connected and interdependent we truly are.

I have written this book to honor the fraught journey, recognizing that honor accomplishes two things at once—it is the purpose I carry in my heart and history *and* the way I pay respect and hold someone or something in high regard. Both noun and verb. When we acknowledge and celebrate how the most vivid portrait of America's so-called melting pot is its food, then we can look beyond the constructed divisions of race and class and arrive at a true American cuisine. We can never examine the fullness of the American story nor embrace that common memory unless we recognize and respect how deeply entwined it is with West African culture, techniques, and customs.

Like most things in late 2020, the Museum of Food and Drink exhibition *African/American: Making the Nation's Table* was postponed because of the COVID-19 pandemic. When it was safe enough for me to embark on the long-delayed research and personal exploration for this cookbook, my first stop was the Africa Center, just on the edge of Harlem and Central Park, where the exhibit was on display.

During a private, masked, socially distant tour with curatorial director Catherine Piccoli, I was not prepared for the scale of the fourteen-foot-tall and thirty-foot-wide Legacy Quilt, the brainchild of lead curator and food historian Dr. Jessica B. Harris. Each of the 406 squares, designed by artist Adrian Franks and stitched by Harlem Needle Arts, represents an individual African American contribution to American cuisine, all the way back to the 1600s.

On one square, a copper pot: a nod to James Hemings, the enslaved French-trained personal chef of Thomas Jefferson, who wrote down the first recipe for what is essentially macaroni and cheese and who introduced copper cookware to America. On another, a wooden barrel for Nathan "Uncle Nearest" Green, the African American whiskey distiller in Tennessee who introduced charcoal filtration and is finally getting recognition as the man who taught Jack Daniels. Other squares illustrate Black innovators in fishing, seed distribution, and catering. Then there are the twentieth century pioneers Edna Lewis, Joe Randall, Leah Chase, and Darryl Evans, who paved the way for today's chefs and scholars like Adrian Miller, Deborah VanTrece, Erick Williams, Kevin Mitchell, and Mashama Bailey. And then, a square or two later, there am I, my likeness quilted into the context of history.

Six squares remain blank, tributes to those souls who made significant contributions but whose names we will never know, perhaps even an ancestor I will never be able to trace.

I walked quietly through the rest of the exhibit, still under construction at the time. In the telling of this story, I saw that the story of Africa and America, seen through the lens of food, was not one of suffering and shame, but one of celebration, endurance, and self-sufficiency.

All I could say was, finally, amen, and hallelujah. I am African American, and the journey of the ancestors is woven through my own.

About This Book

The Recipes

The recipes in this book follow my own origin story from West Africa to the Caribbean to Mexico to the American South and beyond, just as the rice, okra, grilling, and braising migrated—forced and otherwise—with my kinfolk. By traversing the globe through my own DNA, I also illuminate the profound influences of Afro cuisine in the Americas.

Almost all the recipes are envisioned as contemporary interpretations of full, hearty meals that balance proteins, vegetables, and starches—with flavors. I have consciously and intentionally balanced the sour, bitter, salt, and sweet, so I encourage you to prepare the recipes as written, at least once, to absorb the fullness of their story, then feel free to pull out one dish, mix and match, and interpret them through your own tastes and lenses. I have organized the recipes, too, with a flow and order to streamline prep time. Serving portions are easily scaled up or down, depending upon the number of people you are feeding.

These are not restaurant-style recipes, although they certainly are of a quality to make them suitable for a place on any restaurant table. Instead, they are built upon family traditions, shaped by place and history and movement. To have the best success in preparing these recipes, read them fully before beginning, then organize your workspace with the ingredients and tools you'll need.

Even though some of these recipes are rooted in other countries, the ingredients are easy to find in most grocery stores and specialty food markets. I recommend substitutions in the recipe notes if certain ingredients may be difficult to source or might be out of season, depending on where you live and the time of year. At the end of this book, I also provide a list of resources, including online shops and other books that were meaningful to my research. But, just as these dishes are inspired by the humble hands that made them, the ingredients and tools needed are simple and most often staples of any well-stocked pantry—although you may find you need to stock more spices and a greater variety of chilies and peppers. Remember, though, the most important ingredients in any kitchen are love and curiosity. You can never overuse either one. In fact, the flavor of a dish only grows deeper the more you use.

A Soundtrack for *Roots, Heart, Soul*

If we were in my home or one of my restaurants, there would be music. The best kitchens operate in rhythm. They move to a beat. The refrain, "Yes, Chef!" is like an "amen," a call-and-response.

When I was coming up, music played throughout our house. For my mom, who was in the kitchen with her sisters, Nina Simone was the high priestess. For my dad, grilling out in the yard, it could be anything from Motown soul to Chicago blues. In high school, I started deejaying parties, leaning on the funky backbeats of the Philadelphia sound—that 1970s Gamble and Huff conga tempo that was birthed centuries before on the African continent, sharpened by its confluence with Latin rhythms in Cuba, which ultimately found me as a teenager through disco.

Music puts me in a creative frame of mind, helps me express myself. Just like those wood-frame, one-room praise houses sprinkled throughout the South and the Black churches that sprung up in storefronts all along the booming industrial corridors of the Northeast and Midwest, music sets the tone for the message to follow. My message springs not from a pulpit but from the blessings of my table.

Cooking and eating are sensory experiences, and it's essential to involve all the senses to absorb the many cultural, social, and temporal nuances of a cuisine—taste, sight, smell, touch, and hearing. We often don't think of the role our ears play in our encounters with food. There's the clink of a fork against a knife, the chop against a wooden cutting board, the whir of a blender, the crunch of a flaky crust. Kitchens and tables have a melody.

So, too, does this cookbook, as it moves from continent to continent, island to island, region to region. To deepen your experience with these recipes and to set the mood of each place, I have compiled a soundtrack that follows the journey in this book. If you listen to it in the order the songs are presented, you'll find yourself tapping into the fusion of African beats, Latin rhythms, and the poetry of the streets. These songs capture the melding of musical traditions the same way these dishes highlight the blending of flavors and techniques.

Pharoah Sanders ft. Phyllis Hyman	"Love Is Here"
Rufus ft. Chaka Khan	"Hollywood"
Gladys Night & the Pips	"On and On"
Stevie Wonder	"Too High"
El Búho	"Cumbia de Tototl"
Bueno Vista Social Club	"Chan Chan"
Celia Cruz ft. Willie Colón	"Usted Abusó"
Combo Chimbita	"Yo Me Lo Merezco"
Systema Solar and Puerto Candelaria	"Mi Kolombia"
Orchestre Meridional des Cayes	"Manman Zo"
Orchestre Tropicana D'Haiti	"Ingratitude"
Trombone Shorty and Orleans Avenue	"St. James Infirmary"
Wynton Marsalis	"Cherokee"
Dee Dee Bridgewater	"Lonely Disco Dancer"
Gabor Szabo	"Keep Smiling"
Super Value 13	"Money Is Tight"
Bobby Womack	"Across 110th Street"
Robert Glasper	"Always Shine"
Chance the Rapper	"The Highs & the Lows"
Kamasi Washington	"Freeze Tag"
Groove Theory	"Tell Me"
Jade	"Don't Walk Away"
Alexander O'Neal and Cherrelle	"Saturday Love"
Dennis Edwards and Siedah Garrett	"Don't Look Any Further"
Ice Cube	"It Was a Good Day"

Part I
The Middle Passage
(1500-1865)

From West Africa to the Caribbean to Mexico to the American South

The planters brought so many people from tribes in Sierra Leone and surrounding countries that they soon outnumbered everyone else in the Sea Islands, and they stamped these islands with their culture. But first, they had to learn a common tongue and common ways.

What they learned to speak is called Creole, and that's a lot like throwing everything into a huge pot, blending it together and simmering it into a delicious soup served over rice. It was based on the English language, yes, and it included bits and pieces from the French and Portuguese and all the other Europeans that the Africans had come in contact with, but the onions, the okra, and the black pepper in it—the seasonings that gave it an exciting taste—came from African words, speech patterns, and grammar.

—Cornelia Walker Bailey with Christena Bledsoe

God, Dr. Buzzard, and the Bolito Man: A Saltwater Geechee Talks About Life on Sapelo Island, Georgia

West Africa

Even Though I was born and raised on the South Side of Chicago, my story begins in West Africa.

Among the Igbo people: masterful farmers of yam, cassava, and millet, and cultivators of palm oil and kola nut, who were ripped from Nigeria and shipped to what is now Brazil, the Dominican Republic, and Mexico to work on sugar and coffee plantations and mine precious metals. They brought with them a deep faith in Mother Earth and the divine protection of their ancestors. Music and food formed the center of their religious life.

Among the artisans of the Yoruba: weavers and wood carvers, poets and storytellers; growers of red and gold rice, okra, melons, sorghum, green plantains, and groundnuts.

Among the expert foragers and fishers of the Western Bantu people: snatched from Cameroon and shipped in the early 1600s to the Virginia colonies.

Among the Aja of Benin and Togo: practitioners of Vodun, later called voodoo, who were forced to labor on the sugar plantations of Haiti, Cuba, and later the American South.

Between the early 1500s and 1880s, the European colonization of the Americas enslaved more than twelve million Africans from the western and central part of the continent. They represented more than fifty different ethnic groups, each with their own language, expertise, societal structures, and spiritual traditions. My ancestors held fast to their faith and survived the Middle Passage, the brutal Atlantic crossing that was the middle leg of a three-part journey from Europe to Africa to the Americas and back to Europe again.

In Haiti's sugar fields, Mexico's mines, on Sapelo and St. Helena islands, their toil, the seeds they brought with them, and their knowledge of the land fed new nations. In every place, they forever altered the foodways, leaving gold rice, purple ribbon sugarcane, red field peas, burnished spices, and seasonings as indelible as their fingerprints upon the landscapes and the cultures.

Bringing all their knowledge, customs, faiths, traditions, and fortitude with them, West African slaves shaped and influenced what came afterward. Their struggle and the alchemy of heat and pressure created something stronger, new, and vital. Black hands plowed the soil, grew the food, led the kitchens, made do with what was available, and absorbed from the Spanish, Portuguese, French, English, and Indigenous peoples the ingredients and techniques that ultimately created the cuisine we call our own today. This is the very essence of *Creole*.

I have not yet traced my heritage back far enough to know their names or exactly where and when they arrived, but I've taken that first step of understanding the blood and stories that course through my veins. I have traced the food and the music to better understand myself and what drives me in the kitchen, why even flavors new to me seem deeply embedded and familiar.

Peanut *and* Mustard Greens Soup *with* Ginger *and* Tomato

2 tablespoons peanut or vegetable oil

1 large yellow onion, chopped

1 red bell pepper, chopped

2 medium rutabagas or yellow turnips, peeled and chopped

4 garlic cloves, roughly chopped

2 serrano peppers, thinly sliced

1 (4-inch) knob ginger, peeled and roughly chopped

1 tablespoon kosher salt

1 tablespoon freshly ground black pepper

1 (16-ounce) can plum tomatoes

6 cups root vegetable stock (page 6)

1 tablespoon ground turmeric

1 teaspoon cumin seeds

1 pound mustard greens, washed and roughly chopped (see note)

1 tablespoon natural unsalted peanut butter

1 cup roasted salted peanuts, roughly chopped

1 bunch cilantro, roughly chopped

1 lime, cut into wedges

One of the great gifts of West African cooking is the one-pot meal. Born out of both scarcity and necessity, hearty bowls chock-full of color, spices, and powerful nutrients stretched ingredients to meet need. Peanuts, rather than fish or chicken, provide the protein and earthy goodness, much like lentils or other types of peas do in soups and stews. For my interpretation of this Senegalese staple, I chose the serrano pepper because of its bright grassy flavor, which plays well with the peppery greens, the sharp jolt of ginger, and the sweet rutabaga.

Heat the oil in a dutch oven over medium heat. Add the onion, bell pepper, rutabaga, garlic, serrano pepper, and ginger and season with the salt and black pepper. Cook, stirring, for 5 minutes, until the vegetables soften.

Stir in the tomatoes and stock and bring the soup to a simmer. Add the turmeric, cumin, and mustard greens, then let the soup simmer for 20 minutes. Stir in the peanut butter and continue cooking for another 15 minutes, or until the greens are tender.

Serve the soup in large bowls, garnished with the roasted peanuts and cilantro. Serve each bowl with a lime wedge to squeeze over the soup for extra zest and brightness just before eating.

Notes

- Outside of fall and winter seasons, turnips, rutabagas, and mustard greens may be hard to find. You can substitute Yukon gold potatoes for the turnips or rutabagas, and kale or chard for the mustard greens. In a pinch, spinach—while not as peppery—works well, too. It gives the stew a sweeter essence.
- If you can't find fresh ginger, you can use 4 rounded tablespoons of jarred ginger here. If the taste is not sharp and pungent, feel free to increase the minced ginger to 5 tablespoons.

Root Vegetable Stock

Makes 1½ gallons

1 celery root, small grapefruit-size, peeled and cut into 8 pieces

4 medium parsnips, peeled and cut into 2-inch pieces

2 medium white onions, peeled and quartered

2 carrots, cut into 2-inch pieces

2 tomatoes, quartered

8 whole garlic cloves, peeled

2 tablespoons vegetable oil

3 gallons cold water

2 tablespoons vegetable gelatin powder

4 bay leaves

12 whole black peppercorns

2 sprigs fresh thyme, stems removed

Preheat the oven to 350°F.

Place the celery root, parsnips, onions, carrots, tomatoes, and garlic in a roasting or aluminum foil pan, then toss with the oil. Roast the vegetables for 30 minutes or until they have caramelized.

While the vegetables cook, fill a large stockpot with the water and bring it to a simmer over medium-high heat.

Add in the gelatin and stir until dissolved.

Add the bay leaves and peppercorns and continue to simmer until the vegetables are ready to add.

Once the vegetables have caramelized, remove the pan from the oven, add them to the stockpot, and bring the stock back to a simmer. Cook for 1 hour.

Add the thyme and cook for 15 minutes more. Use a ladle to skim off any impurities floating to the top.

Turn off the heat and let the stock rest for an hour.

Strain the stock through a fine mesh sieve into airtight containers and refrigerate for up to 2 weeks or freeze for up to 6 months.

The Proud Peanut

Christopher Columbus is purported to have encountered runner peanuts on Hispaniola. Yet it's the Portuguese who are credited with introducing the peanut plant to Africa during the 1600s, most likely from Brazil. The peanut, or the *nguba* in Bantu language, has flourished in the subtropical climate ever since, especially in Senegal, where it's a staple of the comforting creamy peanut stew, *maafe*. Because Africans already were experts in the cultivation of groundnuts, peas, and beans, the peanut became an adopted part of their regular diet.

The peanut returned to the western hemisphere through the transatlantic slave trade. West Africans enslaved throughout the South planted peanuts as both sustenance and hog feed. It took George Washington Carver's regenerative agricultural research at the Tuskegee Institute in the early 1900s, including using peanuts as a rotation crop to restore cotton-depleted soils, to raise the lowly peanut's profile. His list of three hundred uses for the peanut helped cash-strapped farmers reconsider the legume, so much that peanuts grew into one of the top ten crops of the 1940s. To this day, most of the United States' peanut-growing states are in the South, with Georgia ranked as the number-one producer of peanuts, accounting for nearly half of the entire national yield.

West African Fish Stew *with* Smoked Trout *and* Snapper

Serves 4 to 6

¼ cup vegetable oil

6 brussels sprouts, halved

1 medium sweet potato, peeled and chopped

1 medium yellow turnip, peeled and chopped

1 tablespoon kosher salt, divided

1 tablespoon freshly ground black pepper, divided

2 yellow onions, finely diced

2 (4-ounce) smoked trout fillets

2 okra pods, cut into ½-inch pieces

1 large carrot, peeled and cut into small dice

4 garlic cloves, smashed and roughly chopped

1½ cups short-grain rice, such as Arborio or bomba

4 cups root vegetable stock (page 6)

1 (16-ounce) can plum tomatoes

1 to 2 serrano peppers, thinly sliced

4 bay leaves

4 tablespoons (2 ounces) Maggi seasoning

2 tablespoons tomato paste

1 tablespoon white miso

2 pounds snapper fillets, cut into 4 pieces

Let's dispel the myth that African food is protein heavy and fat laden. In fact, it's vegetable-forward, with scarce and often salt-preserved meats used more as a way of flavoring and enhancing a dish rather than leading it. Seafood is plentiful along the coast and punctuates soups meant for main courses. Variations on this rustic, rust-hued stew, often made with hefty hunks of white fish like cod, pop up in ports from Rio de Janeiro to Mount Pleasant, South Carolina, wherever African hands commanded the kitchens and used what was available to them. For extra depth of flavor in this thick stew, I add smoked fish as well as brussels sprouts for their bright green crunch. The miso heightens the savoriness and imparts a silky texture.

Preheat the oven to 350° F.

Warm the oil in a dutch oven over medium heat. Add the brussels sprouts, sweet potato, and turnip, season with 1 teaspoon salt and 1 teaspoon black pepper, and sear until the vegetables are golden brown on all sides, 5 to 7 minutes. Transfer the vegetables to a bowl and set aside.

Add the onions, trout fillets, okra, carrot, and garlic to the pot, breaking apart the smoked trout. Sauté the aromatics and trout for about 5 minutes, until the aromatics have softened.

Return the root vegetables to the pot and add the rice. Cook for an additional minute, then add the stock, tomatoes, serrano peppers, bay leaves, Maggi seasoning, tomato paste, and miso and bring to a simmer. While the soup simmers, season the snapper pieces on all sides with the remaining 2 teaspoons salt and 2 teaspoons black pepper, then place the snapper on top of the rice, flesh side down if the fish has skin.

Turn off the heat, cover the pot, transfer to the oven, and bake for 30 minutes or until the rice is cooked through. Let the stew rest for 15 minutes, then fish out the bay leaves before serving.

The Gift of Maggi

While I was writing this book, a couple of chefs and I got into a debate about whether Maggi seasoning, a wheat-based flavor enhancer, was necessary. One friend argued that many folks overuse Maggi because they don't know how to cook with fresh herbs, spices, and aromatics anymore. I agree, but...

I also believe cooks should use whatever methods help them serve the most delicious food. This notion that if it's not fresh, it's not pure discounts the authenticity with which many folks learned to cook using Maggi or Accent or other packaged seasonings. It's totally appropriate to use Maggi sparingly to enhance a dish's umami, that overarching savoriness. If you can't find Maggi or just want to up the umami ante, feel free to substitute dark soy sauce for heavier, meatier dishes and light soy sauce, tamari, or Worcestershire Sauce for fish or poultry one-to-one for the Maggi called for in a recipe.

Chicken Yassa *with* Crispy Rice *and* Dandelion Salad

Serves 2 to 4

FOR THE BRINE

8 cups warm water

½ cup kosher salt

½ cup sugar

1 lime, quartered

1 garlic clove, peeled and smashed

3 to 4 pounds chicken pieces, or 1 whole chicken cut into 8 pieces

FOR THE YASSA

1 batch Sazón (page 15)

4 garlic cloves, thinly sliced

Grated zest and juice of 2 lemons, plus another lemon, halved and seeded

2 tablespoons dijon mustard

2 sprigs fresh thyme

1 cup water, plus more if needed

1 bunch Italian parsley, stems removed and leaves chopped

1 whole habanero pepper

Kosher salt and freshly ground black pepper

6 tablespoons vegetable oil

2 cups chicken stock (page 14)

4 yellow onions, halved and then sliced ¼-inch thick

6 green olives, pitted and sliced into rounds

Crispy Rice (page 12)

Dandelion Salad (page 14)

A humble French-influenced country dish popular in southern Senegal, chicken yassa is a staple on every menu in the family-owned Senegalese restaurants peppering 116th Street in Harlem. Although Sazón is a seasoning blend most closely identified with Puerto Rican dishes, the spices that comprise Sazón are rooted in the ancient spice trade routes that came through Africa and became a hallmark of West African cooking. Brining the chicken infuses it with extra juiciness and depth of flavor. I encourage you to make brining chicken and even fish a regular practice in your kitchen from now on. The tangy sauce offers a complex interplay of flavors and textures: sweet, caramelized onions are sharpened by the bite of the mustard and temper the heat of the habanero. This dish is also good with Jolloff Rice (recipe on page 18).

TO BRINE THE CHICKEN: Fill a large pot or food container with the warm water, salt, and sugar, then stir until the salt and sugar dissolve. Toss in the lime and garlic. Let the liquid cool to room temperature, then submerge the chicken pieces in the liquid. Cover with plastic wrap and set the brine in the refrigerator for at least 4 hours or overnight.

TO MAKE THE YASSA: Preheat the oven to 375°F.

Remove the chicken from the brine and pat it dry. Slather the pieces all over with the Sazón, then set the pieces aside in a large bowl.

Put the garlic, lemon zest and juice, dijon mustard, thyme, and water in a blender or food processor and blend until smooth. Toss in three quarters of the parsley and blend until smooth, adding a little more water if needed.

Pour half of the dijon-herb mixture over the chicken, then add the whole habanero pepper. Stir gently to coat the chicken without breaking the pepper. Let the chicken marinate for 30 minutes. Discard the habanero, then sprinkle the chicken with the salt and pepper.

Heat 3 tablespoons of the oil in a 12-inch cast-iron or other oven-safe skillet over medium heat. Set the chicken skin side down in the heated oil and brown for 7 to 10 minutes. Turn the chicken over, then transfer the skillet to the oven and cook for 10 minutes. Turn the chicken pieces once more and cook for an additional

< recipe continues >

8 minutes, or until cooked through and the internal temperature is 165°F. Transfer the chicken onto a plate to rest.

Set the skillet over medium heat and char the lemon halves in the skillet until brown and caramelized. Set the lemons on the plate with the chicken.

Into the skillet over medium heat, add 1 cup of the chicken stock. Gently scrape the bottom with a wooden spoon to gather up the crusty bits. Pour into a measuring cup and reserve.

Add the remaining 3 tablespoons oil to the skillet, followed by the onions. Cook the onions for 3 minutes, or until they are lightly browned. Add the remaining dijon-herb mixture to the onions and cook for 6 to 8 minutes, until the onions are slightly softened. Add all the stock, including the reserved cup, to the skillet. Top the onions with the chicken and put the skillet back in the oven for 5 minutes, until the liquid is almost completely reduced. Remove the pan and allow it to stand for 2 minutes before serving. Top the chicken with the olives and remaining chopped parsley. Serve the chicken with the Crispy Rice, Dandelion Salad, and charred lemons for squeezing on top.

Notes

- This recipe requires some planning as the chicken must brine overnight. You can cook the rice and the chicken in the oven at the same time. While they bake, make the salad.
- To save time, feel free to use store-bought sazón.

Crispy Rice

Serves 4

2 tablespoons Greek yogurt

1 teaspoon curry powder

1 teaspoon kosher salt

½ teaspoon granulated onion

½ teaspoon granulated garlic

2 cups cooked white rice, cooled to room temperature

2 tablespoons vegetable oil

1 habanero pepper, seeded and finely diced (optional)

Preheat the oven to 375°F.

Stir the yogurt, curry powder, salt, and granulated onion and garlic together in a medium bowl. Fold in the cooked rice until thoroughly mixed.

Heat the oil in a large oven-safe skillet over medium heat. When it's hot, press the rice firmly into the skillet. Cook for 4 to 5 minutes, until the bottom starts to brown. Using a heatproof spatula, spread the rice around the skillet, then set the skillet in the oven. Cook the rice for 20 minutes, shaking the skillet and re-forming the rice at the 10-minute mark. When the rice is caramelized around the edges, remove the skillet from the oven and let it rest for a few minutes. To serve, place a plate over the pan and turn out the rice onto the plate. Garnish with the diced habanero, if using, and serve alongside Chicken Yassa.

Caramelization Equals Flavor

Before I ever thought of becoming a chef, I was into science—specifically physics. That's what brought me to Georgia from Illinois in the first place. I was headed to Georgia Tech, but I was depressed, still grieving the loss of my mother, living in a new place where I didn't really know anyone. I made a detour to the butcher shop at Kroger for a job and took off in another direction.

It's not such a stretch between science and cooking, though, because cooking is all chemistry, mathematics, and thermodynamics—whether the home cook thinks of it that way or not. The grandmother who knew through trial and error how humidity would affect her cake was instinctively practicing science. And those kinfolks who cooked solely by fire definitely understood the power of caramelization.

Caramelization is the complex breakdown of sugars and proteins that happens when their molecules meet high heat. Chicken Yassa and Crispy Rice are prime examples of how you can add layers of flavor by caramelizing in stages: browning the chicken skin, sweating the onions, crisping the rice. Together they transform the fats and sugars into sweet, nutty notes that deepen the dish's complexity and heighten the contrast between its crispy and soft textures.

Dandelion Salad

Serves 4

1 pound dandelion leaves, washed and patted dry

1 shallot, peeled and finely diced

2 tablespoons apple cider vinegar

1 tablespoon extra virgin olive oil

1 teaspoon dijon mustard

¼ teaspoon kosher salt

¼ teaspoon freshly ground black pepper

Put the dandelion greens in a large bowl. In a small bowl, stir together the shallot, vinegar, oil, mustard, salt, and pepper until thoroughly combined. Gently toss the greens with the dressing, then serve with the chicken and rice.

Note
You can substitute arugula for the dandelions.

Chicken Stock

Makes 10½ cups

2 pounds chicken bones and necks, from 2 (4-pound) chickens

1 gallon (8 cups) water

1 large carrot, cut into 1-inch pieces (about 2 cups)

2 small yellow onions, peeled and cut into 1-inch pieces (about 1½ cups)

2 celery stalks, cut into 1-inch pieces

2 sprigs fresh thyme

½ teaspoon whole black peppercorns

½ teaspoon kosher salt

Rinse the chicken bones and necks in hot tap water for 3 minutes.

Combine all ingredients in a large stockpot and bring to a boil over high heat. Reduce the heat to medium-low and simmer the stock until the liquid is reduced by one-third, approximately 2 to 3 hours.

Strain the mixture through a fine-mesh sieve into airtight containers. Discard the solids. Store the stock in airtight containers in the refrigerator for up to 1 week, or in the freezer for up to 6 months.

Sazón

Makes ¼ cup

1½ teaspoons cumin seeds

1½ teaspoons coriander seeds

½ teaspoon annatto (achiote) seeds

2 teaspoons granulated garlic

1 teaspoon granulated onion

2 teaspoons dried oregano

1 teaspoon sea salt

½ teaspoon cracked black pepper

¼ teaspoon dried thyme

With a medium-size mortar and pestle, coarsely break up the cumin, coriander, and annatto seeds to release their aromas. Add the garlic, onion, oregano, salt, black pepper, and thyme. Grind the spices and herbs together until you have a thoroughly mixed blend with a vibrant color and texture.

Notes

- Sazón literally means "seasoning" in Spanish. This earthen, smoky blend is ubiquitous in Puerto Rican food as a rub for fish and meat. The deep fiery orange annatto seeds come from the achiote tree and are used more often as a food coloring for cheddar cheese than as a spice. It gives this seasoning a slight bittersweet note. By starting with whole seeds and granulated rather than ground spices, you get a much more fresh, fragrant, and potent flavor from the blend. Of course, you can use store-bought sazón, such as the Goya brand, if you'd prefer.
- If you cannot find annatto seeds, you may substitute smoked paprika or turmeric.

The Spice Roads

Long before the Portuguese and Spanish took to the seas, commencing the Columbian Exchange, Asian, African, and European merchants carried goods and foodstuffs across land by caravans. But by the first century, the port city of Alexandria, Egypt, had become the center of commerce, the first bridge between the East and West. The Moors and Romans used cakes of salt for currency. Through its waters passed coffee and fenugreek from the Ethiopian plateaus; sesame oil and cotton from Somalia; cumin and paprika from Morocco; grains such as millet, rice, and sorghum, as well as seeds, beans, and peas from the West African coast—on their way to Europe. In turn, traders returned from the East with spices and seasonings for the West Africans' cooking, medicinal, and religious practices: onions from the areas around Pakistan and Iran; cinnamon from Sri Lanka; cassia and garlic from China; ginger, turmeric, and cardamom from Indonesia; nutmeg, cloves, and alligator peppers from what is now New Guinea; hot peppers from the Pacific Islands.

Le Petit (Little) Senegal, New York

In the 1970s, when New York City teetered on the brink of bankruptcy and developers pulled their investments out of Harlem, a renaissance was born on 116th Street with the arrival of Senegalese immigrants seeking refuge from environmental and economic drought. Over the next thirty years, they sponsored friends and family to join them. The Senegalese were followed by waves of immigrants from neighboring Sierra Leone, Guinea, and Côte d'Ivoire. The blocks between Frederick Douglass and Malcolm X boulevards filled with people wearing brightly patterned tunics and robes called bou-bous, the sounds of rapid-fire French and Wolof, Halal markets stocked with dried hibiscus flowers and gallons of red palm oil, and narrow storefronts spilling the scents of lamb, peppers, and peanuts onto the streets, beckoning you to come inside for a spell.

Today a quick stop in a local market called Adja Khady turns into an hours-long exploration of spices, seasonings, and herbs not available at a typical supermarket. The adjacent butcher shop sells whole sides of goat, and the air is heavy with the sharp, coppery scent of blood and flesh. At Africa

Traditional West African fare at Africa Kine restaurant on Adam Clayton Powell Junior Boulevard in Harlem includes thiebu djen (fish stewed with carrots, eggplant, and cassava), lamb mafe (in a creamy peanut sauce), and crispy scored fish that illustrates the shallow frying techniques indicative of African cuisine.

During our research in Little Senegal, we tried different versions of jollof rice (pictured here, Pikine on 116th Street) and often found ourselves fighting for the crispiest bits.

Kine and Pikine restaurants, the pace of cooking and service is leisurely, and it's never certain whether the thiebu djen (fish and rice) or the lamb mafe will be ready for lunch or an early dinner. So, you order what's available and you fight good-naturedly—sort of—with your fellow diners over who gets the crispy bits of rice. If you're lucky and jollof is being served, you savor it and recognize its ancestral connection to paella and shrimp Creole. When you've eaten so much you can barely stand, you meander a block west to Lolo's Seafood Shack to quench your thirst on an unseasonably warm afternoon with a coconut rum–laced punch of sorrel and ginger. And you forget you are in New York instead of Dakar, until your cab arrives and shakes you out of your fever dream.

Jollof Rice

Serves 4 to 6

¼ cup vegetable oil

4 poblano peppers, finely diced

2 celery stalks, finely diced

2 shallots, thinly sliced

2 garlic cloves, thinly sliced

1 serrano pepper, thinly sliced

1 (1-inch) knob ginger, peeled and finely diced

6 cups chicken stock

1 (16-ounce) can plum tomatoes

3 tablespoons tomato paste

2 sprigs fresh thyme, chopped

2 bay leaves

1 tablespoon smoked paprika

2 teaspoons curry powder

2 teaspoons kosher salt

¼ teaspoon cayenne pepper

4 cups long-grain rice, rinsed in cold water

1 bunch fresh cilantro, stemmed and leaves roughly chopped

Since my lineage goes back to Ghana and Nigeria, both of which claim this dish as their own, I must tread lightly here, as I have no desire to fight the so-called Jollof Wars over the history and preparation of this prized dish—one that is the centerpiece of community and holiday celebrations and the first dish to disappear after the guests have arrived. (I will say that I opt for long-grain rice, a hallmark of Nigerian jollof.) The fragrant, peppery one-pot dish dates as far back as the 1300s and is the mother of Cuban paella, New Orleans jambalaya, and Savannah red rice. Jollof can be eaten as a hearty main or a side to Grilled Catfish (recipe on page 109) or Chicken Yassa (recipe on page 9).

Heat the oil in a large saucepan over medium heat. Add the poblanos, celery, shallots, garlic, serrano, and ginger and cook, stirring, for 3 to 4 minutes, or until the shallots start to soften.

Add the chicken stock, tomatoes, and tomato paste to the pan and bring to a simmer. Stir in the thyme, bay leaves, paprika, curry powder, salt, and cayenne pepper. Simmer for another 5 minutes, then add the rice to the pot and bring to a simmer. Cover and cook for 15 minutes, or until all the liquid has evaporated. Turn off the heat and let stand for 10 minutes. Garnish the rice with cilantro and serve.

Note

To honor the homeland and make this dish more substantial, add a medley of blanched, steamed, or roasted vegetables, such as diced carrots, corn, green peas, and chopped green beans. Some Nigerian jollofs incorporate stewed beef, so feel free to experiment with or without meat.

Coconut Puff-Puff *with* Rum-Coconut Syrup

Serves 3 to 4

1 (¼-ounce) packet active dry yeast

2 cups warm water (120°F)

3½ plus ¼ cup cups all-purpose flour

½ cup sugar

½ teaspoon kosher salt

½ cup unsweetened shredded coconut

4 cups vegetable oil

1 recipe Rum-Coconut Syrup (page 21)

The sweet fried dough of the French beignet, the Spanish sopapilla, and the puff-puff, ubiquitous in Nigeria and Sierra Leone, must share the same origin story because they are so similar in taste and texture. Food historians have found descriptions for fried dough paste dating to the 1300s. Even Ancient Romans ate an unleavened donut hole, of sorts, called globi. With Alexandria as a trading crossroads, it makes sense then that fried dough passed from Europe to Africa, or vice versa. Puff-puff is a satisfying end to a light meal. Make the syrup first so that it is ready to drizzle on the puff-puffs while they are fresh and hot. The rum in the sauce was the currency by which many enslaved humans were purchased.

In a large bowl, dissolve the yeast in the water and let it rest for 5 minutes. Stir the 3½ cups flour, the sugar, and salt into the yeast, then fold in the shredded coconut. Cover the bowl with a damp towel, then let it rest in a warm place for at least 1 hour or until the dough has doubled in size.

Heat the oil in a large dutch oven over medium-high heat to 350°F.

Dust a cold work surface with the remaining ¼ cup flour and turn out the dough onto it. Using a pastry scraper or knife, cut golf ball–size pieces of dough and roll them into balls.

Use a slotted spoon to gently drop each dough ball into the oil, then cook the puffs until they are golden brown all over, approximately 4 minutes. Work in batches, if necessary.

Drain the puffs on a paper towel and serve immediately, drizzled with the rum syrup or with syrup on the side for dipping.

Notes

If you prefer instant yeast to active dry yeast, simply add the instant yeast to the dry ingredients, mix them together, then add the water.

Rum-Coconut Syrup

Makes 1½ cups

1 (13.5-ounce) can
    coconut milk
1 cup dark rum (see notes)
½ cup sugar
1 tablespoon cornstarch
2 teaspoons kosher salt
½ teaspoon vanilla bean
    paste (see notes)

Stir together all the ingredients in a medium saucepan. Bring the syrup to a simmer over low heat, stirring often, and cook for 5 minutes, or until it has thickened enough to coat the back of a spoon. Remove from the heat and let steep for 10 minutes. Drizzle the syrup over the puffs.

Notes

- Vanilla bean paste can be found in the spice aisle at many grocery stores, including Trader Joe's and Whole Foods. The paste is a combination of both the scraped seeds of a vanilla bean pod and vanilla extract. It has a richer floral taste than scraping the vanilla bean, plus it's more convenient. If you can't find vanilla bean paste, substitute the scraped seeds from 1 vanilla bean.
- If you only have light rum on hand, substitute it for the dark rum but use only ¾ cup.

A Perfect Package

Filled with nutrient-rich water to quench a thirst, sweet meat, and milk to satisfy hunger, oil with a high smoke point for frying, and fibrous shells for rope making and charcoal burning, the coconut is perfect for a tropical climate. Because it is ubiquitous in African and Caribbean cooking, you might think it was indigenous there. But, coconut originated in the Pacific Rim and the Indian Ocean Basin.

Portuguese traders first brought coconuts from Sri Lanka, the Maldives, and Madagascar to their plantations in Benin and Brazil during the 1500s. Spanish traders carried coconuts from the Philippines and Malaysia to Mexico's Baja Peninsula. Once the English, French, and Spanish colonized the Caribbean Islands, coconuts traveled with them and grew abundantly in the humid, salt-encrusted climate. The sandy coral rock keys around South Florida became coconut plantations, tended by Bahamian immigrants.

The Caribbean

When we pulled into the parking lot of an industrial strip on the frontage of State Road 826 in Miami Gardens, we weren't sure we were in the right place for a great Dominican eating experience. Once we opened the doors to Yarumba, however, it felt like we had arrived at a nightclub with pulsing Latin beats and neon lights bouncing off shiny black furnishings. Soon, we were sipping rum cocktails and devouring plates of tostone cups stuffed with shrimp creole; fried cheese and salami; Lebanese-inflected kibe; bowls of beef tripe and sancocho; and a whole crispy snapper filled with spicy Asian shrimp and rice and swimming in a savory coconut sauce. Every dish spoke to the complicated and tangled story of the Dominican Republic's foodways.

When Christopher Columbus set foot on the beaches of Hispaniola (what is now Haiti and the Dominican Republic), imagining he had found a quicker route to India, he set off the greatest exchange of flora and fauna the world has ever known. The world, in effect, shrank. Portuguese explorers gathered tomatoes, peanuts, cassava, and cacao from South America and returned with sugar, rice, coffee, and tea. Spaniards collected pumpkins, maize, potatoes, squash, tobacco, and chili peppers from Mexico, Central America, and the Caribbean and left cattle, pigs, horses, and rice in their wake. Throughout the world, foodways and diets were forever adapted and altered. In Africa, corn and cassava from the Americas joined (and eventually overtook) millet as a starch for stews and fufu, chickens expanded the protein options, and chili peppers induced euphoria and raised the spirits.

But the Columbian Exchange also spelled doom for the native peoples of the "West Indies" and set in motion the Atlantic slave trade. Within one hundred years of Columbus's first voyage, nearly 90 percent of the Taíno and Arawak who inhabited and traded among the islands, South America, and Mexico—and who gave the world *barabicue*, the practice of rubbing meat and fish with spices and peppers, then grilling them on green wood grates set over open firepits—had been wiped out by massacre, disease, and enslavement. In their place, millions of West Africans—cheap labor for coffee, sugar, and rice plantations—were enslaved to enrich the empires and colonial ambitions of Portugal, Spain, France, and Great Britain.

Through the struggle and the suffering, new cuisines and faiths were born. Hispaniola was divided by the French and the Spanish into Haiti and the Dominican Republic. Black Haitians developed a cuisine based on long, slow cooking methods to tenderize meats and vegetables. They employed their own culinary traditions, such as serving double starches like cornmeal and rice, as well as those of the French, such as dressing their dishes in gravies or the five mother sauces of France. After the slave revolt in 1804, which yielded the first Black republic, French landowners absconded with their enslaved humans to New Orleans. Rice and beans, a combination ubiquitous among the enslaved, became as much a touchstone dish of Louisiana as of Haiti.

In the Dominican Republic, African influences are apparent in concón (crispy white rice) and the breakfast dish mangú (mashed plantains). The drumming, stomping, call-and-response dances in the countryside bear a striking similarity to both the Sub-Saharan music traditions and ring shout singers of the United States' Sea Islands.

Cuba, with its 780,000 enslaved Africans, assumed the role of the primary sugar producer by 1840. When Cuba sought its own independence from Spain, an Afro-Cuban—"The Bronzed Titan" Antonio Maceo Grajales—led its liberation army. But colorism endured and Black culture, Santería, and Son music were forced underground. Yet the African hallmarks of its cuisine—grilled and pan-sautéed meats, especially pork, infused with abundant aromatics such as garlic and onions; inventive use of starches such as yuca, and the acid of oranges and limes—could not be subdued.

In Jamaica, callaloo and ackee, goat and oxtail, and Rastafarian vegetarianism all spring from the Afro-Jamaican culture that arose from waves of slavery and indentured servitude among Africans, East Indians, and Chinese. Throughout the islands, Christianity and Catholicism intermingled with the Yoruban gods of nature and the mystical spirits of Vodun to create a pidgin form of Vodou in Haiti, Vudú in the Dominican Republic, and Santería in Cuba that still is practiced today. I believe these practices endure because people live longer when they trust in something bigger than the moment they are living in.

Haiti

Soup Joumou
(Peppered Beef and Pumpkin Soup)

Serves 4 to 6

FOR THE STEW

½ cup vegetable oil

2 pounds flat iron steak, cubed and seasoned with salt and pepper to taste

6 large brussels sprouts, quartered, or 12 small brussels sprouts, halved

2 white onions, cut into 1-inch pieces

4 medium carrots, peeled, cut into 1-inch pieces

2 celery stalks, leaves removed, cut into 1-inch pieces

2 rutabagas, peeled, cut into 1-inch pieces

1 small sugar pumpkin, or kabocha or butternut squash, peeled, seeds removed and reserved, cut into 1-inch pieces

6 garlic cloves, roughly chopped

1 cup red wine, preferably pinot noir or merlot

1 cup white wine, preferably dry riesling or sauvignon blanc

½ cup Maggi seasoning

¼ cup kosher salt

2 tablespoons freshly ground black pepper

Soup joumou is usually reserved for Haitian Independence Day, celebrated every January 1. The first day of the calendar year marks the end of the decade-long slave rebellion that freed enslaved humans from French colonial rule in 1804. Prior to that, soup joumou—prepared by Black cooks—was eaten by French slaveowners but rarely by the enslaved. Making it and eating it honors all of those who never got a chance to taste it.

I use butternut squash or sugar pumpkin in my version, because the traditional kabocha squash is harder to find. I also braise flat iron steak instead of stew meat. Flat iron has grown commercially popular as a steak but braising the flat iron cut like a pot roast produces one of the most tender, flavorful meats you'll ever have the pleasure to savor. I top my stew with a swirl of epis and a garnish of the Haitian slaw pikliz, because I like the way the cool pickled brussels sprouts juxtapose with the warm, caramelized ones in the stew.

TO MAKE THE STEW: Heat a dutch oven over medium heat, then add the vegetable oil. Brown the steak cubes on all sides, in batches if necessary, then transfer to a plate and set aside.

Brown the brussels sprouts on their cut sides only, then transfer to another plate and set aside. Pour off any remaining oil. Add the onions, carrots, celery, rutabagas, pumpkin, and garlic, then return the steak to the pot. Cook for 5 minutes, until the onions and the vegetables begin to soften. Add both wines, the Maggi seasoning, salt and pepper, and continue cooking until the liquids reduce by half, approximately 15 minutes.

Add the beef stock and potatoes to the pot and bring the soup to a simmer.

Make a cheesecloth packet of the peppers, thyme, bay leaves, and peppercorns, tie the bundle tightly, then place it in the pot. Cover and cook the soup for 40 minutes, until the beef is tender, stirring the soup and tasting the broth for the balance of salt and

4 cups beef stock, store-
bought or homemade
(page 26)

4 Yukon gold potatoes, cut
into 1-inch pieces

FOR THE SPICE SACHET

1 Scotch bonnet pepper

1 jalapeño pepper

6 sprigs fresh thyme, or
1 tablespoon dried thyme

4 bay leaves

1 tablespoon whole black
peppercorns

FOR THE GARNISH

1 recipe Chef Stephan's Epis
(page 28)

1 recipe Pikliz (page 32)

pepper and adding more if needed. Once the beef is tender, add the brussels sprouts to the pot, turn off the heat, and let the soup rest for at least 20 minutes prior to serving.

Ladle the soup into bowls and garnish with a swirl of Epis and a dollop of Pikliz.

Beef Stock

Makes 1½ gallons

2 pounds beef knuckle or
   femur bones

4 celery stalks, cut into 2-inch
   pieces

2 medium white onions,
   peeled and quartered

2 large carrots, peeled and cut
   into 1-inch pieces

2 tomatoes, quartered

8 garlic cloves, peeled

2 tablespoons vegetable oil

3 gallons cold water

1 tablespoons beef gelatin
   powder

4 bay leaves

12 whole black peppercorns

4 sprigs fresh thyme

Preheat the oven to 400°F.

Place the bones in a roasting or aluminum foil pan and roast for 30 minutes.

Toss the celery, onions, carrots, tomatoes, and garlic with the oil, then place on top of the bones. Continue roasting the bones and vegetables for 30 minutes more or until they have caramelized.

While the vegetables cook, fill a large stockpot with the water and bring it to a simmer over medium-high heat.

Add in the gelatin and stir until dissolved.

Add the bay leaves and peppercorns and continue to simmer.

Once the vegetables and bones have caramelized, add them to the stockpot and bring the stock back to a simmer. Cook for 2 hours.

Add the thyme and cook for 30 minutes more. Use a ladle to skim off any impurities floating to the top.

Turn off the heat and let the stock rest for an hour.

Strain the stock through a fine-mesh sieve into airtight containers and refrigerate for up to 2 weeks or freeze for up to 6 months.

Stephan Berrouet Durand

My family comes from many different places. Haiti was first inhabited by the Taíno, who were pretty much wiped out on the island. You can still find traces of the Taíno in the Dominican Republic, Puerto Rico, and Cuba. My paternal grandmother is a descendant of the Taíno. My paternal grandfather's ancestors are from Spain and the northern side of France, in Bretagne. I also have Lebanese in my family. The food at my maternal grandmother's home always reflected those influences, including the deep-rooted influence from Africa.

Haiti is deeply rooted in tradition both historical and cultural. It's important that I tell that story. When people eat my food, I want them to have an experience. I want to take them to a place where their next question or conversation has to be about wanting to find out more about Haiti, even wanting to visit Haiti.

My job as a culinary ambassador, as a chef, is to speak about Haiti's rich cultural and historical heritage. There is another story to tell, much more interesting than what is out there. This is a country that has opened its arms to immigrants fleeing persecution elsewhere. We are a resilient people, and that resilience is in the lasting influence of our cuisine.

—Chef Stephan Berrouet Durand, President and cofounder of the Haitian Culinary Alliance

You can find no greater ambassador of Haiti's culinary contributions to the world than Chef Stephan Berrouet Durand. He splits his time between Orlando, Florida, and Brooklyn, New York, but he travels frequently and has taken many chefs, including me, to Haiti to share the rich culinary history of his homeland. Word to the wise, though: if he ever invites you to Haiti, don't let him drive.

Chef Stephan's Epis

Makes 1½ cups

3 heads roasted garlic (see
note)

2 green bell peppers, roughly
sliced

3 scallions, finely chopped

1 shallot, roughly chopped

1 Scotch bonnet pepper,
roasted and seeded (see
note)

1 bunch fresh Italian parsley,
finely chopped

1 bunch fresh fresh chives

5 sprigs fresh thyme

1 stalk lemongrass, tough
outer leaves removed, cut
into 1-inch sections

2 teaspoons ground cloves

2 teaspoons sea salt

3 tablespoons sour orange
juice (see note)

1 tablespoon Creole or spicy
brown mustard

¼ cup extra virgin olive oil

The aromatic base of most Haitian dishes begins with epis, a finely honed blend of herbs, spices, and vegetables that is used for marinating meats by adding sour orange juice (naranja agria) or for creating the roux for stews, gravies, and rice and beans. Here is Chef Stephan's blend.

In a blender or food processor, purée all the ingredients *except* the olive oil until they are a bright green paste. Slowly drizzle the olive oil through the blender top opening as the mixture continues to purée on low speed until you have a smooth consistency. Store, covered, in the refrigerator for up to 3 weeks.

Notes

TO ROAST GARLIC HEADS: Preheat oven to 400°F. Remove the dry papery outer layers of skin from the garlic bulbs, leaving the clove skins intact, then slice off about a ¼ inch off the top of the bulb. Set the bulbs on a piece of aluminum foil, big enough to tightly wrap around the whole bulb. Drizzle the bulb with a little olive oil and sprinkle with salt and freshly ground black pepper. Wrap the bulbs in the foil, place in a baking pan or individually in muffin tins, and roast for 30 to 40 minutes, until the bulbs are tender and squishy. Remove from the oven. When the bulbs are cool enough to handle, unwrap them, and squeeze the roasted garlic from the bulbs into dish.

TO ROAST THE SCOTCH BONNET PEPPER: You can roast the pepper while you roast the garlic. Lay the pepper on its side in the baking pan or muffin tin. Roast uncovered for 20 to 30 minutes, or until the pepper skin is charred and puffy. Remove the pepper from the oven and let cool; it will deflate and wrinkle. Wearing gloves, peel the skin then cut the pepper open, discarding the seeds. Be sure to not touch your face while handling the pepper.

SOUR ORANGE JUICE: Naranja agria, or sour orange juice, is available at Latin grocery stores and in some supermarkets. It is also available online.

If you don't use the whole piece of lemongrass, save the remainder by wrapping it in plastic wrap, placing it in a sealed plastic bag, then storing it in the freezer until you need another piece.

Mayi Moulen

(Cornmeal Porridge with Stewed Black Trumpet Mushrooms and Pickled Okra)

Serves 4

FOR THE STEWED MUSHROOMS

2 tablespoons vegetable oil

1 yellow onion, finely chopped

1 garlic clove, thinly sliced

4 ounces black trumpet or shiitake mushrooms

2 tablespoons dry white wine

1 (16-ounce) can plum tomatoes

Kosher salt and freshly ground black pepper

1 bunch fresh Italian parsley, stems removed and leaves chopped

2 sprigs fresh thyme, leaves removed and chopped

FOR THE PORRIDGE

1 teaspoon unsalted butter

1 small white onion

2 cloves garlic, chopped

1 jalapeño pepper, seeded and finely diced

1 red bell pepper, finely diced

4 cups chicken stock

Kosher salt and freshly ground black pepper

1 cup yellow or white cornmeal

FOR THE GARNISH

4 pods pickled okra, sliced in half lengthwise

When you first plunge into this dish, you may think of polenta or stone-ground grits and you wouldn't be wrong: those dishes are reminiscent of this creamy porridge, which is enriched by the funkiness of mushrooms—usually dried djon in Haiti—and the bite of piquant pickled okra. In both Africa and the Caribbean, grains and root vegetables are mashed to create sweet and savory starchy bases for stewed meats and roasted vegetables. They include millet porridges in Central Africa and the spongelike cassava-mash known as fufu from Ghana. In Jamaica, the cornmeal is cooked with okra and called coucou. In Mexico, it is steamed in husks for tamales.

TO MAKE THE MUSHROOMS: Heat the oil in a large skillet over medium heat. Add the onion and garlic, and cook for 2 minutes, or until softened.

Add the mushrooms and cook for 5 minutes, until they release their juices and start to darken. Stir in the white wine. Continue to cook until the liquid is reduced by half, 12 to 15 minutes.

Add the tomatoes, season with salt and pepper, and cook for 20 more minutes, until the mushrooms and tomatoes have coalesced into a rich, dark stew. Remove from the heat and stir in the parsley and thyme.

TO MAKE THE PORRIDGE: Melt the butter in a large saucepan over medium heat. Add the onion, garlic, jalapeño pepper, and bell pepper, and cook, stirring, for 2 minutes, or until softened. Add the chicken stock and bring to a simmer. Season with salt and black pepper.

Stir in the cornmeal and bring to a simmer. Cover and cook for 15 minutes, stirring occasionally until the cornmeal is tender and creamy.

TO SERVE: Scoop the porridge into bowls and top with the stewed mushrooms. Garnish with the pickled okra.

Haitian Oxtail in Beef Broth *with* Pikliz

Serves 2 to 4

2 pounds oxtails

2 tablespoons kosher salt

1 tablespoon freshly ground
   black pepper

1 teaspoon ground allspice

1 cup vegetable oil

4 celery stalks, chopped,
   including leaves

2 medium carrots, peeled and
   chopped

2 yellow onions, chopped

6 garlic cloves, minced

1 stalk lemongrass, tough
   outer leaves removed,
   chopped

4 bay leaves

1 cup dry red wine

2 tablespoons tomato paste

6 cups Beef Stock (page 26 or
   store-bought)

1 Scotch bonnet or habanero
   pepper

1 serrano pepper

Pikliz (page 32) for serving

Throughout the Caribbean and American South, African slaves transformed the tails of oxen or other cattle, the discards of wealthy plantation owners, into a delicacy by slow-braising them in rich, fragrant stews. In Haiti, oxtail is served with pikliz, an intense peppery and sour slaw tart enough to make your jaws clench, similar in taste and texture to the Southern condiment chow chow. Pikliz is most often made with green cabbage, but I use red cabbage, which is prettier and slightly sweeter, and brussels sprouts, which have a hint of nuttiness. Serve with your favorite white rice.

Preheat the oven to 350°F.

Rinse and pat dry the oxtails. Trim the fat with a sharp knife to a maximum of a ¼ inch, then generously season the oxtails all over with the salt, black pepper, and allspice.

Heat the oil in a dutch oven over medium heat. Working in batches, put the oxtails in the dutch oven and brown them on all sides, about 8 minutes total, then transfer to a paper towel–lined plate and set aside. Drain off the fat from the dutch oven.

Return the dutch oven to the stove and add the celery, carrots, onions, garlic, lemongrass, and bay leaves. Cook the vegetables over medium heat, stirring, until they start to brown, 4 to 6 minutes on each side. Add the red wine and tomato paste and bring to a boil. Return the oxtails to the pot and stir in the stock and the peppers. Bring to a simmer, then remove from the heat, cover, and transfer the pot to the oven.

Cook for 1½ hours, or until the oxtails easily pull away from the bone. Fish out the bay leaves and peppers and serve with pikliz on the side.

Pikliz

Serves 4

8 brussels sprouts, shredded on a box grater or purchased pre-shredded

¼ head purple cabbage, thinly sliced

2 tablespoons kosher salt

1 carrot, peeled and shredded

1 red bell pepper, thinly sliced

1 serrano pepper, thinly sliced

2 garlic cloves, thinly sliced

1 shallot, thinly sliced

1 (½-inch) knob ginger, peeled and minced

4 cups water

2 cups apple cider vinegar

1 cup sugar

2 bay leaves

1 Scotch bonnet or habanero pepper

Put the brussels sprouts and cabbage in a large mixing bowl, cover with the salt, and let stand for 4 hours at room temperature. The sprouts and cabbage will release water but remain crisp. Drain off excess water. Stir in the carrot, bell pepper, serrano pepper, garlic, shallot, and ginger.

In a medium saucepan, bring the water, vinegar, sugar, and bay leaves to a simmer over medium heat, stirring to dissolve the sugar. Toss in the whole Scotch bonnet pepper and simmer for 2 minutes. Remove the pan from the heat and let stand for 10 minutes. Add the vegetables and let the pikliz sit, covered, for 5 minutes.

Ladle the vegetables into a glass container or, if storing for longer than 7 days, divide among sterilized canning jars. Top the slaw with the pickling liquid, removing the Scotch bonnet pepper. Refrigerate, covered, until cold before serving; store in the fridge for up to 2 weeks.

ROOTS, HEART, SOUL

Dominican Republic

Chayote *and* Codfish Frittata *with* Plátanos al Caldero (Caramelized Plantains) *and* Avena Caliente (Hot Spiced Oat Milk)

Serves 4 to 6

2 ounces (1 center-cut fillet) dried salted cod

4 large eggs, beaten

¼ cup heavy cream

1 sprig fresh thyme, leaves separated from stem

2 tablespoons unsalted butter

1 chayote squash, peeled, seeded, quartered, and cut into ¼-inch pieces

1 shallot, thinly sliced into rounds

⅔ cup grated cheddar cheese (2 ounces)

Plátanos al Caldero (page 37), for serving

Avena Caliente (page 37), for serving

Salt cod, or bacalao, has been a part of the Caribbean diet since the 1500s, when Spanish and British ships traded pickled and salted cod from Novia Scotia and Iceland in exchange for sugar, salt, and rum. So, even with the abundance of seafood down island, bacalao remains a centerpiece of Dominican cooking. This hearty brunch features a delicious interplay of flavors and textures. The salty codfish baked into the frittata is moderated by the mild fruitiness of the chayote squash and the sweetness of the caramelized plantains. Served with a hot oatmeal drink that is both nutty and spicy, this meal is the ideal balance of sweet and savory.

Soak the cod in cold water to cover, pouring off and refreshing the water every 20 minutes, for 1 hour. When the cod is rehydrated, remove it from the water, pat it dry, peel the skin away, and flake the flesh apart with a fork, removing any bones as you go.

Preheat the oven to 375°F.

Whisk together the eggs, cream, and thyme in a large bowl, then gently fold in the flaked cod.

Melt the butter over medium heat in a large ovenproof skillet until it foams. Pour the egg mixture into the skillet, then scatter first the squash and shallot and then the grated cheese evenly over the eggs.

Bake the frittata for 30 minutes, or until the eggs have just set and the cheese is melted. Serve with a side of Plátanos al Caldero and the Avena Caliente.

Notes

The frittata can be served at room temperature. So, once you remove the frittata from the oven, you can let it rest while caramelizing the plantains and making the hot spiced oat milk.

Shown at top:
Ham-Hock
Mofongo with
Fried Eggs,
Pork Broth, and
Pickled Red
Onion
(page 45)

Plátanos al Caldero
(Caramelized Plantains)

Serves 4 to 6

2 tablespoons salted butter

2 ripe, black-skinned
  plantains, peeled and cut
  into ½-inch-thick coins

4 tablespoons sorghum
  (see Note) or maple syrup

1 cinnamon stick

¼ cup dark rum

Melt the butter in a large cast-iron skillet over medium heat. Arrange the plantains in an even layer in the melted butter. Cook for 4 to 5 minutes on each side until golden brown.

Transfer the plantains to a plate. Pour off the butter, then return the skillet to the heat. Pour the sorghum or syrup in the skillet and add the cinnamon stick and the rum.

Reduce the syrup by half over medium heat, 3 to 5 minutes. Return the plantains to the pan and baste them in rum syrup. Remove the cinnamon stick, then serve warm with the frittata.

Note

• Sorghum syrup is derived from an ancient grain marked by a tall stalk topped with a plume of gold- to rust-colored berries. Archaeologists have dated sorghum to the Sudan-Egypt border nearly 8,000 years ago. In 1757, Ben Franklin first wrote about sorghum's usefulness in the making of brooms. It gained purchase in the United States because it was cheaper and easier to grow than sugarcane, which made it especially attractive to folk in poor rural regions such as Appalachia. Although often compared to molasses, sorghum syrup is made from crushing the stalks and heating the green juice into a thick, dark elixir chock-full of nutrient-rich proteins and antioxidants.

• The plantains also make a luscious topping for ice cream or pound cake or a sweet accompaniment to roast pork tenderloin.

Avena Caliente
(Hot Spiced Oat Milk)

Serves 4

2 cups oat milk

4 cloves

1 cinnamon stick

1 teaspoon light brown sugar

⅛ teaspoon nutmeg, freshly
  grated or ground

⅛ teaspoon kosher salt

Ground cinnamon

Bring the oat milk, cloves, cinnamon stick, sugar, nutmeg, and salt to a simmer in a saucepan over medium heat, stirring until the sugar and salt have dissolved.

Remove from the heat. Pull out the cinnamon stick and cloves, then evenly divide the milk among 4-ounce glasses or small café cups and sprinkle with the ground cinnamon.

Espaguetis *with* Salami (Beach Spaghetti)

Serves 4 to 6

1 tablespoon extra virgin
 olive oil

8 ounces peppered salami,
 sliced into ½-inch discs,
 then quartered

1 (3.75-ounce) can smoked
 clams (optional)

12 cherry tomatoes, halved

12 pimiento-stuffed olives,
 halved

1 tablespoon capers, drained

1 teaspoon dried oregano

½ teaspoon dried thyme

1 cup frozen green peas (do not
 thaw)

1 pound spaghetti, broken
 in half

1 recipe Salsa Criolla (page 40)

Notes
- Make the sauce first, then
 the spaghetti.
- Because you will need
 the stuffed olives for both
 the spaghetti sauce and
 Salsa Criolla, buy at least a
 21-ounce jar.

Only recently did I learn of a connection between my Chicago childhood and the Dominican family tradition of taking big pots or aluminum foil pans of spaghetti to the beach. It may sound strange, to take hot food that requires bowls and forks and spoons to eat on leisurely sunny days in the sand, but you'll find spaghetti served on New York and Florida beaches where Dominican immigrants congregate, and around Lake Michigan in Chicago where Black families gather. A big pot of spaghetti feeds the multitudes inexpensively and travels well, something the elders learned when they rode trains north out of the South and packed meals to sustain them past the Mason-Dixon Line. Before that crossing, which could take hours or days, they were not welcome in the whites-only dining cars.

The Dominican Salsa Criolla, a spicy creole red sauce, offers rich layers of flavor from caramelized herbs and spices and a classic sofrito foundation. The myriad culinary influences—African, Italian, Jewish, and Spanish—are braided through the layers and history of this dish. With smoked clams, this interpretation evokes the salted sea. As a nod to my own heritage, the spaghetti is broken so that it is easier to serve and eat, especially for children.

Heat the oil in a large skillet over medium-high heat. Sear the salami for approximately 3 minutes on each side. Add the clams, tomatoes, olives, capers, oregano, and thyme and cook, stirring occasionally, for 15 minutes. Set aside.

Meanwhile, bring two large pots of salted water to a boil over high heat. Add the peas to one and cook for 2 minutes, just until the peas have turned a vibrant green. Drain and stop their cooking by plunging them into a bowl of ice water. Drain and set aside. In the other pot, cook the broken spaghetti in the boiling water for 7 to 8 minutes, until al dente. Drain the spaghetti, reserving 1 cup of the water to loosen the sauce if needed.

Return the spaghetti to the pot, fold in the peas, then stir in the salami mixture. Ladle in the Salsa Criolla, 2 cups at a time, and fold it into the spaghetti until the pasta has soaked up the sauce and all the ingredients are well mixed. Cover the pot and head to the beach.

Salsa Criolla

Makes 4 cups

2 tablespoons vegetable oil

¼ cup Classic Sofrito (page 51)

8 sprigs fresh cilantro, roughly chopped

2 bay leaves

½ teaspoon dried oregano

¼ teaspoon ground cumin

2 small sweet peppers, such as ají dulce or cubanelle, chopped

1 yellow onion, chopped

4 garlic cloves, roughly chopped

1 cup dry white wine

1 (28-ounce) can plum tomatoes

16 pimiento-stuffed olives

1 tablespoon kosher salt

1 teaspoon freshly ground black pepper

1 teaspoon tomato paste

Heat the oil in a large saucepan over medium heat. Add the sofrito, cilantro, bay leaves, oregano, and cumin and cook, stirring frequently, until caramelized, 3 to 5 minutes. Stir in the peppers, onion, and garlic and cook, stirring, until softened, 3 to 5 minutes more. Stir in the white wine, then cook until the wine is reduced by at least half, 5 to 7 minutes. Add the tomatoes, olives, salt, pepper, and tomato paste, and simmer for at least 15 minutes, until the sauce is thickened. Serve on pasta.

The History Behind Beach Spaghetti

Spaghetti with red sauce came to the Dominican Republic during the 1880s with Sicilian immigrants. By the 1950s, pasta had become so popular that the DR established its own pasta factory. Beach spaghetti, or *empaguetadas*, became such an institution that in Miami and New York, the scent of spicy tomato sauce perfumes the air at the shore wherever there are multifamily Dominican gatherings.

As for salami, it emerged as a staple of Dominican cuisine during and after World War II. It's part of daily breakfast, served with eggs and mashed plantains. Its origins, however, are less associated with Italians and more with the thousands of Jewish immigrants who, fleeing the rise of the Third Reich in Germany, made their home and livelihood on a former banana plantation on the DR's northern coast. There they set up a meat and dairy cooperative called Productos Sosúa, which made popular nonkosher cheeses and a unique beef-and-pork salami. According to a 2017 BBC Travel article, written by Pippa Biddle, the Jewish immigration was spurred by Dominican dictator Rafael Trujillo during the early years of the Holocaust—not as a humanitarian gesture, but to bring lighter-skinned immigrants to the island to further his ethnic cleansing of the Haitians who had descended from Black slaves.

Danny Dominguez

In the Dominican Republic, in the culinary schools, they start to build professionals by studying French, Spanish, Italian cooking, but you're not from France or Spain or Italy—they grew up eating the dishes we were just learning to cook. We're never going to feel the passion for that food as much as our own.

We have to start teaching students to appreciate their own foods. It's always good to learn the classic techniques, but I feel passionate about the food I grew up eating. Everybody craves their own food. You want your own sancocho from time to time or your yuca-cassava empanadas.

—Chef Danny Peñaló Dominguez
Head Chef
Yarumba, Miami Gardens

Helming Yarumba's kitchen is a young firebrand determined to elevate his native Dominican cuisine by highlighting the amalgamation of influences on the island, from indigenous Taíno and Arawak tribes and Spanish conquerors to enslaved West Africans and later Asian, Italian, and Jewish immigrants. Danny's menu offers a true reflection of all the peoples who have contributed to a unique island gastronomy developed over generations of cultural coalescence.

Puerto Rico

Tostones with Yam, Red Chili Salsa, and Smashed Avocado

Serves 4

FOR THE SALSA

1 yam or sweet potato, peeled and cut into ¼-inch pieces

1 tablespoon kosher salt

1 red bell pepper, finely diced

2 jalapeño peppers, finely diced

8 cherry tomatoes, quartered

1 shallot, finely diced

¼ bunch fresh cilantro, stems removed and leaves roughly chopped

2 tablespoons red wine vinegar

1 tablespoon extra virgin olive oil

Pinch of crushed red pepper flakes

FOR THE TOSTONES

4 green plantains, peeled and cut into ½-inch pieces

1 cup vegetable oil

Kosher salt

FOR THE AVOCADO

2 avocados, pitted and peeled

Grated zest and juice of 1 lime

1 teaspoon kosher salt

In the South, we have fried green tomatoes. In the Caribbean, it's fried green plantains, sturdy little saucers served as a side for dipping into garlic sauce or loading with pulled pork or other savories. Here, I've reimagined the tostones as an appetizer layered with a salsa that speaks to the marriage of old world and new. Tomatoes play second fiddle in this version, with yams and red chilies sharing the starring role. The velvety texture of the avocado counters the crunch and heft of the tostones and salsa. Breakfast treat or finger food, these are satisfying any time of day.

TO MAKE THE SALSA: Place the yam or sweet potato in a medium saucepan, cover with water, add salt, and set over medium heat. Bring to a boil, then reduce heat and simmer until fork-tender, 15 to 20 minutes. Drain and set aside in the refrigerator until chilled, approximately 20 minutes.

Combine the peppers, tomatoes, shallot, cilantro, vinegar, oil, and red pepper flakes in a medium bowl. Stir the chilled yam or sweet potato into the salsa.

TO MAKE THE TOSTONES: Soak the plantains in cold water for 20 minutes, then drain and dry on paper towels.

Heat the oil in a large skillet over medium heat. Working in batches, cook the plantains until lightly browned, then turn and brown on the other side, approximately 4 minutes per side. Transfer to a paper towel–lined plate to drain. Repeat until all the plantains are cooked.

When the plantains have slightly cooled, place them on a flat surface. Using a saucer, lightly smash each plantain, then season each with a pinch of kosher salt. Set aside for a few minutes, then fry the smashed plantains in the same skillet for approximately 1 to 2 minutes on each side, until golden brown.

TO MASH THE AVOCADO: Combine the avocados, lime zest and juice, and salt in a bowl, mashing with a fork.

< recipe continues >

TO ASSEMBLE THE DISH: Top each tostone with a teaspoon each of avocado and salsa and place on a platter. Or put the tostones on the platter with the salsa and avocado in small bowls alongside and let guests help themselves. Serve warm or at room temperature.

Note

Although tostones are traditionally made with plantains, you can use cooked yam or sweet potato as a substitute. Scoop cooked yam or sweet potato with an ice cream scoop and lightly mash each scoop into a round using a saucer on a flat surface. Heat 1 cup vegetable oil in a large skillet over medium heat. Working in batches, cook the yam/sweet potato tostones until golden brown, then turn and brown on the other side, approximately 4 minutes per side. Transfer to a paper towel–lined plate to drain. Repeat until all the tostones are cooked, then sprinkle with kosher salt.

Plantains Are Not the Same as Bananas

Plantains are meant to be cooked, never eaten raw, and they are more likely to be used in savory dishes than sweet ones.

For tostones and mofongo (recipes on pages 42 and 45), use green plantains. They are starchy, have a firm texture, and their flavor is more savory than sweet—closer to a yam or potato. For desserts or sweeter dishes, use plantains whose skins have turned almost solidly black; they will be perfectly ripe, soft, and sweet for caramelizing and mashing to use in quick breads. If you can't find perfect black plantains, you can buy green plantains, separate them, and set them on a sunny window ledge for 10 days. Don't touch them. Just let their skins turn yellow, then speckled brown, then black. They will remain dry and firm with just the right amount of starch to peel, sear, and caramelize.

Ham Hock Mofongo *with* Fried Eggs, Pork Broth, *and* Pickled Red Onion

Serves 4

FOR THE PICKLED RED ONION

1 red onion, halved and thinly sliced

½ cup red wine vinegar

½ teaspoon kosher salt

½ bunch fresh cilantro, stems removed and leaves roughly chopped

FOR THE HAM HOCK (PORK) BROTH

1 teaspoon olive oil

½ small yellow onion, chopped

1 garlic clove, thinly sliced

2 bay leaves

1 tablespoon whole black peppercorns

1 ham hock

8 cups cold water

FOR THE MOFONGO

4 green plantains, peeled and cut into 1½-inch-thick pieces

1 cup vegetable oil

1 small yellow onion, chopped

1 garlic clove, thinly sliced

¼ bunch fresh cilantro or Italian parsley, stems removed and leaves finely chopped

FOR THE FRIED EGGS

2 tablespoons unsalted butter

4 large eggs

Kosher salt and freshly ground black pepper

Cilantro or parsley leaves for garnish

Mofongo is a literal mashup of garlicky green plantains studded with fried pork. Like its African predecessor fufu (made from mashed boiled plantains or cassava), mofongo is meant to be sturdy and filling. If not prepared with enough moisture and fat, however, the dish can turn out heavy, starchy, and dry. It takes practice to strike that balance between airy and leaden. That's why you soak the plantains as well as employ a shallow-frying technique ubiquitous throughout Caribbean cookery. New York–based chef Gabriela Ramos became my sounding board as I attempted variations on this traditional breakfast, which bears some resemblance to Dominican mangú, or mashed plantains. For this recipe, I float balls of mofongo in broth, top it with a fried egg, and garnish it with quick pickled red onion. The liquid-to-fat ratio keeps the mofongo moist and creates a creamy texture once the egg yolk is broken.

TO MAKE THE PICKLED RED ONION: Stir together the red onion, vinegar, salt, and cilantro in a bowl. Set aside for at least 30 minutes.

MEANWHILE, MAKE THE BROTH: Heat the oil in a large saucepan over medium heat. Once the oil has warmed, add the onion, garlic, bay leaves, and peppercorns to the pot. Cook, stirring occasionally, for 2 minutes to quickly brown and soften the aromatics.

Add the ham hock to the pot and cook for 2 minutes, or until the fat starts to melt. Add the cold water to the pan and bring the broth to a simmer. Simmer for 45 minutes, or until the meat pulls away from the bone.

Remove from the heat and take the ham hock out of the pot. Pull off the skin and freeze for 20 minutes to cool and crisp it at the same time and make it easier to cut. Remove the meat from the bone, then discard the bone. Reserve the meat in the refrigerator until you're ready to make the mofongo.

TO MAKE THE MOFONGO: Soak the plantains in a bowl of cold water for 20 minutes.

Meanwhile, heat the oil in a large skillet over medium-high heat. Remove the ham hock skin from freezer and cut it into thin strips.

< recipe continues >

Once a drop of water skitters on top of the oil, fry the skins until crispy, approximately 4 minutes. Drain on paper towels.

Strain the broth into another pot and place on the stove on low heat. Using a ladle or a spoon, remove any excess fat floating on the top.

Remove the plantains from the water and dry them on paper towels. In the skillet you fried the skins in, reheat the oil to medium and, working in batches, cook the green plantains until lightly browned, approximately 4 minutes per side. Drain the plantains on paper towels.

Place the plantains in a medium bowl and, using a potato masher, mash them coarsely. Add the onion and garlic and stir to combine. Add the ham hock meat and cilantro and stir to combine. Crumble the ham hock skins into the plantain mixture and stir well. Form the plantain mixture into approximately 12 to 16 golf ball–size balls.

TO MAKE THE FRIED EGGS: In a nonstick skillet, melt the butter over medium heat. Crack the eggs into the pan and fry for 4 minutes, without turning, for sunny side up. (Depending on the size of your pan, you may need to work in batches.) Season the eggs with salt and pepper and set aside on a paper towel–lined plate.

TO ASSEMBLE: Place 3 or 4 mofongo balls in each of four bowls. Pour the hot broth over the mofongo. Scatter the pickled onions across the mofongo, top each bowl with an egg, and garnish with the cilantro or parsley leaves.

Note

To streamline the process, soak the plantains before you begin making the broth.

Sustaining Starches

Until the Columbian Exchange, bananas, plantains, and cereal grains were not part of the diet of Native people in the western hemisphere, who mostly relied on ground corn or mashed pumpkin for complex, filling starches. The arrival of plantains and bananas, which thrived in similar subtropical climates, added new flavors and textures and were familiar to Africans enslaved as part of mining and sugar operations. Their reliance on porridges and stews was not only to make do but to create sustaining, energy-giving meals to fuel them for long days of labor and deprivation while tilling soil and extracting metals. By mashing and pounding starches, like fufu in West Africa and coucou in the Caribbean, less energy was expended on digestion and more on work.

Bistec Encebollado

(Puerto Rican Steak, Onions, and Salsa)

Serves 4

4 (6-ounce) flat iron steaks

¼ cup Classic Sofrito or Sofrito with Roasted Jalapeño (page 51)

4 tablespoons vegetable oil

1 tablespoon Sazón (page 15)

1 large yellow onion, cut into ½-inch-thick rings

1 (28-ounce) can plum tomatoes

2 cups beef stock (page 26 or store-bought)

¼ cup red wine vinegar

2 sprigs fresh oregano

1 tablespoon kosher salt

4 sprigs fresh cilantro

Traditionally, bistec encebollado is a one-pot stew made with cube steak. This interpretation is less stew and more a saucy steak. Sofrito provides the aromatic base, both as a marinade for the beef and as a seasoning for the tomato sauce. Searing the beef, then braising it, creates the added layer of caramelization plus tenderizes the steaks. Crispy Rice (recipe on page 12) makes an ideal accompaniment.

Rinse and pat the steaks dry. Pour half the sofrito on a plate, then set the steaks onto the sofrito to coat the bottoms. Pour the remaining sofrito over the steaks and marinate them for at least 1 hour, but no more than 2 hours, at room temperature.

Preheat the oven to 350°F.

Heat the oil in a large cast-iron skillet over medium-high heat. Press the sofrito firmly into the steaks, then season both sides of the steaks with the Sazón. Sear the steaks for 3 to 4 minutes on each side, then transfer to a platter or cutting board.

Add the onion rings to the skillet and brown them on one side to get some caramelization, 3 to 5 minutes. Transfer the onions to the platter with the steaks.

In a 9-by-13-inch casserole dish, combine the tomatoes, stock, vinegar, oregano, and salt. Heat the casserole dish in the oven for 20 minutes.

Remove the casserole dish from the oven, then lay the steaks in the dish in a single layer and cover with the onions. Return the dish to the oven and cook for about 1 hour, or until the steak is fork-tender, basting the steaks with the tomato sauce every 15 minutes.

Let the steaks rest for 15 minutes. Serve each steak topped with a generous helping of sauce from the dish and a sprig of cilantro.

Note

If you cannot find flat iron steak, substitute flank steak.

Sofrito

In France, you begin with mirepoix. In Haiti, you start with epis (recipe on page 28). In Puerto Rico, the Dominican Republic, and other Latin American countries, the aromatic foundation of all sauces, rice dishes, and stews is sofrito. When you consider this culinary-narrative thread, it is not a long stretch to arrive at the Holy Trinity, the basis of dishes from New Orleans to Savannah to Charleston—port cities all. New York–based chef Gabriela Inez Ramos, who comes from both Puerto Rican and Dominican lineage, insists there are no hard-and-fast rules, other than that a respectable sofrito must include garlic, onions, peppers, and an acid—either citrus or vinegar—and that the consistency must be relish-like. If it's overprocessed into a purée, the ingredients will release too much liquid, lose their flavor, and change the composition of the resulting dishes.

Classic Sofrito

Makes 2 cups

16 garlic cloves, roughly chopped

2 cubanelle or Anaheim peppers, seeded and chopped

2 yellow onions, chopped

1 red bell pepper, chopped

1 bunch fresh cilantro

¼ cup sour orange juice (see page 28)

¼ cup lime juice

2 tablespoons extra virgin olive oil

Combine all the ingredients in a food processor, cover, and pulse to a relish-like consistency. Store in an airtight container in the refrigerator for up to 1 week or freeze for up to 6 months.

SOFRITO WITH ROASTED JALAPEÑO VARIATION: Preheat the oven to 400°F.

Cut 2 jalapeño peppers in half lengthwise. Put the jalapeño in a small baking dish, add the oil, roll the jalapeño in the oil, and season with salt and pepper. Roast in the oven for 15 minutes, or until the pepper is tender. Remove from the oven. When it has cooled, chop the jalapeño and put it in a food processor along with the remaining ingredients. Pulse to a relish-like consistency. Store in an airtight container in the refrigerator for up to 1 week or freeze for up to 6 months.

Coconut Pudding *with* Chicharron *and* Coconut Cracklins

Serves 4 to 6

FOR THE PUDDING

2 (13.5-ounce) cans coconut milk

⅔ cup turbinado sugar

½ cup cornstarch

2 tablespoons dark rum

1 cinnamon stick

½ teaspoon vanilla bean paste or 1 vanilla bean, scraped

½ teaspoon sea salt

6 gratings fresh nutmeg

FOR THE CRACKLINS

1 (8-ounce) package pork rinds (chicharrones)

⅔ cup (2 ounces) unsweetened shredded coconut

1 cup granulated sugar

Grated zest and juice of 1 lime

Using a savory ingredient, such as pork rinds, in a dessert used to be considered nouvelle cuisine. Nowadays, something as simple as sea salt sprinkled on chocolate chip cookies marries two cravings—sweet and salty—and heightens the richness of the chocolate. Here, the mouthwatering chicharron melds with the feathered feel of sweet coconut to create a savory-sweet crunch enrobed in a velvety pudding.

TO MAKE THE PUDDING: Combine the coconut milk, turbinado sugar, cornstarch, rum, cinnamon stick, vanilla, and salt in a large saucepan. Cook over medium heat until simmering but not boiling. Stir constantly for 4 to 6 minutes, until thickened.

Remove the cinnamon stick from the pan, then add the nutmeg. Pour the warm pudding mixture into six 4-ounce ramekins or espresso cups, leaving room at the top. Place the cups uncovered in the refrigerator to chill for at least 2 hours.

While the pudding chills, preheat the oven to 350°F. Line a baking sheet with parchment paper or a nonstick baking mat.

Place the pork rinds in a plastic bag, close the bag, and use a rolling pin or the bottom of a pot to crush the pork rinds.

Place the crushed pork rinds in a bowl and combine with the coconut, sugar, and lime juice. Spread in an even layer on the prepared baking sheet and bake for 15 minutes, or until the mixture is melted evenly. Remove from the oven and let cool completely.

Once cool, break into small pieces. To serve, sprinkle the cracklins generously over the tops of the chilled puddings and garnish each pudding with a pinch of lime zest.

Cuba

The Cubano (Cuban Sandwich) with Yuca Fries

Serves 4

12 cornichon pickles or
   3 whole dill pickles, finely
   diced

1 cup whole grain mustard

1 tablespoon red wine vinegar

4 Cuban bread loaves, split
   lengthwise

8 slices Swiss cheese

1 pound Black Forest ham,
   thinly sliced

1 cup Ham Hock Jelly
   (page 55)

¼ teaspoon dried oregano

¼ teaspoon kosher salt

¼ teaspoon coarsely ground
   black pepper

2 tablespoons unsalted butter

1 tablespoon coffee extract
   (optional)

A true workhorse in both sustenance and flavor, the lineage of the meaty Cuban sandwich is purported to date back more than 500 years to the Taíno people, who stuffed fish and fowl between two crackers made of yuca flour. But to tobacco field hands living on the Caribbean's largest island some 300 years later, the pork-laden sandwich served as a hearty breakfast or an easily transportable lunch.

On the island, where it is simply called a sandwich, mojo-marinated roast pork, sugar-cured ham, Swiss cheese, mustard, and pickles are pressed and toasted between crispy slices of Cuban bread. (The similar medianoche is made with sweet egg bread.) In Tampa, where the Cubano first made its way on American soil during the 1800s, the sandwich also includes Genoa salami—a nod to the Italian immigrants who helped build Ybor City's cigar manufacturing industry.

With the influx of Cuban refugees into Miami after the 1959 revolution, the Cubano, sans salami, grew in popularity. I pay homage to both the Miami and Tampa versions by pulling in a bit of the American South with a ham hock jelly that imparts citrusy notes with a hint of Italian herbs and spices.

In a medium bowl, fold the pickles into the mustard and vinegar. Spread the mixture on each half of the Cuban bread.

Lay a slice of Swiss cheese on each half of bread. Divide the Black Forest ham equally among the sandwich halves on top of the Swiss cheese, followed by approximately 2 tablespoons Ham Hock Jelly per slice.

Stir together the oregano, salt, and black pepper in a small bowl, then sprinkle it over the jelly.

Close up the sandwiches. Melt the butter in a large cast-iron skillet or griddle over medium heat. Place the sandwiches in the skillet or griddle, then set a heavy skillet or pan on top of the sandwiches, pressing down to flatten. Cook the sandwiches for 4 minutes, remove the pan, flip the sandwiches, return the pan and press, then cook for 4 minutes more, until the bread is browned and the cheese is melted.

Remove the top skillet from the top of the sandwiches and move the sandwiches to a cutting board. Brush the tops with a thin coat of coffee extract, and cut crosswise to reveal all of the layers of goodness. Serve with a side of Yuca Fries (recipe on page 56) or plantain chips.

Notes

If you want to save time but still enjoy a homemade Cuban sandwich, substitute thinly sliced, store-bought mojo-marinated roast pork loin for the ham hock jelly.

If you cannot find Cuban bread, you can substitute 6-inch baguettes or focaccia.

Ham Hock Jelly

Makes 4 cups

2 tablespoons lard or vegetable oil

2 pounds ham hock

1 yellow onion, chopped

8 garlic cloves, finely diced

4 bay leaves

1 tablespoon cumin seeds

8 cups water

¼ cup dark rum

Juice of 1 sour or navel orange

Juice of 1 lime

2 tablespoons whole grain mustard

1 tablespoon dried oregano

½ teaspoon crushed red pepper flakes

½ teaspoon dried mint

Heat the lard in a large stockpot over medium heat.

Sear the ham hock on all sides then transfer to a large bowl and set aside. Add the onion, garlic, bay leaves, and cumin seeds to the stock pot. Sauté for 3 to 5 minutes, until the onion softens. Return the ham hock to the pot, then pour in the water, rum, fruit juices, mustard, oregano, red pepper flakes, and mint.

Reduce the heat to medium-low and bring the broth to a simmer. Cover and cook for 2 hours, or until the ham hock meat pulls away effortlessly from the bone.

Turn off the heat and let the broth rest for 30 minutes. Remove the hock from the broth, pull the meat from the bone, and set aside in a large bowl. Return the ham bone to the pot and cook over medium-high heat for 30 more minutes, until the broth is reduced by half.

Turn off the heat and strain the broth over the pulled meat. Let the meat rest for 30 minutes or until it comes to room temperature, then cover and refrigerate for at least 4 hours or overnight.

Yuca Fries

Serves 4

2 pounds yuca (see Notes)

1 quart lard, coconut oil, or
  vegetable oil

Kosher salt

Remove the ends of the yuca and cut into 4-inch sections. With a sharp knife, make a cut down the length of the rough, bark-like skin and peel it away from the flesh.

Bring a large saucepan of salted water to a boil over high heat. Drop the peeled yuca into the boiling water and boil for 20 to 30 minutes, or until the yuca can be easily pierced with a fork. Drain in a colander and transfer it to paper towels to drain further.

Heat the lard in a dutch oven over medium-high heat until it reaches 375°F. Line a plate with paper towels and set it aside.

Cut the yuca sections into ½- to 1-inch sticks, then drop the sticks into the oil in batches and fry them until they are golden brown and crispy. Remove with a slotted spoon and drain them on the paper towel–lined plate.

Sprinkle salt over the fries and serve.

Notes

- Yuca is the starchy root of the cassava plant. By the time West Africans arrived in the Caribbean, they had been cooking with cassava and other tubers for hundreds of years and used yuca not just as a base for fufu but also as a digestive to settle stomach issues.
- To save time, you can use a 16-ounce package of frozen yuca fries, preferably the Goya brand. Prepare according to package directions.

Why Pork Is So Plentiful

On his second voyage to the Americas, Columbus brought Iberian pigs to the Caribbean islands to be used for breeding stock. Dropping pigs on islands all along the routes, including the southeastern coast of what would become the United States, was standard practice for Spanish explorers, because the pigs needed little to no care to thrive and would provide food during lean times. Therefore, pork has become a staple of Cuban and Puerto Rican cuisine as well as critical to the foodways of the American South.

Cubano Sauce

Serves 4

1 tablespoon vegetable oil

1 tablespoon whole black peppercorns

½ teaspoon cumin seeds

½ teaspoon coriander seeds

4 bay leaves

1 cup dry white wine

1 ham hock

4 cups chicken stock (page 14 or store-bought)

1 celery stalk, chopped

1 medium white onion, quartered

4 garlic cloves, smashed

1 tablespoon bacon fat or vegetable oil

4 tablespoons dijon mustard

4 tablespoons mayonnaise, preferably Duke's

1 teaspoon white vinegar

2 sprigs fresh curly parsley, chopped

1 dill pickle, finely diced

2 slices Swiss cheese, finely diced

Grated zest of 1 lime

For a variation on the traditional Cubano, make a layered dip for crunchy yuca fries. The Cubano Sauce has all the elements of a deconstructed sandwich: salty meat, pungent mustard, mild cheese, and tart pickles.

Heat the oil in a small saucepan over medium heat. Add the peppercorns, cumin, and coriander and fry for approximately 2 minutes, stirring frequently, until they are fragrant and toasted. Add the bay leaves and wine and simmer until the wine is reduced by half, 5 to 7 minutes.

Add the ham hock, stock, celery, onion, and garlic and bring the stock to a boil. Reduce the heat to low and simmer the stock for 1 hour, or until the meat pulls away from the bone.

Remove the stock from the heat and remove the ham hock to a plate with a slotted spoon. When it has cooled, peel away the skin and reserve it for another use. Pull the meat from the bone and place in a bowl. In a small saucepan, melt the bacon fat, then pour the fat over the ham hock meat.

Strain the stock through cheesecloth into a heatproof container, cool, and refrigerate or freeze for another use.

Put the mustard, mayonnaise, vinegar, and parsley in a blender and blend until you have a silky sauce.

Spoon one quarter of the mustard-mayonnaise sauce into the bottom of a clean 16-ounce Mason jar, followed by one quarter of the ham hock meat, 1 teaspoon of the dill pickle, and 1 teaspoon of the Swiss cheese, repeating the layers until almost to the top of the jar. Finish with a dollop of the mayonnaise, the ham hock, then the lime zest. Serve as a dip for the Yuca Fries.

Ham Steak *with* Red-Eye Gravy, Mango de Bizcochuelo *and* Pepper Relish, *and* Tostada Cubana

Serves 4

FOR THE RELISH

2 tablespoons honey

2 tablespoons apple cider vinegar

2 tablespoons extra virgin olive oil

½ teaspoon kosher salt

Pinch of freshly ground black pepper

2 ripe mangos, peeled, seeded, and cut into small dice

1 red bell pepper, cut into small dice

1 jalapeño pepper, seeded and cut into small dice

1 serrano pepper, seeded and cut into small dice

½ cubanelle pepper, seeded and cut into small dice

1 shallot, thinly sliced

FOR THE HAM STEAK AND GRAVY

1 tablespoon bacon fat or vegetable oil

4 bone-in ¼-inch-thick ham steaks

2 shallots, thinly sliced

1 celery stalk, finely diced

2 garlic cloves, crushed

2 cups strong brewed coffee, such as espresso

½ cup chicken or pork stock (page 14 or store-bought)

1 tablespoon sugar

Since coffee arrived in the Caribbean from Ethiopia, dark-roasted, finely textured espresso has become central to the Cuban culture. It gives new meaning to the concept of café society. Early in the mornings, graying ladies hand sweetened cafés con leche along with advice and wax paper–wrapped tostadas through storefront pass-throughs, only to serve up cordatitos to the same patrons for a midafternoon kick.

The bread has its own character, similar to a French baguette but not quite. Although similarly concocted from white flour, yeast, and water, traditional Cuban bread is made with lard and rises around a fresh palmetto leaf, giving it a distinctive split down the middle and a grassier flavor. The lard makes the thin crust crisp and fills the soft insides with an airy texture. Although, if you don't have easy access to Cuban bread, a French baguette makes a worthy substitute.

The relish sparkles with tang and heat, an ideal counterbalance to the salt and fatty richness of the ham. As with any of the recipes calling for peppers, use as little or as much to suit your taste.

TO MAKE THE RELISH: Whisk together the honey, vinegar, oil, salt, and black pepper in a large bowl. Stir in the mangos, peppers, and shallot, and set aside.

TO MAKE THE HAM STEAK AND GRAVY: Heat the bacon fat over medium heat. Sear the ham steaks one at a time until brown, then brown the other side, approximately 2 minutes on each side. Set aside on a platter.

Cook the shallots and celery in the fat remaining in the skillet for 2 minutes, or until softened. Add the garlic and cook for 1 minute. Stir in the coffee, stock, and sugar, and continue cooking until the gravy is reduced by half. Sprinkle the black pepper, salt, oregano, and cumin over the gravy then cook for another minute. Stir in the cream and continue cooking and stirring until the gravy has reduced by half. Remove from the heat.

½ teaspoon freshly ground
  black pepper

¼ teaspoon kosher salt

¼ teaspoon dried oregano

Small pinch of cumin seeds

½ cup heavy cream

1 loaf Cuban bread or French
  baguette, sliced lengthwise,
  toasted and buttered

Put a ham steak on each plate, spoon over some of the gravy, and top with a dollop of mango relish. Serve with Cuban bread for dipping in the gravy.

Notes

If you are using a premade stock, taste first for the level of sodium. If it's salty, cut back the salt called for in the recipe.

If you have access to a Latin grocer, try to find a Bizcochuelo mango, a Toledo, or another variety common to the islands. With skin the shade of a Meyer lemon, the small- to medium-size Bizcochuelo is grown in and around the city of Santiago de Cuba, and it can be found throughout South Florida. It is juicy, less fibrous, and sweeter than the large and ubiquitous blushed green-gold Tommy Atkins varietal found in most US grocery stores.

You can make your own pork stock or buy it at the grocery store. There are a number of brands available, including Knorr Pork Bouillon, Better Than Bouillon Ham Base, and Minor's Pork Base. Follow the package directions for the amount of broth called for in the recipe.

Café Society

Our pilgrimage to Little Havana's Versailles began at the bakery. Our guide, Merari Hall Fortún, who runs a travel service and website called Dreaming in Cuban, encouraged us to order one of everything from the cases—spicy beef empanadas, creamy-crunchy croquetas de jamón, shattering pastelitos de guayaba, along with steaming cortaditos and cafés con leche. We sat on a sunny covered porch overlooking Calle Ocho, the artery to the heart of Miami's Cuban exile community for more than fifty years.

Merari spoke of Versailles' cultural significance to South Florida and how the atmosphere reflects Cuba's storied café society—how no local, state, or national politician could get elected unless they connected with the people here; how demonstra-tions for Cuban independence, pro-democracy marches, rescue efforts for people braving the Straits of Florida were planned around these tables. In fact, two weeks after we visited Versailles, Calle Ocho filled with Miamians, most of Cuban descent, marching in solidarity with people still on the island, who were protesting the communist government because of ongoing shortages of food and medical supplies.

At a nearby table, two older women were involved in a passionate and demonstrative discussion with a younger gentleman. Cup after cup of café consumed and replenished along with baskets of Cuban bread pressed into buttery tostada. I wondered, "Is it the coffee that makes the ritual or is the ritual drinking coffee?"

Grilled Shrimp Mojo *with* Black Bean Purée *and* Toasted Rice *with* Cumin Seeds *and* Mint

Serves 4

FOR THE BLACK BEAN PURÉE

2 tablespoons vegetable oil

1 pound pork bones, such as smoked pork neck bones

4 garlic cloves, roughly chopped

2 celery stalks, roughly chopped

1 yellow onion, roughly chopped

4 bay leaves

1 pound dried black beans, soaked overnight and drained

2 quarts pork or chicken broth (page 14 or store-bought)

4 sprigs fresh thyme

4 sprigs fresh oregano

2 teaspoons kosher salt

1 teaspoon freshly ground black pepper

¼ teaspoon crushed red pepper flakes

2 tablespoons lard or unsalted butter, melted

FOR THE SHRIMP MOJO MARINADE AND MOJO

½ cup sour orange juice (see page 28)

½ cup orange juice

½ cup lime juice

½ cup extra virgin olive oil

1 tablespoon molasses or 1 teaspoon sugar

1 tablespoon dijon mustard

4 garlic cloves, finely chopped

4 sprigs fresh oregano

Just off the northwestern coast of Africa, an archipelago of volcanic islands serves as the crossroads of East and West, old and new, Europe and Africa. The Canary Islands are the birthplace of mojo, a garlic-citrus concoction with a flash of heat that acts as both a marinade and a sauce for meats and vegetables. The Canary Islands are where the oranges and limes of Southeast Asia meet the aromatics of the Middle East and Africa to be transformed by the Portuguese and Spanish into one of the most versatile sauces adopted by West Africans and carried to the Caribbean.

My interpretation of this Cuban dish is constructed in a way that allows you to grab all the flavors at once—the sweet-tart notes of the shrimp and the nutty earthiness of the rice. The mint gives it a brightness, and the herbaceous black bean purée acts as a dip for the shrimp and rice. Although it has moving parts, each one is simple to prep and even easier to cook. Perfect for a quick dinner on a hot weekend evening.

TO MAKE THE PURÉE: Heat the oil in a large stockpot over medium heat. Put the pork bones in the pan and caramelize the bones and meat on all sides, approximately 4 minutes per side. Stir in the garlic, celery, onions, and bay leaves and cook, stirring, for 2 minutes.

Add the black beans and broth, then bring to a simmer. Stir in the thyme, oregano, salt, black pepper, and red pepper flakes, and continue cooking for 1 hour, or until the beans are soft.

Turn off the heat and let the beans cool for 30 minutes. Remove the bones and bay leaves from the pot. Put some of the beans and liquid in a blender (no more than halfway up the blender because the beans will expand as they purée). Blend the beans until smooth. Pour the purée into a large bowl and set aside. Repeat the process until all the beans have been puréed.

Return the beans to the stockpot and bring to a simmer. Turn off the heat and stir in the lard until well incorporated.

TO MAKE THE MARINADE AND MOJO SAUCE: Combine the citrus juices, oil, molasses, mustard, garlic, spices, and salt. Blend until all the ingredients have thoroughly incorporated.

Pour half the marinade in a large bowl. Stir in the onion, then toss the shrimp in the marinade. Set aside for at least 20 minutes but

< recipe continues >

½ teaspoon freshly ground
  black pepper

¼ teaspoon cumin seeds

¼ teaspoon smoked paprika

¼ teaspoon sea salt

½ small white onion, cut into
  ¼-inch-thick rings

16 head-on or 32 shell-on
  jumbo or colossal shrimp

Grated zest of ½ orange

Grated zest of 1 lime

2 tablespoons mayonnaise

½ teaspoon dijon mustard

2 tablespoons dark rum

2 sprigs fresh curly parsley

Toasted Rice with Cumin
  Seeds and Mint (see below)

no more than 30 minutes or the citrus will begin "cooking" the shrimp.

Add the orange and lime zest, mayonnaise, mustard, rum, and parsley to the reserved marinade in the blender. Mix on medium-high speed until smooth.

TO GRILL THE SHRIMP AND ASSEMBLE THE DISH: Preheat a gas or charcoal grill to medium-high (375°F).

Remove the shrimp and onion from the marinade and place them on the grill. Cook until the shrimp turn bright red, 2 to 3 minutes on each side. Cook the onions until they are slightly charred on both sides, 3 to 5 minutes.

Reheat the black bean purée. Layer the onions on a platter, set the shrimp on top, and serve alongside Toasted Rice and the black beans. Encourage guests to peel a shrimp and run it through the rice and purée to enjoy all the flavors and textures together.

Note
While the black beans cook, make the mojo sauce and marinade. Once you've returned the black beans to the pot to simmer, marinate the shrimp, then cook the rice. Grill the shrimp and onions once the rice is cooling. Let the shrimp sit at room temperature while you toast the rice.

Toasted Rice with Cumin Seeds and Mint

Serves 4

4 tablespoons vegetable oil,
  divided

1 cup Carolina Gold rice or
  other long-grain rice

1 shallot, thinly sliced

1 garlic clove, finely chopped

8 cumin seeds, or ¼ teaspoon
  ground cumin

6 whole black peppercorns

1 bay leaf

4 cups vegetable stock
  (page 6 or store-bought)

½ teaspoon ground turmeric

Pinch of sea salt

1 sprig fresh mint, leaves
  chopped

Heat 2 tablespoons of oil in a medium saucepan over medium heat. Add the rice, shallot, garlic, cumin seeds, peppercorns, and bay leaf. Cook the rice, stirring, for 3 to 4 minutes, or until the rice and shallot start to brown slightly. Stir in the stock, turmeric, and salt, then cover and simmer for 20 to 25 minutes over medium-low heat, or until the liquid is fully absorbed. Remove the rice from the heat and let it steam off the heat for 5 to 10 minutes. Fluff the rice with a fork, then spread it on a platter to cool for 5 to 10 minutes. Pull out the cumin seeds, peppercorns, and bay leaf, sprinkle the mint onto the rice, and continue to cool until ready to toast in the skillet.

Heat the remaining 2 tablespoons oil in a large skillet over medium heat. Return the rice to the skillet and toast the rice until it is crispy all over, 5 to 7 minutes. Serve it atop the black bean purée with the shrimp or as a side to grilled fish or roasted chicken.

Note
If turmeric is unavailable, substitute ½ teaspoon curry powder.

Carolina Gold Rice

So-called for its brilliant, unhulled hue, Carolina Gold rice also could have been named for the way it made many a South Carolina and Georgia plantation owner wealthy in the years before the Civil War. Botanical research reveals that the first non-Indigenous rice in the Americas was of African origin and planted as part of subsistence gardens by slaves who hailed from the continent's Rice Coast, between Senegal and Cameroon. (Later, Asian rice, already grown abundantly in West Africa, would become the predominant cultivar.)

By the 1700s, in fact, enslaved Africans from this region were imported specifically to cultivate rice in the tidal estuaries and semi-tropical swamps from North Carolina to North Florida. According to research by culinary historian Michael Twitty, each enslaved person in this region was responsible for producing more than 2,000 pounds of rice annually. Among the rice growers were my ancestors.

After the Civil War, the rice economy plummeted and heirloom varieties of beans, seeds, and grains—such as Carolina Gold rice—fell out of favor until the 1980s. That's when a Savannah eye surgeon showed that the historic varietal could be grown again—although he was just trying to attract ducks to his hunting grounds. But he caught the attention of food scholars, who have revived Carolina Gold rice production throughout the Carolina Lowcountry. It is a versatile grain, both fluffy and creamy, and known for its sweet almond flavor.

Stewed Chicken with Cuban Okra and Sweet Plantains and Pickled Baby Corn

Serves 4 to 6

FOR THE STEW

Grated zest of 1 lime

1 tablespoon kosher salt

1 teaspoon dried oregano

1 teaspoon ground cumin

1 teaspoon sugar

1 teaspoon smoked paprika

1 teaspoon freshly ground black pepper

½ teaspoon dried thyme

3 to 4 pounds chicken pieces (or 1 whole chicken, cut into 8 pieces), brined (page 9)

2 tablespoons vegetable oil

4 okra pods, cut into ½-inch pieces

2 garlic cloves, roughly chopped

1 yellow onion, chopped

1 cubanelle pepper, seeded and sliced into ¼-inch rings

2 bay leaves

1 cup white wine

4 cups chicken stock (page 14 or store-bought)

1 (28-ounce) can plum tomatoes

24 pimiento-stuffed olives (21-ounce jar)

¼ cup golden raisins

2 sprigs fresh curly parsley, finely chopped

4 sprigs fresh cilantro, finely chopped

Sweet Plantains and Pickled Baby Corn (page 68)

Crispy Rice (page 12)

To my tastes, this sublime one-pot stew is the epitome of Afro cuisine. The infusion of flavors from the brine harkens back to old-world curing and tenderizing methods for older hens that no longer produce eggs. The okra, of course, is a thickener, but also a nutrient powerhouse packed with vitamins A and C for immunity support, vitamin K for blood clotting, and antioxidants that can help fight cancer. The broth of this stew alone, just like the potlikker for stewed collards, can be a medicinal drink for body and soul.

TO MAKE THE STEW: Mix the lime zest, salt, oregano, cumin, sugar, paprika, black pepper, and thyme in a small bowl. Rub the chicken pieces on all sides with the seasoning mixture. Reserve any leftover seasoning.

Preheat the oven to 350°F.

Heat the oil in a dutch oven over medium heat. Working in batches, if necessary, cook the chicken pieces, skin side down so they are not touching, until golden brown on the first side, about 5 minutes. Turn and brown on the other side, 3 to 5 minutes.

Transfer the chicken to a plate and set aside. Add the okra, garlic, onion, pepper, and bay leaves and cook, stirring, until the vegetables are brown on all sides, 5 to 7 minutes.

Return the chicken to the pan. Add the wine and simmer until reduced by half, 5 to 7 minutes, scraping up the tasty brown bits with a wooden spoon.

Add the stock and tomatoes and bring the stew to a simmer. Add the olives, raisins, parsley, cilantro, and any remaining seasoning mixture.

Cover, place in the oven, and cook for 30 minutes. Remove the cover and continue to cook for 15 minutes, or until the chicken is fork-tender.

Once the stew is done, let it rest for 10 minutes, then serve it with Sweet Plantains and Pickled Baby Corn (page 68) and Crispy Rice (page 12).

Sweet Plantains *and* Pickled Baby Corn

Serves 4

2 tablespoons vegetable oil

2 ripe plantains, peeled and cut in half crosswise, then cut in half lengthwise

4 ears pickled baby corn, cut in half lengthwise

1/2 red bell pepper, chopped

1 sprig fresh curly parsley, chopped

1 sprig fresh cilantro, chopped

Heat the oil in a large cast-iron skillet over medium heat. Lay the plantains on their flat sides in the skillet without touching. Cook the plantains, working in batches, if necessary, until they are caramelized to a golden brown, 3 to 5 minutes. Turn and brown the other side for another 3 to 5 minutes.

Add the baby corn and pepper, and cook until the corn has lightly browned, approximately 3 minutes. Garnish with the parsley and cilantro and serve with the chicken.

Note
You can find pickled baby corn in the Asian food aisle at the grocery store.

Jamaica

Jerk Chicken Wings *with* Lime Dipping Sauce

Serves 4

16 jumbo chicken wings

4 cups pineapple juice

2 cups water

½ cup Maggi seasoning

½ cup Worcestershire Sauce (page 72 or store-bought)

6 garlic cloves, coarsely chopped

3 medium scallions, chopped

2 Scotch bonnet peppers, seeded and chopped

2 sour oranges, quartered, or 1 cup sour orange juice (see page 28)

1 medium onion, coarsely chopped

1 lemon, quartered

4 sprigs fresh thyme

2 cinnamon sticks

Kosher salt

1 tablespoon vegetable oil, plus more for rubbing the wings

1 tablespoon five-spice powder

1 tablespoon allspice berries, smashed, plus more whole berries for the grill

1 tablespoon whole black peppercorns

1 teaspoon freshly grated nutmeg

1 tablespoon kosher salt

2 teaspoons freshly ground black pepper

Lime Dipping Sauce (page 73), for serving

A Jamaican, a Haitian, a Dominican, and an African American walk into a bar and get into a heated discussion about jerk.

Is jerk simply a seasoning or is it also a grilling technique? All of us agreed it was more than a seasoning. Two of the four agreed that true jerk is grilled with a base of charcoal, a layer of pimento logs (pimento is the tree on which allspice berries grow), and the meat sits right on top of the wood. But most home cooks can't get their hands on pimento wood. The alternative is to throw whole allspice seeds into the charcoal or use alderwood, maybe hickory or pecan, depending upon where you live. The smoke, however, is incidental. The real flavor comes from the seasonings.

Does it include citrus or pineapple or soy sauce? No, said the Haitian, but the Jamaican said his grandmother used to put soy sauce in everything . . . he just couldn't remember if she used it in her jerk paste, which must—no exceptions—include allspice, Scotch bonnet, and thyme.

Pat the chicken wings dry.

In a large bowl or plastic food storage container, stir together the pineapple juice, water, Maggi seasoning, Worcestershire Sauce, garlic, scallions, peppers, sour oranges, onion, lemon, thyme, cinnamon sticks, 2 tablespoons salt, oil, five-spice powder, allspice, peppercorns, and nutmeg. Place the chicken wings in the marinade, cover with plastic wrap, and refrigerate for at least 8 hours or up to 16 hours.

Preheat a gas or charcoal grill to medium heat (325°F). If using charcoal, toss in a handful of allspice seeds, if desired. Remove the chicken wings from the marinade, pat them dry, and rub the wings with oil so that they won't stick to the grill grate. Sprinkle each wing with salt and black pepper.

Grill the wings, turning occasionally to char, until the internal temperature reads 165°F on an instant-read thermometer and there is no red at the bone, approximately 12 minutes. Serve with the dipping sauce.

Note
Make the dipping sauce while the wings marinate.

Coconut-Fried Spiny Lobster Tail
with Rum-Soy Dipping Sauce

Serves 4

FOR THE LOBSTER MARINADE

1 can (13.5 ounce) light coconut milk

Grated zest and juice of 1 lime

Grated zest of 1 lemon

1 tablespoon hot sauce

1 teaspoon Maggi seasoning

1/8 teaspoon crushed red pepper flakes

1/8 teaspoon ground ginger

4 (6-ounce) spiny (Florida) lobster tails, split in half, shelled (see note)

FOR THE COCONUT COATING

2 cups panko breadcrumbs

1/4 cup unsweetened shredded coconut

1 teaspoon granulated onion

1 teaspoon granulated garlic

1/2 teaspoon chili powder

4 to 6 sprigs fresh curly parsley, stems removed and leaves finely chopped (3 to 4 tablespoons)

1 teaspoon sea salt

1/2 teaspoon freshly ground black pepper

1/2 cup coconut oil

2 1/2 cups vegetable oil, for frying

Rum-Soy Dipping Sauce (page 73)

As foods moved from the islands to the mainland of the American South, frying often became laden with animal fats and butter, creating a myth that African-inspired dishes are intrinsically unhealthy. But, when you dig into the origins of the West African cooking methods that shaped the cuisine, you don't find that excess. Instead, you discover shallow frying techniques that add texture and flash-cooking methods that enhance, rather than disguise, the ingredients. This spiny lobster—often called Florida lobster—is an ideal example of this shallow frying technique, where the rich buttery notes of the lobster meat complement the sweet-savory crunch of the coating. This dish makes an ideal appetizer or it can be paired with Bistec Encebollado (recipe on page 48) for a spicy surf and turf.

TO MAKE THE MARINADE: Stir together the coconut milk, lime zest and juice, lemon zest, hot sauce, Maggi seasoning, red pepper flakes, and ginger in a bowl. Add the lobster tails and marinate in the refrigerator for at least 15 minutes but no longer than 30 minutes.

MEANWHILE, MAKE THE COATING: Combine all the ingredients in a large bowl, using your hands to slightly crush the breadcrumbs.

TO FRY THE LOBSTER: Heat the oil in a large cast-iron skillet or dutch oven over medium heat until it reaches 325°F.

While the oil is heating, remove a lobster tail from the marinade, allowing the excess to drip off. Place the tail in the crumb mixture and coat by pressing it into the crumbs. Repeat until all the lobster tails are coated.

Working in batches if needed, fry the tails on one side for 4 minutes, then turn and cook for an additional 2 to 4 minutes. (The tails will float slightly when they are ready.) Transfer the tails to either a dripping rack set over a baking sheet or paper towel–lined plate to drain. Serve hot with the dipping sauce.

Notes
- Florida spiny lobster tails are available for shipping across the United States, but you can substitute Maine lobster tails. Increase the frying time by 2 minutes per side.
- Make the dipping sauce while the lobster tails marinate.

Worcestershire Sauce

Makes 1½ cups

¾ cup apple cider vinegar

½ cup dark brown sugar

¼ cup balsamic vinegar

¼ cup soy sauce

½ teaspoon dry mustard

½ teaspoon ground ginger

½ teaspoon granulated onion

½ teaspoon granulated garlic

½ teaspoon kosher salt

¼ teaspoon ground anise

¼ teaspoon ground cinnamon

¼ teaspoon cracked black
  pepper

Combine all ingredients in a medium saucepan and bring to a simmer over medium heat, stirring continuously until the sugar dissolves.

Remove the sauce from the heat and let it rest for 30 minutes.

Transfer the sauce to an airtight container and store in the refrigerator for up to 2 weeks.

The Flavor of Freedom

As far back as 400 years ago, the Maroons were escaped slaves who hid among the indigenous people of Jamaica's Blue Mountains. There, they preserved wild boar with a seasoning crafted from hot peppers, pimento (allspice), and thyme. They would pierce—or "jook"— the meat to imbue it with these flavors before roasting the boar in dirt-covered pits in the ground. As the technique migrated down from the mountains into the cities, the "jook" spices became known as "jerk."

Lime Dipping Sauce

4 fresh chives, finely chopped
Grated zest of 1 lime
½ cup mayonnaise
1 tablespoon dijon mustard
1 teaspoon Maggi seasoning
1 teaspoon dark brown sugar
Pinch of ground ginger

Whisk all the ingredients in a bowl and serve alongside Jerk Chicken Wings.

Rum-Soy Dipping Sauce

2 shallots, minced
1 serrano pepper, seeded and finely diced
Grated zest of ½ orange
Grated zest of ½ lemon
½ cup light soy sauce
¼ cup dark rum
1½ tablespoons honey
1 tablespoon rice wine vinegar
Pinch of ground ginger

Combine all the ingredients in a bowl. Let stand for 15 minutes so the flavors meld. Serve alongside the lobster.

Pepper Crawfish Cocktail *with* Hibiscus Punch

Serves 4

FOR THE COCKTAIL SAUCE

1 small cucumber, peeled, seeded, and finely diced

1 shallot, finely diced

1 garlic clove, minced

Grated zest and juice of 1 lime

1 cup ketchup

2 tablespoons Jamaican tamarind sauce or 1 teaspoon tamarind paste

1 tablespoon bottled horseradish

1 teaspoon whole grain mustard

1 teaspoon Maggi seasoning

1 teaspoon hot pepper sauce

¼ teaspoon sea salt

FOR THE CRAWFISH COCKTAIL

2 tablespoons vegetable oil

4 celery stalks, chopped

4 shallots, thinly sliced

4 garlic cloves, thinly sliced

1 (2-inch) knob ginger, peeled and cut into small dice

4 sprigs fresh thyme

2 cups seafood stock or vegetable stock (page 6 or store-bought)

6 allspice berries

2 Scotch bonnet peppers

2 tablespoons kosher salt

2 bay leaves

1 teaspoon smoked paprika

1 teaspoon Jamaican hot curry powder

1 pound fresh or frozen crawfish, washed and drained

1 tablespoon ghee or clarified butter (see note)

1 lemon, quartered

Hibiscus Punch (page 75), for serving

This appetizer bridges the flavorful Jamaican street food of pepper shrimp with the classic shrimp cocktail sauce, for a zesty start to any party. Pepper shrimp is usually made with janga, or freshwater crayfish, stewed with aromatics. I've opted to use Louisiana crawfish here. The spiciness of the crawfish and the zing of the cocktail sauce is brightened by the gingery punch, an homage to a traditional Jamaican sorrel drink.

TO MAKE THE COCKTAIL SAUCE: Combine all the sauce ingredients in a medium bowl.

TO MAKE THE CRAWFISH COCKTAIL: Heat the oil in a large saucepan over medium heat. Add the celery, shallots, garlic, ginger, and thyme and cook, stirring, for 2 minutes, then pour in the stock. Add the allspice, peppers, salt, bay leaves, paprika, and curry powder and bring the stock to a simmer. Simmer for 5 minutes, then add the crawfish and simmer for 8 minutes, or until the crawfish turn bright red.

Transfer the crawfish to a bowl with a slotted spoon and toss with the ghee until the crawfish are lightly coated and shimmering. Serve warm on a platter with cocktail sauce and lemon wedges, accompanied by Hibiscus Punch.

Notes

Crawfish are available for purchase online fresh or frozen and shipped to your home.

Clarified butter is melted butter with the milk solids removed. To make it: melt 1 stick of butter without stirring in a small saucepan over low heat for 10 to 12 minutes, or until the butter has melted and the solids separate from the fat. Turn off the heat and set the saucepan aside to cool for 5 minutes. Skim off the foam using a spoon, then pour off the clear yellow liquid in a separate bowl. The milk solids will have settled into the bottom of the pan. What you don't use immediately, cool completely and store in an airtight container in the refrigerator for up to 6 months.

Hibiscus Punch

Serves 4

4 cups cold water

1 cup sugar

1 (4-inch) stalk lemongrass, tough outer leaves removed, roughly chopped

1 (1-inch) knob ginger, peeled and thinly sliced

1 cup (8 ounces) dried hibiscus flowers

½ cup dried white hibiscus flowers (see note)

¼ cup Jamaican white rum

¼ cup freshly squeezed lemon juice

Club soda

1 lemon, quartered

8 pieces candied ginger

Heat the water in a medium saucepan over medium heat. Add the sugar, lemongrass, and ginger and bring to a simmer. Remove the pan from the heat, then sprinkle both types of hibiscus flowers in the water and steep them for 20 minutes. Strain the liquid into a pitcher and refrigerate.

When you're ready to serve the punch, fill four 12-ounce highball glasses with ice cubes. Pour 2 cups of the hibiscus tea, the rum, and half the lemon juice into a cocktail shaker and top with ice. (Reserve any leftover tea and juice for a second round.) Cover the shaker and shake the cocktail until it is mixed well. Strain into the glasses. Top with club soda, then garnish with a skewer of a lemon wedge and 2 pieces of candied ginger. Cheers!

Note

If you cannot find dried white hibiscus flowers at your local health food store, they are available online through my-greenheart.com or you can use the same amount of red hibiscus.

A Word or Two on Red Drink

As we toured Brooklyn's Little Caribbean community, in just about every homespun bakery, mom-and-pop restaurant, and corner market dotting Flatbush, Church, Utica, and Nostrand avenues, we sampled nearly every magenta-colored, hibiscus-infused tea or syrup we encountered. Known as bissap in Africa and sorrel throughout the Caribbean, this red drink with a centuries-old history is purported to be both a tonic and an anti-inflammatory, good for whatever ails you. Naturally tart from the dried calyxes, sorrel's flavor profile is sharpened by fresh ginger and sour orange, sweetened by cane sugar, and deepened by cloves and nutmeg. It also makes one fine rum punch.

Brooklyn's own Jackie Summers, the creator of Sorel Liqueur, believed so deeply in the drink's rich heritage, he distilled it into a successful liqueur that was the toast of the cocktail crowd . . . until it wasn't because he couldn't secure long-term financing. That all changed when Fawn Weaver, the founder of the distillery that brought both the whiskey and story of Uncle Nearest to the masses, helped Sum-

mers relaunch Sorel, which now is available nationwide through reservebar.com.

What Is the History of Sorrel?

All Black families have this ancestral memory of red drink. It goes back to West Africa. Our medicine was in plants and roots and trees that have natural antimicrobials, natural antioxidants. Hibiscus flowers have more vitamin C than most citrus fruit. It's an antimicrobial. It's an aphrodisiac. West Africans used it for all these great medicinal purposes.

And then, 500 years ago, when the slave trade started, they were stealing human bodies and importing these spices alongside the bodies. So, the knowledge of what this flower can do traveled, literally, alongside—in the bodies next to it. These bodies and this knowledge go to the Caribbean, and it takes root there. All the places that were ports for slavery are places where this beverage, this red drink, took root.

Are All Red Drinks the Same or Do They Have Regional Differences?

Depending on where you were in the spice trade, you would get different influences. In Jamaica, for example, you might get ginger and cardamom and rum. In Trinidad and Tobago, you might get Indonesian influences like cassia cinnamon, nutmeg, and clove. Every island did it a little differently. Every family definitely thinks theirs is the best. This knowledge has traveled for centuries—this thing with deep cultural significance that survived colonization.

What Do You Want People to Understand When They Sip Sorel?

Sorel Liqueur represents a culture that couldn't be killed. It represents the blood and the sacrifice of all those we lost on the way. That dramatic red color that is imprinted in our epigenetic memory.

Grilled Whole Snapper *with* Mango Slaw

Serves 4

FOR THE MARINADE

3 scallions, chopped

2 garlic cloves, coarsely chopped

2 sour oranges, quartered, or 1 cup sour orange juice (see page 28)

2 cinnamon sticks

1 medium onion, coarsely chopped

1 Scotch bonnet pepper, seeded and chopped

1 lemon, quartered

4 sprigs fresh thyme

1 (12-inch) piece lemongrass, tough outer leaves removed, cut into 4-inch pieces

2 cups pineapple juice

1 cup water

¼ cup soy sauce

2 tablespoons kosher salt

1 tablespoon freshly ground black pepper

1 tablespoon vegetable oil

2 (1½- to 2-pound) red snappers, scaled and cleaned, with heads (see note)

FOR THE SEASONING

2 tablespoons vegetable oil

1½ teaspoons kosher salt

½ teaspoon freshly ground black pepper

½ teaspoon granulated garlic

½ teaspoon granulated onion

⅛ teaspoon dried thyme

Mango Slaw (page 79)

Scarcity forces people to stretch ingredients, to use everything available from nose to tail. And leaning into scarcity reveals there are far more flavors and textures to enjoy than we realize. Whole fish cooking unveils so much more beyond the fillets along the spine—the sweetness of cheek meat to the firmer flesh near the tail to the crunchiness of the tail itself. You get a different bite from mouth to fin. Here the acid of the pineapple juice and citrus in the marinade and the sweetness and heat of the mango slaw play up the mild flavor of the snapper.

TO MARINATE THE SNAPPER: Combine all the marinade ingredients in a bowl. Pour half the marinade into a large baking dish, add the red snapper, pour the remaining marinade over the fish, then cover the dish with plastic wrap. Let the fish marinate at room temperature for 30 minutes or up to 8 hours in the refrigerator.

Preheat a gas or charcoal grill to medium heat (350°F).

In another bowl, whisk together the oil, salt, pepper, garlic, onion, and thyme for the seasoning. Remove the fish from the marinade, pat dry with a paper towel, and rub the fish inside and out with the seasoning mixture.

You can use a grilling grid or basket, or place the fish flat directly on the grill. Cook on one side for 10 minutes, until the skin is brown and flaky. Turn the fish over and continue to cook for another 8 minutes. Transfer the fish to a large platter and serve with the slaw.

Notes

Make the slaw while the fish marinates.

If you think your guests will be squeamish about the head, you can remove it after cooking (be sure to scoop out the sweet cheek meat and serve it with the rest of the fish). Or you can remove it before cooking and save it for making fish stock.

Mango Slaw

Serves 4

1 head red cabbage, thinly
sliced or shredded

1½ teaspoons kosher salt

1 orange, zested, then peeled
and segmented

Grated zest of 1 lime

2 tablespoons rice wine
vinegar

1 tablespoon red wine vinegar

1 tablespoon honey

2 jalapeño peppers, seeded
and thinly sliced

1 red bell pepper, thinly sliced

½ red onion, thinly sliced

1 mango, peeled, seeded, cut in
half lengthwise, and thinly
sliced

Pinch of crushed red pepper
flakes

Combine the cabbage and salt in a large bowl and let sit for
20 minutes.

Combine the orange segments and zest, lime zest, vinegars, and
honey. Pour over the cabbage and toss until the cabbage is evenly
coated.

Add the peppers, onion, mango, and red pepper flakes. Toss, then
let sit for 15 minutes before serving with the fish.

Little Caribbean

Brooklyn, New York

Shelley Worrell is a force of nature.

A first-generation daughter of Trinidadian parents, Worrell led the charge in 2017 to get the New York City mayor's office to officially designate the blocks between Nostrand, Flatbush, Utica, and Church avenues in Brooklyn as "Little Caribbean," the only such designation in the United States. For sixty years or more, immigrants from down island have transformed the twelve-block neighborhood adjacent to Prospect Park into a hub of cultural and social celebration among the Caribbean diaspora, a diverse mix of descendants of African, East Indian, Asian, European, and Indigenous peoples. This neighborhood is the largest concentration of West Indians outside of the islands.

Worrell founded and now directs the nonprofit arts, culture, and events organization CaribBEING. CaribBEING began as a film festival but has morphed into an incubator for Afro-Indo-LatinX artisans, entrepreneurs, and artists. She's also a helluva food tour guide.

She's got the owner of Labay Market on speed dial to see what provisions owner Big Mac has brought up from his sixty-acre family farm in Grenada and if he will have ready-mades such as bammy, accra, and ginger juice for the weekend.

"When you come here on the weekend," she says, "the lines are wrapped around the corner."

When she walks into Culpepper's Restaurant for a Barbadian take on oxtails or Allan's Bakery for a coconut roll, she catches up on the lives and loves of families who have helmed these businesses for three or more generations. At the new café Hibiscus Brew, she speaks to the nuances of sorrel.

We sample accra, or fish cakes, from four different places and all are slightly different in density,

Culpepper's Restaurant

Accra, or fish cakes

saltiness, and shape, but they have a lightness unlike the ones I've found in Atlanta, which are heavier, doughy, and the size of golf balls.

"Whether you're in Guadeloupe, Martinique, if you're in Barbados and Trinidad—like all across the entire Caribbean, you'll find them around," Worrell explains. "It's like street food. Or, if you're having a party, a delicacy."

Worrell keeps a close eye on the creeping gentrification beginning to push out the one-of-a-kind restaurants, boutiques, markets, and galleries that give the community its character and authenticity. Acting as an advocate for those small businesses, she helped rally neighbors to support a forty-year-old Jamaican ice cream and vegetarian eatery on Flatbush Avenue called Scoops, helping to raise funds so that it could stay in business after a new landlord raised the rent threefold.

As we walk from one end of the neighborhood to the other, Worrell points to new condominiums where houses used to be. "I called one of my friends," she says, "and I said, 'Can you drive around and just let me know if these places are still there where we used to eat?' And she was like, two of them are not. They're gone now."

Hibiscus Brew café

Saltfish Cakes *with* Chilled Ackee Soup *and* Mango Salsa

Serves 4

FOR THE SALTFISH CAKES

1 pound salted codfish

2 Yukon gold potatoes, peeled and cubed

2 large eggs, beaten

2 teaspoons kosher salt

1 white onion, chopped

2 garlic cloves, finely chopped

Grated zest of 1 lemon

1 jalapeño pepper, seeded and finely diced

6 stems fresh Italian parsley, stems removed and leaves chopped

4 sprigs fresh thyme, leaves removed

4 fresh chives, minced

½ teaspoon freshly ground white pepper

Pinch of crushed red pepper flakes

1 cup vegetable or coconut oil

Ackee Soup (page 83)

Mango Salsa (page 84)

When I travel, I frequent the hole-in-the-wall places and street vendors before a fine-dining establishment. If someone is on the side of the road, cooking in some remote spot, all the better. That's how I happened upon Jamaica's national dish: saltfish and ackee. I literally pulled over and sat there watching this man make this dish again and again. It is typically served for breakfast in the country, since the fruit of the ackee tree tastes uncannily like scrambled eggs. The rehydrated cod and ackee fruit are sautéed with peppers and onions and served alongside boiled rice or plantains.

For my saltfish cakes, I used as a cultural touchstone those served in the Little Caribbean neighborhood in the Flatbush section of Brooklyn, where bakeries, restaurants, and markets offer potato-codfish cakes that double as street food. Instead of mixing the ackee into the cakes, I created a cool, creamy, and mildly nutty-tasting soup brightened by the sweet-citrusy hit of mango.

Because the saltfish requires at least 8 hours of soaking, some preplanning is necessary.

TO MAKE THE SALTFISH CAKES: Soak the cod in a bowl of cold water in the refrigerator for 8 hours, draining the water and covering the fish in fresh water again after 4 hours. Repeat the process, draining and adding fresh water at the halfway point. Set aside.

Boil the potatoes in salted water in a large saucepan over medium-high heat, then turn the heat to medium-low and let the potatoes simmer for 15 minutes, until fork-tender. Drain, return to the pan, and return to medium heat for 30 seconds to dry the potatoes.

Using a potato masher, mash the potatoes coarsely until the lumps are about the size of small peas.

Flake the drained salted cod into the potatoes, then fold in the eggs and salt. Stir in the onion, garlic, lemon zest, jalapeño, herbs, white pepper, and red pepper flakes. Mix until thoroughly combined.

Using a small ice cream scoop or two spoons, scoop the saltfish mixture into golf ball–size rounds, then flatten them into disks. Place the saltfish cakes on a baking sheet, then freeze for 15 minutes.

In a large skillet, heat half the oil on medium heat until a bit of water sizzles in the pan. Fry the patties in batches, until golden brown, turning once, 3 to 5 minutes per side, adding the rest of the oil as needed. Remove the cakes from the skillet and set them on a paper towel–lined plate to dry. Serve them warm with a side of the salsa and a bowl of ackee soup.

Note

The soup and the salsa can be made a day ahead, while the saltfish soaks.

Ackee Soup

Serves 4

1 tablespoon unsalted butter

1 white onion, chopped

1 leek, white and light green parts only, rinsed well, and thinly sliced

2 Yukon gold potatoes, peeled and cut into 1-inch pieces

2 garlic cloves, smashed and finely chopped

1 (19-ounce) can ackee, drained

4 cups chicken stock (page 14 or store-bought)

2 teaspoons kosher salt

1 cup heavy cream

Fresh nutmeg, for grating

Melt the butter in a saucepan over medium heat until the butter foams and then clarifies, 2 to 3 minutes. Add the onion and leek and cook for 3 to 4 minutes, stirring. Add the potatoes and garlic and cook for another 3 to 4 minutes, until the onions are lightly browned.

Add the ackee and cook for 5 more minutes, then add the chicken stock and salt. Bring the soup to a simmer. Cover the pan and cook for 15 minutes, until the potatoes are cooked through. Remove from the heat and stir in the cream.

If using an immersion blender, blend the soup in the pan until smooth then transfer to a large bowl or container. If using a countertop blender, let the soup cool slightly, then transfer half the soup to the blender and blend until smooth. Pour the soup into a large container, then repeat with the other half. Grate fresh nutmeg over the soup and refrigerate. Serve cold with the saltfish cakes and salsa.

Note

Ackee is the fruit of an evergreen tree native to West Africa that grows lush throughout the Caribbean and South America. Unripe, ackee is deadly poisonous. Once fully ripened, the ackee's scarlet pods "yawn" open to reveal four black olive–shaped seeds surrounded by pale-yellow fleshy arils. The arils have a similar taste and consistency as garbanzo beans. They can be found frozen in Caribbean markets or canned online.

Mango Salsa

2 jalapeño peppers, seeded and finely diced

1 red bell pepper, finely diced

1 mango, peeled, seed removed, cut in half lengthwise, then diced into ¼-inch pieces

½ red onion, finely diced

Grated zest of 1 lime

2 tablespoons rice wine vinegar

1 tablespoon red wine vinegar

1 tablespoon honey

½ teaspoon kosher salt

Pinch of crushed red pepper flakes

4 fresh chives, finely diced

Stir together the peppers, mango, onion, lime zest, vinegars, honey, salt, and red pepper flakes in a bowl. Let sit for at least 10 minutes before serving, or you can make ahead and store in an airtight container in the refrigerator for up to 3 days. Just before serving, garnish the salsa with the chives.

Collard Greens *with* Boiler Potatoes Braised in Coconut Milk *and* Curry

Serves 4 to 6

2 tablespoons vegetable oil

1 white onion, finely diced

2 teaspoons kosher salt

1 teaspoon freshly ground black pepper

1 red bell pepper, cut into small dice

2 jalapeño peppers, seeded and finely diced

4 garlic cloves, chopped

1 tablespoon peeled minced ginger

4 bay leaves

¼ teaspoon dried thyme

1 tablespoon curry powder

¼ teaspoon chili powder

¼ teaspoon ground cumin

4 cups root vegetable stock (page 6 or store-bought)

1 (13.5-ounce) can coconut milk (not light)

Pinch of crushed red pepper flakes

8 to 10 small boiler potatoes (about the size of golf balls or smaller)

1½ to 2 pounds of collard greens, stemmed, leaves cut into 1-inch ribbons

2 to 3 scallions, chopped

Sharp nutrient-rich greens pair with small, skin-on potatoes in this filling vegetarian curry. The rich coconut milk imparts a non-dairy creaminess (many Africans are lactose-intolerant), while the addition of curry reflects the influence of the East Indians who were indentured into servitude by the English beginning in 1845. East Indians remain the largest ethnic minority in Jamaica today.

West Africans were accustomed to eating greens year-round in stews and juices as a mainstay of their diet, so when they arrived in the western hemisphere and found spinach, collards, and mustard greens, they knew how to use them.

Heat the oil in a dutch oven over medium heat. Add the onion and season with a pinch of salt and black pepper. Cook, stirring occasionally, for 4 to 6 minutes, until the onions have lightly browned.

Add the bell pepper, jalapeños, garlic, ginger, bay leaves, thyme, curry powder, chili powder, and cumin to the pot and cook for 2 minutes more.

Stir in the stock and coconut milk and bring the liquid to a simmer. Add the red pepper flakes and simmer for 5 more minutes. Add the potatoes and cook for 5 minutes, then add the greens.

Cook for 25 minutes, or until the greens are tender and a knife easily pierces the potatoes. Fish out the bay leaves. Once the greens are done, turn off the heat and let the greens rest for 15 minutes before serving.

Ladle the greens into bowls and garnish with the scallions.

Notes
- Other garnishes: pickled jalapeño, chow chow, or other pickled vegetables.
- As with all vegetables, cooking times can vary slightly. Check the potatoes for doneness halfway through the cooking process. If they are ready, remove them, finish cooking greens, and return them to pot just before serving.
- Winter collard greens may require longer cooking time than spring collards. More stock may be needed if the stock reduces too much, and greens may require longer to cook

North America

Mexico

The 1 percent of my DNA attributed to "Indigenous Americas-Mexico" was the most unexpected revelation in my ancestry, a clue that seven generations back, a great-great-great-great-great-great-grandparent was abducted from the Congo during the early 1600s and shipped as cargo to Heroica Veracruz. From there, he or she was sent to the silver mines in Guanajuato, or the sugar plantations of Morelos, or the textile factories of Oaxaca.

By the early 1800s, African descendants comprised 10 percent of Mexico's population. But only in the past twenty years have significant strides been made to recognize Africans as the "third root" of Mexican cultures and cuisines. Mexico long ago adopted a narrative that its darker citizens were the progeny of runaway slaves from the United States and the Caribbean—the "maroons"—escaping to a free Mexico, which had liberated itself from Spain in 1821 and abolished slavery eight years later.

As always, the truth is far more complicated.

Spanish conquest of North Africa conscripted primarily Islamic Africans as auxiliary soldiers and workers to aid in the colonization and mineral extraction of "New Spain." This invasion led to the decimation of Indigenous peoples, who numbered in the tens of millions but were reduced by more than 90 percent through wave upon wave of disease to which they had no immunity and forced into labor to which they had no recourse. In the years between 1520 and 1640, upward of 200,000 enslaved Africans were transported through the port at Veracruz.

Despite generations of quashing Afro-Mexican culture, Afromestizos have left an indelible mark on Mexican foodways, religion, and music. The sopas de chaya made of ground cornmeal and pulverized leaves recalls starchy provisions such as fufu. The heavily seasoned tomato-accented Spanish rice honors jollof. Meat-filled empanadas are the kissing cousins of Jamaican patties. Stewed and steamed chaya harkens back to callaloo, collards, and moringa. The whirl of the fandango mirrors the mystical dervishes of Northern Africa. The maracas, drums, and jaranas of the Costa Chica region's Son Jarocho folk music owe their history to djembes and koras, instruments played by ancient tribes along the equatorial coast of Africa as part of celebrations and rituals. Just like the venerable mole poblano, what is claimed as so authentically Mexican did not come to be without struggle, sacrifice, and transcendence.

The first time I tasted a mole poblano was on a chicken taco at a South Side Chicago restaurant. This mole had layer upon layer of smoke, but it was lighter than the ones I would encounter later in adulthood during those first excursions to Mexico, where pure chocolate and cinnamon darken its color and flavor it with a hint of bitterness. As an adult, when I began to experiment with making mole poblano, I recognized the ingredients—peanuts and seeds—and the smoking techniques of the ancho and chipotle peppers that came out of West African preservation methods. There are Arabic and Asian influences as well, and although the mole is identified with Mexico, where it has been perfected and refined, it represents all the confluences of Mexico's colonial history.

Mogo-Mogo: Smashed Plantain Porridge *with* Black Pepper *and* Sesame Seed Bacon

Serves 4

FOR THE BACON

1 teaspoon grapeseed or canola oil

8 strips thick-cut bacon

1 tablespoon cracked black pepper

1 tablespoon sesame seeds

1 tablespoon sugar

FOR THE MOGO-MOGO

1 tablespoon canola oil

2 semi-ripe (yellow, black speckled) plantains, peeled

1½ cups chicken or vegetable stock (page 14 or 6, or store-bought)

1 cup heavy cream

2 tablespoons bacon fat (reserved from cooking the bacon)

Pinch of kosher salt

2 tablespoons crumbled cotija cheese

1 sprig fresh cilantro, stem removed and leaves roughly chopped

With a base of salted mashed plantains, Mogo-Mogo's culinary thread runs straight through mofongo (recipe on page 45) to fufu. Yet Mogo-Mogo is a creamier version—standard breakfast fare for people in eastern Mexico often served with the crisp of pork cracklins and the starchy protein of refried beans. Here, I use thick-cut bacon to bring the salt and the smoke along with sesame seeds for a light nuttiness and crunchy texture. Sesame seeds, called ajonjolí in Latin American nations, are a hallmark of Afromestizo cuisine in and around the southwestern coast near Guerrero, where sesame seeds have been grown on former cotton and sugar plantations since the early 1900s. The cojita cheese imparts a cool burst of salted creaminess to the warm mashed plantains.

TO MAKE THE BACON: Preheat the oven to 350°F. Line a baking sheet with foil and glaze the foil with the oil. Lay the bacon slices on the foil so that they do not overlap.

Mix the pepper, sesame seeds, and sugar in a small bowl. Generously sprinkle each piece of bacon with the pepper mixture.

Bake for 15 to 25 minutes, until the bacon is brown and crispy, even a little charred around the edges.

Transfer the bacon to a paper towel–lined plate to drain. Pour the bacon fat from the baking sheet into a glass measuring cup and reserve for the porridge.

TO MAKE THE MOGO-MOGO: Heat the oil over medium heat in a deep-sided skillet with a lid. Lay the plantains in the skillet and cook until lightly caramelized all around, 3 to 4 minutes per turn.

Pour the stock into the skillet then cover and cook for 10 minutes, or until the plantains are tender. Remove the cover, pour in the heavy cream, then cook uncovered for 5 minutes more.

Remove the skillet from the heat and transfer the plantains and sauce to a large bowl. Using a potato masher, smash the plantains into a fine porridge. Fold the bacon fat into the mixture then season with salt.

< recipe continues >

TO SERVE: Divide the porridge among four bowls and sprinkle with the cotija cheese. Garnish with cilantro leaves and serve with the peppered bacon on the side.

Note

Semi-ripe plantains are a little less sweet and a lot more savory—ideal for a sustaining breakfast. Their firm but malleable texture gives the porridge a full-bodied consistency.

What Is a Benne Seed?

Benne—or sesame—seeds come from hardy, drought-tolerant annuals that produce greens, pods, seeds, and oils—all edible and with multiple benefits, from skin moisturizing to nutrition-packed crunchiness. The plant dates back more than four centuries in Africa and began its migration along with slaves to the Americas. Although the seeds were introduced into South America and Mexico during the 1500s, they didn't take root in the coastal American South until the 1700s, along with the rise in rice cultivation and cookery.

Peanut, Pumpkin, *and* Chile Salsa

Makes 1½ quarts

4 cups water

2 tablespoons kosher salt

1 small (4-pound) sugar pumpkin, such as a Baby Pam or Autumn Gold, peeled, seeded, and diced into small chunks

1 chipotle pepper

Grated zest and juice of 1 lime

¼ cup extra virgin olive oil

3 tablespoons red wine vinegar

1 tablespoon sugar

2 shallots, sliced into thin rounds

2 garlic cloves, thinly sliced

2 jalapeño peppers, seeded and finely diced

1 red pepper, small diced

1 cup roasted and salted peanuts, slightly crushed

Note

If sugar pumpkins are hard to find, you can substitute acorn squash in this recipe.

Salsa is the number one condiment sold in the United States, but we have a narrow view of its versatility beyond the familiar iteration of tomatoes, onions, jalapeño peppers, and cilantro. This salsa made with ingredients from the Americas speaks to the shared story between indigenous Mexican cultures and the influence of West Africans on native foodways. In addition to being refreshingly packed with heat from the layers of peppers, it has a gentle smokiness from the chipotle, a tart sweetness from the pumpkin and vinegar, and an indelible crunch from the peanuts. During pumpkin season, keep this salsa on hand in the refrigerator to garnish fall and winter soups and stews, mix into salads, serve as a dip for toasted pita or roti, or use as a topping on your favorite tacos.

Bring the water and salt to a boil in a large saucepan over high heat. Add the pumpkin and simmer for 5 minutes or until tender but not mushy. Using a slotted spoon, transfer the pumpkin to a bowl and set in the refrigerator to cool for 10 minutes.

Combine the chipotle pepper, lime zest and juice, olive oil, vinegar, and sugar in a large mixing bowl, whisking vigorously to dissolve the sugar. Stir in the shallots, garlic, jalapeño peppers, and peanuts. Toss the pumpkin into the salsa mixture, making sure to coat the pumpkin well without breaking or mashing the chunks.

Pumpkin and Squash

Pumpkins and other squashes originated in Mexico in and around the Oaxaca Valley as far back as 7000 BCE and grew into a cultivated crop a century later. In the sixteenth century, Spanish explorers carried pumpkins all along their trade routes, including to Africa. There, along the subtropical coast, West Africans had been cooking with calabash, young bottle gourds, for centuries after they were brought in by Muslim traders from Asia. So, the pumpkin was easily adapted into the West African diet. When the transatlantic slave trade began, West Africans found familiarity in the pumpkins available in the Caribbean, Latin America, and the American South.

Sweet *and* Spicy Grilled Chicken Tenderloin *with* Chipotle *and* Tamarind Glaze *and* Crushed Peanuts

Serves 4

FOR THE CHICKEN AND MARINADE

1 pound chicken tenderloins

4 cups warm water

1 lime, quartered

1 serrano pepper, cut in half widthwise

1 garlic clove, smashed

½ cup kosher salt

¼ cup sugar

FOR THE GLAZE

½ cup water

2 chipotle peppers

1 jalapeño pepper, sliced into thin rounds

2 garlic cloves, finely diced

1 shallot, sliced into thin rings

Grated zest and juice of 1 lime

½ cup tamarind paste

½ cup honey

¼ cup rum

2 tablespoons Maggi seasoning or soy sauce

½ teaspoon ground ginger

FOR THE CHICKEN SKEWERS

4 tablespoons kosher salt

2 tablespoons smoked paprika

2 tablespoons ground black pepper

2 teaspoons granulated onion

2 teaspoons granulated garlic

2 teaspoons ground cumin

2 teaspoons chili powder

1 teaspoon dried thyme

1 teaspoon ground ginger

This dish reminds me of the magical realism so prevalent among Latin American literature. How something so earthbound, like a bland chicken tenderloin, can be suffused with the fantastical, the zing from peppers and tamarind. The push-and-pull between sweet and spicy in this dish is a flavor combo full of subtleties. The balance of art and science, of faith and alchemy. Something meant to nourish can also play with the endorphins in your brain. The saltiness keeps you coming back for more, and the hint of bitterness aids in digestion. The heat brings excitement. The sweetness, remembrance.

Marinades aren't meant only to infuse flavor, but also to tenderize and preserve, a technique the ancients understood, not because they had backgrounds in food science, but because they lived so deeply in harmony with the land and nature and had come to know through trial and error the energy-giving and medicinal properties of plants. This is an ideal Sunday or celebration dish because it takes a little extra time to prepare and the presentation on skewers makes it a little more special. Serve with Red Rice (recipe on page 98).

TO MARINATE THE CHICKEN: Rinse and pat dry the chicken tenderloin. Set aside while you prepare the marinade.

Stir together the water, lime, serrano pepper, garlic, salt, and sugar in a 2-quart mixing bowl or food storage container. Continue to stir until the sugar completely dissolves. Submerge the chicken tenderloin in the marinade and let it steep at room temperature for no more than 2 hours. If you want to marinate the chicken overnight, cut the salt to ¼ cup and refrigerate the chicken. Remove the chicken from the refrigerator at least 1 hour before cooking to bring it to room temperature.

TO MAKE THE GLAZE: Bring the water to a simmer in a medium saucepan over medium-low heat. Add the peppers, garlic, shallot, lime zest and juice, tamarind paste, honey, rum, Maggi seasoning, and ginger, then simmer for 5 minutes, stirring occasionally, until the tamarind paste is fully melted. Set aside.

TO PREPARE THE CHICKEN SKEWERS: Preheat the oven or prepare your grill for high heat (400°F). If using wooden skewers, soak them in cold water for at least 30 minutes.

½ teaspoon ground turmeric

½ cup vegetable oil

2 sprigs fresh cilantro, chopped

2 sprigs fresh curly parsley, chopped

Remove the chicken from the marinade, pat the tenderloins dry, and place them on a baking sheet. Slide one skewer into each chicken tenderloin.

Mix all the dried spices together in a small bowl. Drizzle the oil over both sides of the tenderloins, then sprinkle the spices generously all over the tenderloins.

Grill the skewers until golden brown, approximately 4 minutes on each side. If cooking in the oven, arrange the skewers on a baking sheet or broiler pan. Bake for 4 to 5 minutes, then turn the skewers to cook for 4 to 5 minutes more.

Pull the skewers from the grill or oven, then brush the tenderloins all over with the glaze and garnish with the cilantro and parsley. Serve the remaining glaze as a dipping sauce on the side should you and your guests want more (they'll want more).

Grilled Quail Tacos on Flour Tortillas *with* Mole Poblano, Pickled Red Onions, *and* Red Rice

Serves 4 to 6

FOR THE TORTILLAS

4 cups all-purpose flour

1 teaspoon white cornmeal

1½ teaspoons salt

¼ teaspoon chili powder

Pinch of cayenne pepper

¼ cup lard

1½ cups hot water

FOR THE QUAIL

12 quail breasts

4 cups water

2 garlic cloves, coarsely chopped

1 shallot, coarsely chopped

1 sour orange, quartered, or ½ cup sour orange juice (see page 28)

1 lemon, quartered

2 tablespoons kosher salt, plus extra

1 tablespoon coarsely ground black pepper, plus extra

1 tablespoon Worcestershire Sauce (page 72 or store-bought)

2 bay leaves

2 tablespoons vegetable oil

1 lime, quartered

FOR THE PICKLED RED ONIONS

1 red onion, halved and thinly sliced

½ cup red wine vinegar

½ teaspoon kosher salt

½ bunch fresh cilantro, stems removed and leaves roughly chopped

I still can taste the mole poblano that sauced the street taco I ate from a South Side Chicago taqueria during my teens. Its earthy intensity was such a striking contrast to the sweet barbecue sauces I was accustomed to, but its smoky complexity held a strange familiarity—probably because our neighborhood backed right up to the Latino enclaves where Mexican and Central American families lived, and I could often smell slow-roasted goat, lamb, or beef wafting over the fences. Although a wee ground scrub bird, quail's rich essence, more akin to dark meat chicken or duck, stands up well to the sauce. The pickled onion brings a sharp acidity to balance the flavors. The texture and flavor of homemade tortillas offers a rustic authenticity to this dish, but feel free to use store-bought tortillas instead of making your own.

TO MAKE THE TORTILLAS: Stir together the flour, cornmeal, salt, chili powder, and cayenne pepper in a large mixing bowl.

Cut the lard into the flour mixture with your fingers until the flour mixture resembles a coarse meal or peas. Fold in the hot water until the dough comes together.

Place the tortilla dough on a cold, flat surface and knead 10 to 15 times, until the mixture is smooth. Separate the dough into 12 evenly sized balls, then, using a rolling pin, roll each ball into a circle about an ⅛-inch thick.

In a cast-iron skillet over medium heat, cook each tortilla about 1 minute per side until lightly brown. Stack the tortillas atop each other and cover them with a damp cloth to keep soft.

When ready to serve, preheat the oven to 300°F. Wrap the tortillas in foil in stacks of six and warm in the oven for 10 to 15 minutes.

TO MAKE THE QUAIL: Wash and pat dry the quail breasts, then set aside.

Bring the water to boil in a medium saucepan over medium heat. Remove the pot from the heat and stir in the garlic, shallot, sour orange, lemon, salt, pepper, Worcestershire Sauce, and bay leaves. Continue to stir until the salt completely dissolves. Let the water cool to room temperature, approximately 30 minutes.

Place the quail breasts in a heavy-duty gallon-size plastic bag with secure seal. Pour the cooled brine over the quail breasts, seal the

< recipe continues >

ROOTS, HEART, SOUL

FOR THE MOLE

3 tablespoons vegetable oil

6 ancho chilies, hydrated in water, stems removed

4 poblano peppers, stems and seeds removed, chopped

2 jalapeño peppers, seeded and chopped

2 white onions, chopped

6 garlic cloves, roughly chopped

6 ounces sun-dried tomatoes, hydrated in water

1/4 cup whole roasted unsalted peanuts, roughly chopped

1/4 cup whole raw almonds, roughly chopped

1/4 cup dried currants or raisins

1 cup dry sherry

4 cups chicken or vegetable stock (page 14 or 6, or store-bought)

6 star anise

6 sprigs fresh thyme, stems removed and leaves roughly chopped

6 sprigs fresh Mexican oregano, roughly chopped

2 cinnamon sticks

1 tablespoon kosher salt

1 teaspoon whole black peppercorns

4 fresh bay leaves or 6 dried bay leaves

1/2 cup Mexican chocolate or 75 percent dark chocolate

bag securely, then set the quail breasts in the refrigerator for at least 1 hour.

While the quail brines, make the pickled red onions, mole, and Red Rice (recipe on page 98).

Heat a grill to medium-high heat, 375°F. Remove the quail breasts from the brine and pat dry with a paper towel. Coat the quail with vegetable oil, season with salt and pepper, then grill the quail for 2 to 4 minutes per side, until firm to the touch and juices run clear.

Place the grilled quail breasts on a platter and garnish with the lime wedges.

TO MAKE THE PICKLED RED ONION: Stir the red onion, vinegar, salt, and cilantro in a bowl. Set aside for at least 30 minutes.

TO MAKE THE MOLE: Warm the oil in a medium saucepan over medium heat, then add the chilies, peppers, onion, garlic, sun-dried tomatoes, peanuts, and almonds. Cook for 6 to 8 minutes, until the onions are caramelized.

Add the currants and sherry to the pot and cook until the liquid is reduced by half, 7 to 10 minutes. Then stir in the stock, anise, thyme, oregano, cinnamon, salt, and peppercorns. Bring the sauce to a simmer. Add the bay leaves, then cook, partially covered, for 20 minutes.

Turn off the heat, then stir in the chocolate. Let the sauce stand undisturbed for 15 minutes.

Remove the anise, cinnamon sticks, and bay leaves. Using an immersion blender, blend the sauce until combined and smooth as silk. (If you do not have an immersion blender, use a regular blender. Fill the carafe halfway full, and start on the lowest speed, gradually increasing the speed until the sauce is smooth. Repeat until all the sauce is blended.) Keep the sauce warm until ready to assemble your tacos.

TO ASSEMBLE THE TACOS: Place a tablespoon of Red Rice (recipe on page 98) in the center of a tortilla, top with a quail breast and a heaping tablespoon of mole poblano sauce. Garnish with the pickled red onion and enjoy.

Notes

You can make the tortillas ahead of time, store them in a plastic bag with a tight seal, and refrigerate until you are ready to use them, up to 1 week. To reheat, preheat your oven to 350°F. Pull the stack of tortillas out of the plastic bag and wrap them in aluminum foil. Heat for 15 to 20 minutes before serving.

To get that same smoky flavor as homemade tortillas while using store-bought, mix 2 tablespoons unsalted butter and ½ teaspoon Sazón (recipe on page 15). Melt a teaspoon of the seasoned butter in a cast-iron skillet over medium-high heat, then lay a tortilla in the skillet and let it slightly char, 1 to 2 minutes. Flip it over and repeat on the other side. Repeat for each tortilla.

Do not substitute regular oregano for Mexican oregano. Mexican oregano imparts citrusy notes, as it comes from the verbena family and is an altogether different plant from regular oregano, which comes from the mint family. You can find Mexican oregano in most grocery stores. If you cannot find it, substitute dried marjoram or dried verbena.

You can find fresh or frozen quail in most supermarkets, but feel free to substitute Cornish game hens if quail is out of season or hard to locate.

Red Rice

Serves 4

3 cups chicken or vegetable stock (page 14 or 6, or store-bought)

4 sun-dried tomatoes

2 tablespoons tomato paste

1 tablespoon vegetable oil

1 yellow onion, finely diced

2 garlic cloves, thinly sliced

2 cups long grain white rice

2 bay leaves

1 teaspoon kosher salt

¼ teaspoon dried Mexican oregano

Bring the stock and sun-dried tomatoes to a simmer in a medium saucepan over medium heat and simmer for 10 minutes. Add the tomato paste and stir until it is dissolved.

In another saucepan, heat the oil over medium heat, then cook the onions and garlic for 4 to 5 minutes, until the onions have grown translucent.

Add the rice, bay leaves, salt, and oregano to the pot. Strain the chicken stock through a fine mesh sieve into the rice, cover, and bring to a gentle simmer. Turn the heat to low and cook for an additional 15 minutes, or until all the liquid is absorbed.

Remove the rice from the heat, keeping it covered. Remove the bay leaves and and let it rest for at least 10 minutes before serving.

Horchata *with* Cinnamon Cookies *and* Ancho Chili-Sugar Rim

Serves 4 to 6

1 cup uncooked short grain white rice

1 cinnamon stick, preferably Ceylon cinnamon

¼ teaspoon vanilla bean paste

¼ teaspoon kosher salt

4 cups hot water

2 cups sweetened almond milk

1 cup cold water

FOR THE SUGAR RIM

Grated zest and juice of 1 lime

1 cup turbinado sugar

½ cup granulated sugar

1 teaspoon ancho chili powder

1 teaspoon kosher salt

½ teaspoon ground cinnamon

This is the ultimate milk-and-cookies dessert, good for an afternoon snack or following a rich and piquant repast. The cool, creamy horchata offers a lightly sweet ending to a meal while also taking the heat down just a notch. Seasoned with Ceylon cinnamon—considered the true cinnamon that came to Mexico in the 1500s—the hit of spice paired with the mild nuttiness of the rice milk evokes the historic ancestry of tiger nut. The pillowy cookies—crisp on the edges, tender in the center—are made for dunking.

Place the rice, cinnamon stick, vanilla bean paste, and salt in a large bowl. Pour the hot water over the rice, then cover the bowl with plastic wrap. Let the rice steep for a minimum of 4 hours or until the rice has softened into rice milk.

Stir the almond milk and cold water into the rice milk until completely incorporated.

Fill a blender carafe halfway with the rice milk mixture, then purée until smooth. Strain the rice milk mixture through a sieve into a quart-size pitcher. Repeat the process until all the rice milk has been puréed. Chill the rice milk until ready to serve.

When ready to serve, make the Ancho Chili–Sugar Rim: In a medium bowl, thoroughly stir together the lime zest, sugars, chili powder, and salt. Dip the rims of four Collins glasses or six lowball glasses in the lime juice, then the sugar mixture. Fill the glasses with ice cubes, followed by the horchata. Sprinkle ground cinnamon on top of the horchata and serve with a chaser of Cinnamon Cookies (recipe on page 101).

Notes

Horchata is not cooked and should always be refrigerated. Horchata will keep for up to 5 days.

If the horchata is too thick after puréeing, stir in up to 1 cup hot water to thin.

History in a Glass

The roots of horchata, the spiced cream agua fresca with ancient origins, run to northern Nigeria, where the tiger nut, or "imumu" in Yoruban, grew—quite literally—like a weed. Not a nut at all, the tiger nut is the tender, brown tuber of the nutsedge plant that, when ground and soaked in water, produces a refreshing, spicy, almond-tasting milk that both quenches thirst and imparts energy for laboring in the hot sun.

During the Islamic conquest of the Iberian Peninsula during the Middle Ages, North African Muslims carried horchata de chufa to Spain, which then was carried to the Americas by Spaniards, conscripted North African soldiers, then by enslaved Africans in the 1500s.

Instead of tiger nuts, rice from Africa, almonds from Iran, and sometimes squash or melon seeds from Mexico became the foundational "milk." Vanilla, indigenous to Mexico, and cinnamon were incorporated, becoming the cornerstone of the horchata most associated with the Texas Mexican cuisine we enjoy today.

Texas Mexican chef, writer, and documentarian Adán Medrano, in an interview with John T. Edge of the Southern Foodways Alliance, described horchata as a story of relationships, a food that "transcends politically imposed borders." In one cool glass, horchata is the embodiment of something created from what Adán terms "need and dispossession."

Cinnamon Cookies

Makes 24 cookies

1 large egg, separated and brought to room temperature

¾ cup sugar

½ teaspoon vanilla extract, preferably Mexican vanilla

¼ teaspoon almond extract

2 cups vegetable shortening

2 cups all-purpose flour

2 cups bread flour

3 teaspoons baking soda

1½ teaspoons ground cinnamon

Whip the egg white in a large bowl on high speed for 4 to 5 minutes until stiff peaks form.

In a separate bowl, stir together the egg yolk, sugar, vanilla, and almond extract until thoroughly combined. Fold the egg yolk mixture into the egg whites, scooping from the bottom to the top until the mixture is light yellow and airy.

In another bowl, whip the shortening on high speed until it is smooth and fluffy, approximately 2 minutes. Gently fold the shortening into the egg whites until all the white streaks are gone.

Stir the flours, baking soda, and cinnamon together in a medium bowl, then fold the dry ingredients into the wet ingredients until together they make a light dough. Set the bowl aside and let the dough rest for 5 minutes.

Turn the dough onto a clean counter surface and knead the dough by pressing it away, then folding it toward you, turning it one quarter, then repeating until you have made one full circle.

Pat the dough into a disk, then roll it with a flour-dusted rolling pin to ¼-inch thickness.

Line two baking sheets with parchment paper, and preheat the oven to 350°F.

Using a two-inch round or scalloped cookie cutter, cut the cookies and lay them about 2 inches apart on a baking sheet. Gather any scraps of dough and shape them into a disk, then reroll the dough and repeat until all the cookies are cut out. Refrigerate for 30 minutes.

Bake one sheet at a time for 8 to 10 minutes, or until the cookies turn a golden brown. For even cooking, turn the sheet halfway through the baking time. Once the cookies are done, let them rest on the baking sheet for 3 to 5 minutes, then transfer them to wire racks to cool completely. Serve alongside the Horchata (recipe on page 99). The cookies can be stored in an airtight container for up to one week.

American South and Appalachia

Strange that the portal through which institutionalized chattel slavery opened in what would become the United States was named Point Comfort. I am certain that the ancestors on my mother's side, who were part of those first Africans, felt no comfort as they came in chains to Virginia and were sold in town squares throughout the Shenandoah Valley, the Carolinas, and into Kentucky. Just how far back my lineage stretches remains unknown, although my auntie Cherie and my sister, Kea, continue searching. They are the genealogical researchers and memory-keepers, and both keep finding new leaves on the branches of our family's tree.

My maternal great-great-great-grandfather, Bentley Childs, is listed in the 1870 Census as a Civil War veteran. He fought for the Union Army, helped hold this nation together, and put an end to legalized slavery—all from the border state of Kentucky where the enslaved numbered more than 225,000 in the decade before his emancipation. There in the bluegrass, my kin mingled with indentured Irish immigrants and Swedish and German settlers—whether by will or by force, I do not know.

I believe I have long held an affinity for Southern foods more aligned with the Appalachian region—roasted root vegetables, stuffed game birds, and cornmeal-crusted freshwater fish; pickled green beans, okra, and spring onions; fresh-fruited cobblers and pies; and caramel-kissed bourbons—because of these ancestral ties. Without my ever fully understanding their pull until now, I know in my heart that my life's work as a chef in Louisville and Atlanta is, in some way, my going back from whence my family came.

My father's people came up out of Louisiana and Alabama, which most likely means my story has links to Haiti, the Dominican Republic, and Mexico. It is why my father's gift to our dinner table included the conviviality of red rice and beans—a Monday dish, just like in New Orleans—spicy shrimp gumbos, and sweet barbecue sauces mopped across tender grilled meats.

On both sides, faith traditions ran deep and evangelical. Just like their foods, my family carried faith through even their leanest moments, and they made room at the table for another seat. And despite a history that, until recently, has diminished the contributions of African Americans, I can attest that my roots in this soil reach as far back as the 1600s, making me as American as any apple pie.

Hoppin' John *with* Turnip Greens *and* Yellow Rice

Serves 4 to 6

1 pound dried Sea Island red peas, or dried black-eyed peas

2 tablespoons vegetable oil

1 medium white onion, finely diced

2 turnips, peeled and cut into 8 equal pieces, greens washed and reserved (you will need ½ pound greens; or substitute kale)

2 teaspoons kosher salt

1 teaspoon freshly ground black pepper

2 celery stalks, washed, cut in half lengthwise, and finely diced

4 garlic cloves, smashed and roughly chopped

4 jalapeño peppers, seeded and finely diced

4 dried bay leaves, or 2 fresh bay leaves

¼ teaspoon dried thyme, or 2 sprigs fresh thyme

3 cups vegetable stock (page 6 or store-bought)

2 tablespoons harissa paste

1 teaspoon smoked paprika

¼ teaspoon ground cumin

Yellow Rice (page 105)

2 to 3 scallions, chopped

It's not hard to trace the lineage of Hoppin' John to jollof (recipe on page 18) or to make a connection to the red rice and beans of Haiti and New Orleans or the moros (black beans and yellow rice) of Cuba. All are rice dishes punctuated with vegetables, legumes, and seasoned with salted meats. All come from places where people of African descent shaped the cuisine. Yet, it's harder to figure out how a dish of mixed rice and peas, served as sustenance on slave ships, became associated with good luck and fortune in the New Year. According to an article by Robert Moss for Serious Eats, Charleston, South Carolina's Hibernian Society served Hoppin' John for good luck at its annual New Year's Day dinner as far back as 1909. Perhaps more practically, a big pot of tender cowpeas, collards, and rice deep into the lean winter months when not much was growing along the coast of Georgia and the Carolinas hinted that spring would come. The version I present here is vegetarian and fired with peppers and harissa paste. Don't hesitate to add sausage, smoked turkey, or shrimp if you desire.

Rinse the dried peas through a fine strainer, then pick through and discard any rocks, dirt, or other foreign objects. Place the peas in a bowl and cover with cold water. Soak the peas for 6 to 8 hours or overnight.

When you are ready to cook the peas, drain them and set aside.

Heat a large dutch oven on medium heat, then drizzle with the oil. Add the onion, turnips, and a pinch of the salt and black pepper. Cook for 4 to 6 minutes, until the onions have slightly browned. Add the celery, garlic, peppers, bay leaves, and thyme, then cook for 2 minutes more. Stir in the peas, remaining salt and black pepper, stock, harissa paste, paprika, and cumin, cover, and bring to a simmer. Turn the heat to low and cook the peas for 45 minutes or until fork tender.

Remove the peas from the heat. Stir in the turnip greens and let stand for 15 minutes so that the greens slightly wilt but retain their color. Remove the bay leaves and fresh thyme sprigs, then serve the peas over Yellow Rice and garnish with the scallions.

Notes

Sea Island red peas are available through mail order from Anson Mills and Marsh Hen Mill.

When searching for turnips, pick ones that have young greens.

< recipe continues >

Traditional Hoppin' John calls for bacon or ham hock, which can be added to this dish once you add the peas and vegetable stock.

Other garnishes can include pickled jalapeño, chow chow, or other pickled vegetables.

Smoked fish such as trout, oysters, or scallops can be added to the dish at the 35-minute mark when cooking the peas. Or add 1 pound of fresh shrimp with the turnip greens.

Yellow Rice

Serves 4

2 tablespoons vegetable oil

1 medium onion, finely diced

2 garlic cloves, smashed and finely diced

2 bay leaves

6 whole black peppercorns

1 cup Carolina Gold rice, or other long grain rice

1 teaspoon ground turmeric

¼ teaspoon sea salt, or slightly less than ½ teaspoon kosher salt

2 cups vegetable stock (page 6 or store-bought)

Heat the oil in a medium saucepan over medium heat. Stir in the onion, garlic, bay leaves, peppercorns, and rice, and cook for 3 to 4 minutes, until the rice and onions start to brown slightly.

Stir in the turmeric and salt, then add the stock and simmer, covered, for 20 to 25 minutes over medium-low heat, or until the liquid has fully absorbed and evaporated.

Remove the rice from the heat and let it rest for 5 to 10 minutes. Fluff the rice with a fork before serving.

Notes

Peppercorns can be fragrant if eaten whole, or they can be removed before serving.

If turmeric is not available, substitute ½ teaspoon yellow curry powder.

Scallion *and* Smoked Cheddar Cornbread Fritters *with* Red Pepper Honey

Serves 6

½ cup all-purpose flour

½ cup yellow cornmeal

1 teaspoon kosher salt

1 teaspoon baking soda

Pinch of cayenne pepper

¼ teaspoon black pepper

¼ teaspoon granulated garlic

½ cup buttermilk

2 large eggs, beaten

2 tablespoons unsalted butter, melted

1 bunch fresh Italian parsley, stems removed and leaves chopped

1 ounce smoked cheddar cheese, cut into small cubes (¼ cup)

2 scallions, white and green parts sliced

4 cups vegetable oil, for frying

¼ cup cheddar cheese powder for dusting (see note)

Coarse sea or kosher salt

At my restaurant Soul: Food & Culture in Atlanta's Krog Street Market, I serve a version of this dish in the form of Collard Green Hushpuppies. Perfect little deep-fried poppers as a starter or side for the Hot Fried Catfish sandwich or Fish and Spaghetti (recipe on page 220). Hushpuppies are essentially street food—dense, ready for travel, and enjoyed hot or room temperature. For this version, I've concocted a light fritter, best served hot alongside the Grilled Catfish (recipe on page 109) with a dip of savory-sweet honey.

Whisk together the flour, cornmeal, kosher salt, baking soda, cayenne pepper, black pepper, and granulated garlic in a mixing bowl. In a separate mixing bowl, stir together the buttermilk, eggs, butter, and parsley. Fold the dry ingredients into the wet ingredients, followed by the cheese and scallions. Mix until well combined, but do not overmix.

Bring the oil to 350°F over medium-high heat in a deep skillet or stockpot. Using a large spoon or a small ice cream scoop, measure about a tablespoon of the fritter batter into the oil and repeat until the surface of the oil is about 75 percent filled. Fry the fritters for 4 minutes on one side, then flip using tongs or a slotted spoon and cook on the other side for an additional 3 to 4 minutes until golden brown.

Transfer the fritters to a paper towel–lined plate to drain.

Place the hot fritters in a bowl and dust them with cheddar cheese powder. To serve, place the fritters on a platter and garnish with a sprinkle of coarse sea salt and a dipping bowl of Red Pepper Honey (recipe on page 108).

Notes

If you don't have buttermilk on hand, add 1½ teaspoons of freshly squeezed lemon juice to ½ cup whole or 2 percent milk for a buttermilk substitute.

For people with gluten sensitivities, substitute the exact same amount of gluten-free for the all-purpose flour.

Experiment with flavor profiles using aged cheddar, white cheddar, or smoked gouda.

You can find a good quality cheddar powder, such as the kind used on cheddar popcorn, from King Arthur Flour. It is available on Amazon, through spice shops, and at most specialty grocery stores.

Red Pepper Honey

Makes ⅔ cup

1 large red bell pepper, finely diced

1 medium onion, finely diced

2 tablespoons whiskey or bourbon

½ cup honey

Pinch of kosher salt

In a dry medium-size saucepan over medium heat, sauté the red pepper and onion for 2 minutes, stirring frequently, until softened.

Turn off the heat, add the whiskey, and let the mixture steep for five minutes. Stir in the honey. Turn the heat back to medium and bring the mixture to a simmer, constantly stirring. Turn off the heat, sprinkle a pinch of salt, then pour the honey into a dipping bowl to serve warm. Store leftovers in an airtight container in the refrigerator for up to 1 week.

Notes

Use a completely dry pan to ensure the honey has no oily texture.

Substitute dark rum if whiskey is unavailable.

Experiment with different honeys for this dish, including wild honey or even black truffle honey. If you can find one that is locally sourced, all the better, because you'll have the added benefit of its healing properties, such as protecting against seasonal allergies.

Grilled Catfish *with* Grilled Spring Onions *and* Creamed Potato Hash *with* Mustard Greens

Serves 4

FOR THE CATFISH BRINE

4 (8-ounce) catfish fillets

4 cups water

1 lemon, quartered

1 lime, quartered

2 sprigs fresh thyme

2 bay leaves

¼ cup sugar

2 tablespoons kosher salt

½ tablespoon whole black
    peppercorns

**FOR THE GRILLED FISH AND
SPRING ONIONS**

2 spring onions, green ends
    trimmed, halved lengthwise

2 tablespoons vegetable oil

2 tablespoons dry rub
    (page 207)

Creamed Potato Hash
    (page 110), for serving

You read that right: *grilled* catfish. Not fried. My grandma stopped frying catfish after my uncle began having health problems. Grilled is the more authentic way to eat fish anyway. Still, most people don't think to brine fish before they sear it. But, once a fish is out of the water, it's already dry. Brining reconstitutes the fish and helps bring it as close to fresh from the sea (or lake) as possible. This is particularly true for oily fish. Once the flesh begins to dry, the skin produces more oil, which can produce an off-putting fishy flavor and flakiness; brining helps prevent this.

TO BRINE THE FISH: Rinse the catfish fillets and pat them dry.

Stir the remaining brining ingredients together in a large mixing bowl or food storage container until the sugar dissolves. Submerge the fillets in the brining liquid and marinate for 1 hour at room temperature.

TO GRILL THE FISH AND SPRING ONIONS: Preheat your grill to medium-high heat (375°F to 400°F).

Remove the catfish fillets from the brine, rinse, and pat them dry. Rub the fillets and onions all over with the oil, then lightly season all sides of the fillets and onions with the rub seasoning.

Lay the onions cut side down on the hottest part of the grill and set the fillets on the grill at least 4 inches away from the heat source.

Once the onions begin to caramelize, turn them over and continue to grill them until they are tender, approximately 4 minutes on each side.

After 5 minutes, turn the fillets over and grill until the fish just starts to flake, approximately 3 minutes.

Transfer the spring onions and fillets to a platter. Serve with the Creamed Potato Hash.

Notes

If you are using previously frozen fish, know that it already has been brined. You may still wish to brine it; even though it won't absorb much more water, it will absorb the flavors.

You can make the Creamed Potato Hash while the fish is brining.

Creamed Potato Hash

Serves 4 to 6

4 cups water

2 teaspoons kosher salt

2 russet potatoes, peeled and diced into ¼-inch cubes

2 tablespoons extra virgin olive oil

2 shallots, sliced into thin rings

2 garlic cloves, smashed and roughly chopped

1 cup chicken stock (page 14 or store-bought)

1 tablespoon dijon mustard

1 cup heavy cream

2 sprigs fresh thyme, leaves removed

Grated zest of 1 lemon

4 mustard green leaves, washed and roughly chopped

Pinch of kosher salt

Pinch of ground black pepper

Pinch of nutmeg

Fill a stockpot with 4 cups of water, add the salt, and bring to a boil over medium-high heat. Add the potatoes and blanch them for 5 minutes. Remove the potatoes from the boiling water, then plunge them in a bowl of ice water to stop them from cooking any further. Drain the potatoes in a colander and set them aside.

Heat the oil in a deep cast-iron skillet over medium heat. Toss in the shallots and sauté until the shallots slightly melt, 5 to 7 minutes.

Stir the blanched potatoes, garlic, stock, and mustard into the shallots. Bring to a simmer and cook, stirring occasionally, until the stock has reduced by half, 7 to 10 minutes. Mix in the heavy cream, thyme, and lemon zest, and cook for 1 minute more. Add the greens and stir another 5 minutes until the leaves have wilted and the potatoes are tender. Season with salt, pepper, and nutmeg. Serve hot, straight from the skillet.

Cola-Braised Ham *and* Onion-and-Smoked-Cheddar Buttermilk Biscuits *with* Arugula *and* Mustard Seed Dressing

Serves 4

4 (8-ounce) pieces of country ham

2 shallots, thinly sliced

1 garlic clove, smashed

1 cup ham hock broth (page 45) or chicken stock (page 14 or store-bought)

1 tablespoon apple cider vinegar

8 whole black peppercorns

1 sprig fresh thyme

1 bay leaf

1 (12-ounce) bottle of Mexican Coca-Cola, made with cane sugar (see note)

½ cup heavy cream

Notes

This recipe calls for country ham, which is a kind of salt-cured ham indicative of Virginia. You may find it marked as Virginia ham or Virginia-style ham in stores.

Make sure you use the glass-bottled Mexican Coca-Cola, which is made with real cane sugar, rather than Coca-Cola from a can or plastic, which is made with corn syrup. They do not cook the same and evaporate differently.

If you are throwing a dinner party or brunch, the ham, biscuits, and arugula make a great sandwich station.

This recipe is a nod to both my West African heritage and Atlanta, the city I now call home, and which sits at a crossroad between the South and the Appalachian region. The kola nut was harvested by the people of Nigeria, Senegal, and Gambia and valued for centuries for its natural energizing properties (caffeine), similar to coffee, tea, and chocolate. By the 1800s, tons of kola nut were shipped by traders to Europe and America, primarily for use in tinctures and medicinal drinks, such as Coca-Cola—created in Atlanta by the chemist John Pemberton. Braising the country ham in the cola tenderizes the dry meat and imparts a sweetness, gifting it a salted caramel glazing that plays beautifully with the gentle smokiness of the biscuits and the tang of the mustard dressing on the arugula greens.

Heat a cast-iron skillet over medium heat. Sear the pieces of ham on both sides until they turn golden brown, approximately 3 minutes per side. Transfer the ham to a plate and set aside.

In the same skillet, sauté the shallots and garlic for 2 to 3 minutes until they caramelize to golden brown. Stir in the broth and vinegar followed by the peppercorns, thyme, and bay leaf. Continue to cook, stirring and making sure to scrape the bottom of the pan, until the liquid has reduced by half, 7 to 10 minutes.

Return the ham to the pan then pour the cola over the ham. Braise until the cola is reduced by half, 7 to 10 minutes. Reduce the heat to medium-low and stir in the cream. Reduce the liquids, stirring constantly and taking care not to scorch or burn the cream, until a glaze has formed over the ham, about 10 minutes. Remove the thyme and bay leaf. Serve with the Onion-and-Smoked-Cheddar Buttermilk Biscuits and the Arugula with Mustard Seed Dressing, both of which can be made ahead of time.

Onion-and-Smoked-Cheddar Buttermilk Biscuits

Makes 12 biscuits

2 ounces smoked cheddar cheese

2 cups all-purpose flour

1 tablespoon baking soda

1 tablespoon light brown sugar

1 tablespoon minced onion flakes

1 teaspoon kosher salt

¼ teaspoon baking powder

6 tablespoons unsalted butter, frozen

1 cup whole buttermilk, chilled

2 tablespoons salted butter, melted

Freshly ground black pepper

Preheat the oven to 375°F. Line a baking sheet with parchment paper and set aside.

Dice the cheddar cheese into pea-size cubes into a bowl, then set the bowl in the freezer.

Gently whisk together the flour, baking soda, brown sugar, minced onion, salt, and baking powder in a large mixing bowl.

Grate the frozen butter into the flour mixture using a box grater, then gently toss the flour with your hands to combine. Make a well in the center of the dry ingredients, then fill the well with the frozen diced cheddar cheese and buttermilk. Using a wooden spoon or your hands, gently mix the dry and wet ingredients until a sticky dough forms.

Turn the dough onto a clean, lightly floured surface. Dust the top of the dough gently with flour. Dust a rolling pin, then roll the dough to ½-inch thick.

Cut the dough into rounds with a 2-inch biscuit cutter and set them 1 inch apart on the parchment-lined baking sheet. Refold the remaining dough and repeat the process until it's all gone.

Bake the biscuits for about 10 minutes, or until they are golden brown. Let rest on the baking sheet for 2 to 3 minutes.

Brush the biscuits with the melted butter and sprinkle with black pepper. Serve immediately.

Note

It is important to freeze the cheddar cheese after cubing so that it will caramelize more evenly during baking.

Arugula *with* Mustard Seed Dressing

Serves 4

8 ounces baby arugula

¼ cup apple cider vinegar

1 teaspoon whole mustard seeds

1 shallot, finely diced

1 tablespoon whole grain mustard

1 tablespoon honey

1 teaspoon kosher salt

¼ teaspoon coarsely ground black pepper

¼ cup extra virgin olive oil

1 sprig fresh thyme, stem removed and leaves reserved

Rinse and thoroughly dry the arugula, then place it in a large bowl.

Stir together the vinegar and mustard seeds in a small saucepan over medium heat. Simmer for 5 minutes.

Remove the pan from the heat, then stir in the shallot, mustard, honey, salt, and pepper.

Whisk in the oil and thyme leaves until just combined.

Pour the dressing over the greens then toss until the greens are lightly coated.

Four-Cheese Baked Mac 'n' Cheese *with* Lobster Variation

Serves 4

1 pound dried macaroni pasta

2 cups (8 ounces) freshly grated cheddar cheese

1 cup (4 ounces) freshly grated pepper jack cheese

½ cup (3 ounces) freshly grated mozzarella cheese

¼ cup (1 ounce) freshly grated parmesan cheese

4 large eggs, lightly beaten

1 cup heavy cream

3 tablespoons sriracha

2 teaspoons kosher salt

½ teaspoon white pepper

1 whole nutmeg, for grating

½ pound cooked lobster (page 117)

This dish represents a paradox. During the Colonial era, lobster was considered a poor man's food fed to prisoners, slaves, and indentured servants, while "macaroni pie" was considered a delicacy of Southern elites. Pasta and cheese imported from Europe were hard to come by, while lobster was ubiquitous along the Atlantic shore. Now, there's not a respectable church potluck, meat-and-three, or barbecue joint without mac and cheese among their offerings.

We can thank James Hemings, Thomas Jefferson's enslaved cook, for introducing macaroni and cheese to American tables. Hemings apprenticed in French kitchens while Jefferson served as ambassador to Paris in the late 1700s. He brought back with him a boiled and baked macaroni casserole layered with cream, butter, and cheese that Jefferson requested frequently. Mary Randolph, the sister to Jefferson's brother-in-law, included the macaroni recipe in *The Virginia House Wife*, the first cookbook published in America in 1824—twenty-five years after Hemings's death. My version evokes Hemings's rich and creamy ideal, while amplifying the flavor quotient with a little heat from jalapeño-inflected cheese and sriracha. The addition of nutmeg and lobster only adds to the indulgence.

Preheat the oven to 350°F.

Fill a large saucepan or crockpot three-quarters full with salted water and bring it to boil over high heat. Once the water reaches a rolling boil, stir in the macaroni, and cook it for six minutes, just slightly undercooked.

While the macaroni boils, combine the cheeses in a medium mixing bowl. In another bowl, whisk together the eggs, cream, sriracha, salt, and pepper.

Once the pasta has cooked, drain the water off the macaroni and return the pasta to the pot but set it away from the heat. Stir in the egg mixture until all the macaroni is coated. Using a Microplane or zester, grate the nutmeg four or five times over the pasta, then fold in the lobster, if using, and three-quarters of the cheese blend.

Pour the macaroni and cheese into a buttered 9-by-13-inch casserole dish. Top with the remaining cheese.

< recipe continues >

Bake the macaroni and cheese for 35 minutes, or until the dish has set and the cheese is caramelized and bubbly. Let it rest for 20 minutes before serving.

Note

Do not use pre-grated cheeses because they are coated with a wood pulp cellulose to prevent them from clumping. The cellulose prevents the cheeses from melting and melding.

If the macaroni has set but the cheese has not browned to your liking, simply turn the oven to broil and caramelize the top.

I lean toward spiny lobster tail for the meat in this recipe because it is far more convenient to source and prepare and is sustainably managed throughout southern waters.

Broiled Lobster Tails

Makes ½ pound meat

2 spiny lobster tails

1 tablespoon unsalted butter, melted

1 teaspoon smoked paprika

1 teaspoon sea salt

½ teaspoon freshly ground black pepper

Preheat the oven broiler.

Line a baking sheet with aluminum foil.

Cut the top side of the lobster shells lengthwise with a sharp knife or kitchen shears. Slightly spread the shells to reveal more of the meat.

Brush the meat with the melted butter, then sprinkle with paprika, salt, and pepper.

Broil the tails for 5 to 10 minutes, or until the lobster meat is opaque and slightly browned.

Set the lobster tails aside until cool enough to handle. Pull the lobster meat from the shells and cut into chunks to fold into the Baked Mac 'n' Cheese.

Roasted Chicken *and* Dumplings *with* Buttered Green Peas *and* Roasted Heirloom Carrots

Serves 4

FOR THE ROASTED CHICKEN

1 whole (4- to 5-pound) chicken

2 quarts warm water

1 cup plus 2 tablespoons kosher salt, divided

1 cup sugar

1 orange, halved

1 lemon, halved

1 shallot, halved

2 teaspoons whole black peppercorns

4 sprigs fresh thyme

2 bay leaves

4 tablespoons vegetable oil

2 sprigs fresh rosemary, stems removed and leaves roughly chopped

1 tablespoon coarsely ground black pepper

FOR THE DUMPLINGS

Skin from roasted chicken

2 cups all-purpose flour

½ teaspoon baking powder

2 tablespoons unsalted butter, frozen

1 cup whole milk

FOR THE CHICKEN AND DUMPLINGS

3 tablespoons vegetable oil

1 roasted chicken carcass

1 white onion, cut into eight wedges

2 bay leaves

12 cups water

When we talk about dishes that stretch sparse ingredients and feed a lot of people, our words can carry the negative undertone of poverty. I would contend, however, that many of those dishes—one-pot stews and casseroles—are now the cornerstone of what we consider comfort food, regardless of one's socioeconomic status. Chicken and dumplings has grown from a rustic stew into a legendary comfort food. For me, though, it also represents a narrative thread from Africa to the Caribbean to the South, picking up elements through time and history. Roasting an older hen that has passed its egg-laying prime tenderizes the meat. The stewing of the chicken bones along with salted root vegetables infuse the stock with nutrients and flavor. The flour-based dumplings, a nod once again to fufu or coucou, provide a starch that holds up the chicken. It's a dish that's both filling and practical. In this version, I employ a three-step process, first brining the hen, then roasting it, followed by stewing the bones to create a lush, nutritious stock layered with flavor upon flavor. It takes extra time, but the subtle hints of citrus and herbaceous goodness are worth the effort as they echo the ingenuity of the make-do spirit of Appalachian foodways. The crisped skin elevates the dumpling from bland to complex and tasty. Altogether, this dish becomes one of comfort and celebration.

TO ROAST THE CHICKEN: Rinse and pat dry the chicken inside and out.

Stir together the water, 1 cup of the salt, and the sugar in a 4-quart food container or large bowl until the salt and sugar dissolve. Squeeze the juice of the orange and lemon into the liquid, then drop the fruit into the water. Add the shallot, peppercorns, 2 sprigs of the thyme, and the bay leaves. Submerge the chicken into the brining liquid and steep the chicken at room temperature for no more than 2 hours.

About 30 minutes before the chicken finishes brining, preheat the oven to 350°F. Strip the leaves from the remaining 2 thyme sprigs. Stir together the oil, thyme leaves, and rosemary, then set aside.

Remove the chicken from the brining liquid and pat it dry. Rub the oil over the skin, then season inside the cavity and all over with the remaining 2 tablespoons salt and pepper. Truss the chicken

2 small heirloom carrots, peeled and cut into ½-inch rounds

2 cups heavy cream

¼ teaspoon crushed red pepper flakes

Grated zest of ½ lemon

1 sprig fresh thyme, stem removed

Kosher salt

Freshly ground black pepper

with butcher twine and set it on a rack in a roasting pan. Bake the chicken for 50 minutes or until it reaches an internal temperature of 165°F. Let the chicken cool long enough to handle.

Remove the skin and set it aside. Debone the chicken and cut the meat into ½-inch cubes. Reserve the chicken carcass for the chicken stock.

TO MAKE THE DUMPLINGS: Preheat the oven to 350°F.

Place the chicken skin on a foil-lined baking sheet and bake for about 15 minutes, until crispy. Let cool completely, then chop the chicken skin into small pieces.

In a large mixing bowl, stir together the flour and baking powder. Using a fork or pastry cutter, cut in the frozen butter until the mixture resembles peas. Pour in the milk and, using your hands, bring the dough together. Gently incorporate the chopped chicken skin, then turn the dough onto a lightly floured surface. With a lightly floured rolling pin, roll the dough to ⅛-inch thick. Use a sharp knife to cut the dough into 1-inch squares. Place on a plate in the refrigerator until ready to make the dish.

TO MAKE THE CHICKEN AND DUMPLINGS: Heat 1 tablespoon of the oil in a large stockpot over medium heat. Place the carcass into the stockpot and cook, turning occasionally, until caramelized all over, 3 to 5 minutes per turn. Stir in the onions and bay leaves, then add the water. Bring the stock to a simmer and cook for 30 minutes, or until the stock has slightly reduced.

While the stock is simmering, heat the remaining 2 tablespoons oil in a cast-iron skillet on medium heat. Sauté the carrots for 2 to 3 minutes on each side until they are slightly caramelized. Transfer the carrots to a paper towel–lined plate to drain. Remove the dumplings from the refrigerator.

Once the stock is done, remove the carcass, onions, and bay leaves from the stockpot. Return the stock to a boil, then stir in the heavy cream. Once the stock boils again, drop in the dumplings, and cook for 2 minutes, stirring occasionally.

Turn the heat down to medium-low, then add the chicken, carrots, and red pepper flakes. Simmer for another minute, then stir in the lemon zest, thyme, salt, and black pepper.

Turn off the heat, cover the pot, and let it stand for at least 5 minutes before serving with a side of Buttered Green Peas (recipe follows).

Buttered Green Peas

Serves 4

1 cup vegetable or chicken
    stock (page 6 or 14,
    or store-bought)
2 shallots, sliced into thin
    rounds
2 cups fresh or frozen
    green peas
2 tablespoons unsalted butter
Coarsely ground sea salt
Coarsely ground black pepper

Heat a large saucepan over medium heat. Pour in the stock and stir in the shallots, then bring the stock to a simmer. Add the green peas, cover the pot, and blanch the peas for five minutes, or until they are bright green and just tender.

Turn off the heat and whisk in the butter. Season the peas with salt and pepper, then serve alongside the Roasted Chicken and Dumplings.

Peach Cobbler *with* Butter Pecan Ice Cream

Serves 4 to 6

FOR THE DOUGH

1 cup all-purpose flour

1 cup sugar

2 teaspoons baking powder

¼ teaspoon salt

¾ cup whole buttermilk

6 tablespoons unsalted butter, room temperature

FOR THE PEACH FILLING

½ cup peach schnapps liqueur

½ cup apple juice

½ cup lightly packed brown sugar

1 teaspoon ground cinnamon

Pinch of salt

2 teaspoons water

1 teaspoon cornstarch

4 medium peaches, pitted and cut into ¼-inch slices

Note

You can substitute other seasonal fruits—apples, blackberries, and cherry—for the peaches. Make sure to adjust your liqueur as well, from peach schnapps to apple schnapps, crème de mûre, and cherry heering, respectively.

Although Georgia, where I live, is called "the Peach State," South Carolina produces three times the number of peaches during the May-through-September growing season. (Both states' production is dwarfed by California, though, which has been growing peaches since the 1700s.) Nevertheless, when summer arrives in the South with its potlucks and picnics, so too do the inevitable peach cobbler competitions. It's the ultimate in seasonal eating. But you've never heard smack talk and signifying like women at a church social. They put *Top Chef*–type competitions to shame. Who used canned peaches? (Sniff.) Was that cinnamon freshly grated? (The nerve.) Are the peaches hard? (Amateur.) Is the crust caramelized? (Not enough.)

Come peach season, you'll find a sweet-spicy cobbler like this one on the menu at my restaurant Soul: Food and Culture. But, if we're in my backyard, it'll be served with another taste of summer: homemade butter pecan ice cream. The Southern pecan is the only native nut tree in America, and it was an important protein source to Native Americans as well as slaves. From pralines to pies, the savory-sweet concoctions the pecan inspires remain staples of the Southern table. This recipe doesn't call for hours of hand-churning, thankfully.

TO MAKE THE DOUGH: Stir the flour, sugar, baking powder, and salt together in a medium mixing bowl. Create a well in the middle of the flour and fill the well with the buttermilk and butter. Using a wooden spoon or your hands, fold the dry and wet ingredients together until a soft dough forms.

Turn the dough onto a clean, lightly floured surface. Using a lightly dusted rolling pin, roll the dough to ½-inch thick.

TO MAKE THE PEACH FILLING: Combine the schnapps, apple juice, brown sugar, cinnamon, and salt in a medium saucepan on medium heat and bring the syrup to a simmer.

Stir the water and cornstarch together in a small bowl, then add it to the syrup. Simmer until the syrup has thickened, 5 to 7 minutes, stirring often. Toss in the peaches and stir over medium heat until they are coated with the syrup.

TO ASSEMBLE THE COBBLER: Preheat the oven to 350°F. Butter a 9 x 9-inch baking dish.

Set the rolled dough into the baking dish, pressing it into the corners of the dish until the surface is covered. Pour the peaches

‹ recipe continues ›

and syrup into the dish, then fold the dough over the peaches. It will not cover the entire mixture.

Bake the cobbler for 30 minutes or until the dough has turned golden brown and the peaches are bubbly. Let cool for 15 minutes before serving with a scoop of Butter Pecan Ice Cream (see below).

Butter Pecan Ice Cream

Makes 1 gallon

2 cups heavy cream

1 cup whole milk

4 large egg yolks

½ cup brown sugar

¼ cup bourbon, or
   1 tablespoon bourbon
   extract

½ teaspoon vanilla bean
   paste

1 tablespoon unsalted butter

1 teaspoon pecan oil

½ cup pecans, chopped

Pinch of sea salt

Note

This recipe is scaled for a 4-quart ice cream maker. You can scale the recipe to the volume of your particular maker.

Combine the heavy cream and milk in a large saucepan over medium heat and bring to a simmer. While the cream heats, stir together the egg yolks, brown sugar, bourbon, and vanilla bean paste in a large mixing bowl.

Once the cream simmers, remove it from the heat. Pour half the cream into the egg mixture and stir mightily to keep from cooking the eggs. Once the mixture is fully incorporated, stir in the remaining cream.

Cover the cream-egg mixture with plastic wrap, adhering the wrap to the surface of the mixture to prevent a film from forming. Set the bowl in the refrigerator to chill.

Melt the butter and heat the pecan oil over medium heat in a cast-iron skillet. Add the pecans and cook 5 to 7 minutes, stirring and tossing often until they are toasted on all sides, 3 to 5 minutes. Remove the pecans from the heat, transfer them to a paper towel, then sprinkle with sea salt.

Once the ice cream base is thoroughly chilled, churn it in your ice cream maker according to the manufacturer's instructions. The ice cream will be soft once it has completed churning, and this is the time to fold in the pecans by hand. Transfer the ice cream to an airtight plastic container and freeze for at least an hour. It will keep in the freezer for at least a week.

Scooped

While working as a porter at a drugstore and hotel in Pittsburg, Pennsylvania, thirty-year-old Alfred L. Cralle received US Patent No. 576395 for his invention: the ice cream mold and disher—the precursor to the modern ice cream scoop. He needed something that would allow servers to scoop ice cream with one hand while holding a cone or cup with the other without the ice cream sticking to the spoon. A square of the Legacy Quilt at the Museum of Food and Drink shows a rendering of his invention.

Watermelon Agua Fresca *with* Spiced *and* Salted Rim

Serves 4

FOR THE AGUA FRESCA

1 (6- to 8-pound) Sugar Baby or similar icebox watermelon, meat cubed, rind removed and reserved for Quick Watermelon Pickles (page 126)

1 cup apple cider

Zest and juice of 1 lime

¼ cup turbinado sugar

FOR THE SPICED AND SALTED RIM

4 tablespoons kosher salt

2 tablespoons turbinado sugar

1 teaspoon paprika

1 teaspoon coarsely ground black pepper

½ teaspoon ground ginger

½ teaspoon chili powder

½ teaspoon curry powder

Pinch of cayenne pepper

Freshly squeezed lime juice

Our ancestors in Northern Africa knew five centuries ago, when they grew and cultivated the first watermelons, that these bright orbs were portable packages of nourishing hydration. They even placed them in the tombs of pharaohs for the long journey into the afterlife. The fibrous qualities of the meat helped alleviate stomach ailments, to boot. Back in Chicago, we grew watermelons in our urban backyard garden. They never grew as large as the ones you found along roadsides or in grocery store produce bins, but ours could fit into the refrigerator with no problem and the seeds were small. Sliced and salted, watermelon was a cool treat on a hot July afternoon—sweet, sticky, the juice running down your fingers and chin. This refreshing and decidedly less messy quencher pays homage to ancient history as well as the back stoop of my youth with just a little kick around the rim. It reclaims the watermelon from a negative Jim Crow–era caricature to a celebratory beverage fit for a king or queen.

TO MAKE THE AGUA FRESCA: Place the watermelon, cider, lime juice and zest, and sugar in a blender and purée on high speed until smooth. Pour the purée through a mesh sieve into a half-gallon pitcher, working in batches if necessary. Chill the pitcher in the refrigerator until ready to serve.

Mix the spiced and salted rim ingredients for at least 2 minutes in a shallow bowl until they are thoroughly combined.

Pour the lime juice in another shallow dish or bowl.

Dip the rim of a chilled pint glass into the lime juice, then dip the rim into the spiced and salted mixture. Repeat with three more pint glasses. Fill the glasses with ice. Pour the agua fresca over the ice and serve.

Note

Feel free to top off the fresca with sparkling cider, champagne, prosecco, ginger beer, or a lemon-lime soda.

Hibiscus Sweet Tea *with* Watermelon Pickles

Serves 4 to 6

2 quarts water

1 cup coconut water

1 cup turbinado sugar

1 (1-inch) knob ginger, roughly
    chopped

12 allspice berries

1 cup dried hibiscus flowers

1 lime, cut in eight wedges

Iced sweet tea has been quenching Southern thirst since the late 1700s, when Charlestonians and Savannahians began serving spiked green tea punches at their balls and galas. It really grabbed hold once refrigeration evolved in the 1800s, and it's been the "house wine of the South" since. This version marries iced sweet tea with the African tradition of red drink by using dried hibiscus flowers rather than dried black or green tea leaves, and the addition of spices offers a nod toward Jamaican sorrel. The pickles as a garnish or side, however you choose to serve them, is my homage to another African American tradition that came up out of the Mississippi Delta—Kool-Aid pickles, created by either dipping pickles in red Kool-Aid powder or adding a packet of red Kool-Aid mix to a jar of pickles. Although there is no Kool-Aid powder in this recipe, the sweet-tart flavor combination reminds me of childhood and those crimson jars of pickles in Chicago's soul food restaurants. The use of the leftover watermelon rind reinforces that nothing went to waste.

In a large saucepan or stockpot, bring the water, coconut water, sugar, ginger, and allspice berries to a simmer over medium-high heat.

Once the water is about to boil, turn off the heat and add the hibiscus flowers; let steep for at least 15 minutes. Taste for strength and steep longer, if preferred.

Strain the tea through a fine mesh sieve into a half-gallon pitcher and chill in the refrigerator until ready to serve.

Fill tumblers with ice and pour the tea into the glasses. Garnish each glass with a lime wedge and a cool, tart Quick Watermelon Pickle (see below).

Makes 1 to 2 pints

2 cups apple cider vinegar

1 cup water

1 cup sugar

Rind of one 6- to 8-pound
    Sugar Baby watermelon,
    green skin removed, and
    cut into 1-inch cubes,
    approximately 6 cups

1 shallot, thinly sliced

12 whole black peppercorns

8 allspice berries

2 bay leaves

1 tablespoon kosher salt

1 teaspoon pickling spice

1 teaspoon ground turmeric

Quick Watermelon Pickles

Bring the vinegar, water, and sugar to a boil in a 2-quart saucepan set over medium heat, stirring until the sugar completely dissolves.

Add the watermelon rind, shallot, peppercorns, allspice berries, bay leaves, salt, pickling spice, and turmeric. Turn the heat to low and simmer for 5 minutes.

Remove the pan from the heat and allow the pickles to come to room temperature. Once cooled, transfer the pickles and brine to an airtight container and chill in the refrigerator for up to 6 weeks.

Serve as a refreshing treat alongside the Hibiscus Sweet Tea.

Stuffed Cornish Hens *with* Rice *and* Field Peas *and* Buttered Cabbage

Serves 4

4 (2-pound) Cornish hens, brined (see page 9)

FOR THE WILD RICE

2 cups cooked wild rice

1 cup cooked or frozen field peas, such as black-eyed peas or Sea Island red peas

4 shallots, thinly sliced

2 celery stalks, peeled and finely diced

Zest and juice of 1 orange

Zest of 1 lemon

½ cup dried cranberries

¼ cup chopped pecans

¼ cup slivered almonds

4 fresh sage leaves, roughly chopped

2 sprigs fresh thyme, stems removed

1 bunch fresh Italian parsley, roughly chopped

1 tablespoon kosher salt

2 teaspoons coarsely ground black pepper

FOR ASSEMBLY

4 tablespoons vegetable oil

2 tablespoons kosher salt

1 tablespoon coarsely ground black pepper

Game birds, such as squab, quail, pheasant, and wild turkey, are leaner and richer tasting than their domesticated counterparts, which is why brining has long been a tradition in rustic cookery to infuse moisture into the meat and temper the gaminess from whatever that bird ate in its lifetime. But I tend to brine all poultry so that the bird does not dry out during the cooking process.

Cornish hens really are a modern invention of crossbreeding begun in the 1950s that produced a young bird with a richer taste more akin to quail or duck than your typical yard bird. It pairs nicely with a stuffing of rice and field peas, a nod to the Southern Appalachian region. The stuffing, of course, can be served as a side on its own, but when cooked inside the hen it helps keep the bird's temperature constant so that it doesn't overcook, steaming the hen from the inside out and suffusing it with subtle layers of flavor.

Served with a side of buttered cabbage, a cornerstone of Appalachian cookery, you get another chapter of the story—in which a green typical of European diets, often boiled or fermented, is instead permeated with nuance through braising.

TO MAKE THE WILD RICE: Stir together the rice and peas in a large mixing bowl. Stir in the shallots, celery, orange juice and zest, lemon zest, cranberries, and nuts until evenly distributed. Add the sage, thyme, parsley, salt, and pepper and stir until thoroughly incorporated. Set aside until ready to stuff the hens.

TO ASSEMBLE THE DISH: Preheat the oven to 350°F. Remove the hens from the brine, pat them dry inside and out, then slather them all over with the oil.

Season the inside cavities with salt and pepper, then stuff each hen with the wild rice, packing the birds full and firmly but not to the point where each bird feels hard to the touch.

Truss the hens with butcher twine. Set the hens in a casserole dish and bake for about 50 minutes, or until the internal temperature of the hens has reached 165°F and the skin is crisp and golden brown. Let the hens rest for 20 minutes before serving with a bowl of Buttered Cabbage (recipe on page 129).

Note

This recipe is based on 8 total pounds of Cornish hens, and it is easily scalable for larger birds, such as pheasant (8 pounds) or turkey (based on size of turkey). In fact, it makes a delicious and herbaceous Thanksgiving meal—my absolute favorite holiday meal.

Yard Birds

Game birds, such as the indigenous guinea fowl, were part of the West African diet well before the time of Christ, and ancient trade routes with Asia introduced domesticated village chickens into the region sometime around 400 to 800 CE. Yard birds weren't just an important source of protein that required little maintenance, they also were vital to sociocultural rituals, including religious ceremonies.

Buttered Cabbage

Serves 4

2 tablespoons extra virgin
  olive oil

2 shallots, thinly sliced

2 bay leaves

1 sprig fresh thyme

1/8 teaspoon caraway seeds

1 (2-pound) head white
  cabbage, shredded

1 cup chicken stock (page 14
  or store-bought)

Sea salt

1 cup water (if needed)

3 tablespoons unsalted butter

Preheat a large cast-iron skillet over medium heat. Drizzle the oil into the pan, then sauté the shallots, bay leaves, thyme, and caraway seeds for 3 minutes to soften. Sprinkle the cabbage over the aromatics, cover, and cook for 5 minutes.

Pour in the stock, season with sea salt to your liking, and continue to cook, covered, for 5 more minutes or until the cabbage softens, but do not let the cabbage caramelize. If the stock has completely evaporated, add the water, cover, and cook for 1 minute more.

Turn off the heat and stir in the butter until it has completely melted into the cabbage. Serve warm, straight from the skillet.

Sweet Potato *and* Squash Casserole *with* Pickled Green Beans

Serves 4 to 6

- 2 tablespoons extra virgin olive oil
- 2 medium sweet potatoes, peeled, cut in half, and sliced into 1/8-inch discs
- 2 yellow squash, cut in half and sliced into 1/2-inch discs
- 1 yellow onion, cut in half and sliced into 1/8-inch discs
- 2 cups grated cheddar cheese
- 6 large eggs
- 4 cups heavy cream
- 2 sprigs fresh thyme, stems removed
- 4 teaspoons kosher salt
- 1 teaspoon freshly ground black pepper
- 1 teaspoon white pepper
- 1/2 teaspoon crushed red pepper flakes
- 1/4 teaspoon freshly grated nutmeg
- Pickled Green Beans (page 132), for serving
- Dandelion Salad (page 14),

This casserole tastes like a throwback to something warm and comforting from childhood while also seeming like a new addition to the family table. Sweet potatoes come together in a hearty dish that can stand alone as a main course for vegetarians or as a side to a larger meal. I think of this for Thanksgiving because it is truly my favorite meal of the year.

Made with eggs, the casserole has a soufflé-like airiness and consistency. The French influence through Haiti and New Orleans is evident in its preparation, but the presence of sweet potatoes and pickled green beans gives it that rustic, down-home Appalachian flair. A salad of dandelion greens (recipe on page 14) and Pickled Green Beans (page 132) on the side finishes it with a peppery bite.

Preheat the oven to 350°F. Brush the bottom and sides of a 9-by-13-inch casserole dish with the oil.

Layer the sweet potatoes, squash, onion, and cheddar cheese in the casserole dish. Whisk together the eggs, cream, thyme, salt, black pepper, white pepper, red pepper flakes, and nutmeg in a medium bowl, then pour the egg mixture over the vegetables. Ensure the vegetables and cream mixture are spread evenly.

Bake the casserole for 35 minutes or until the sweet potatoes are fork-tender and the top of the casserole is bubbly and golden brown.

Let rest for 20 minutes before serving with Pickled Green Beans and Dandelion Salad.

Pickled Green Beans

Serves 4

4 cups water

2 cups apple cider vinegar

1 cup turbinado sugar

2 tablespoons kosher salt

1 tablespoon pickling spice

2 shallots, thinly sliced

1 pound haricots verts
(French green beans), ends
clipped

Bring the water, vinegar, sugar, salt, pickling spice, and shallots to a simmer in a large stockpot over medium heat.

Add the green beans to the pot and continue to simmer for 5 minutes, then remove the beans from the heat.

Ladle the green beans and pickling liquid into a 16-ounce (pint) food storage container, then place that container into an ice bath to stop the cooking and cool the beans rapidly. You can store the beans, covered, in the refrigerator for up to two weeks. Serve as a side or atop a salad.

Note

If you cannot find fresh, tender haricots verts, then you can substitute fresh green beans, string beans, asparagus, wax beans, greasy beans, or yardlong beans.

Pan-Fried Chicken Livers Glazed in Sorghum *and* Shaved Bulb Onions

Serves 4

FOR THE LIVERS AND MARINADE

1 pound chicken livers

1 cup whole milk

2 tablespoons Worcestershire Sauce (page 72 or store-bought)

2 tablespoons hot sauce

1 tablespoon kosher salt

½ tablespoon freshly ground black pepper

1 teaspoon granulated onion

1 teaspoon granulated garlic

FOR THE PAN-FRYING

2 cups all-purpose flour

½ cup yellow cornmeal

1 tablespoon kosher salt

2 teaspoons coarsely ground black pepper

1 teaspoon granulated garlic

1 teaspoon granulated onion

½ teaspoon chili powder

¼ teaspoon yellow curry powder

1 cup vegetable oil

FOR THE SORGHUM GLAZE

1 cup sorghum

½ cup bourbon

Zest of ¼ of a lemon

Pinch of crushed red pepper flakes

Shaved Bulb Onions (page 134)

My grandfather, a former military man, did not cook a lot at home. But when he did, his go-to dish was pan-fried liver. He used beef and he cooked it with a lot of onions. It never had that iron taste that livers sometimes have—it was always perfectly cooked with a lightly pink center. I think I may have been the only kid who ate it. I spent a lot of time in the kitchen with my family. So, whatever they cooked, I ate.

In this homage to him, I use chicken livers, which I glaze with sorghum—an inspiration from a version I tried by Mashama Bailey, the two-time James Beard Award–winning chef-owner of The Grey in Savannah, Georgia. You'll need to plan ahead with this one, because the livers need to luxuriate in a milk bath for at least four hours. You can make the Shaved Bulb Onions while the chicken livers are marinating so that the onions will be nice and pickled when you are ready to serve.

TO MARINATE THE CHICKEN LIVERS: Wash and pat dry the chicken livers, then place them in a large bowl.

Pour the milk, Worcestershire Sauce, hot sauce, salt, pepper, granulated onion, and granulated garlic over the chicken livers and toss together to coat all over. Cover and set the bowl in the refrigerator and chill the chicken livers for at least 4 hours.

TO PAN-FRY THE CHICKEN LIVERS: Stir together the flour, cornmeal, salt, pepper, granulated garlic, granulated onion, chili powder, and curry powder in a large mixing bowl.

Remove the chicken livers from the marinade, shaking off any excess.

Drop the chicken livers in the flour mixture and toss them to coat all over.

Heat the oil over medium heat in a large, deep-sided skillet until it reaches 375°F. Working in batches if necessary to give them room to cook evenly, fry the chicken livers for 3 to 4 minutes on each side until golden brown. Transfer the livers to a paper towel–lined plate to drain.

While frying the livers, heat the sorghum in a medium saucepan over medium heat. As it begins to loosen, stir in the bourbon, lemon zest, and red pepper flakes. Bring to a light simmer and

‹ recipe continues ›

cook until the glaze has thickened to coat the back of a spoon, 5 to 10 minutes.

Remove the sauce from the heat and let it stand until all the livers have been fried and drained.

Set the livers in a large bowl. Pour the sorghum glaze over the livers and gently toss until the livers are thoroughly coated with the glaze. Serve warm alongside the Shaved Bulb Onions (see below).

Shaved Bulb Onions

Serves 2

2 bulb onions, shaved as thinly as possible (see note)

1 tablespoon extra virgin olive oil

2 tablespoons red wine vinegar

½ teaspoon kosher salt

½ teaspoon coarsely ground black pepper

Combine all ingredients in a large mixing bowl. Cover and set the bowl in the refrigerator for at least 1 hour until ready to serve.

Note

A bulb onion is somewhere between a scallion and a leek. It looks like a large green onion bulb with a white bulb that measures about 1 inch in diameter.

Sweet Potato Pie *with* Sorghum Ice Cream

Serves 8

FOR THE PIECRUST

1 cup all-purpose flour, plus another tablespoon for rolling

½ teaspoon salt

8 tablespoons unsalted butter, cut into squares and chilled

½ teaspoon almond extract

3 tablespoons ice water

FOR THE PIE FILLING

2 large sweet potatoes, skin on

8 tablespoons unsalted butter, softened

1 cup packed brown sugar

½ cup heavy cream

2 large eggs, plus 1 egg yolk

½ teaspoon freshly grated nutmeg

½ teaspoon ground cinnamon

¼ teaspoon ground allspice

½ teaspoon vanilla bean paste

The vibrant sienna tubers known as sweet potatoes found purchase in the South by way of South America and the Caribbean thanks to the long hot summers and late frosts conducive to their growth. Because they could be cultivated in small gardens and rocky outcrops, their rich flesh filled many a belly through lean winter months, whether baked, boiled, or roasted. Throughout the Caribbean, Black cooks poured boiling sugarcane over sweet potatoes—the origin story of the candied sweet potatoes that grace autumnal tables. Mashed and spiced, it wasn't much of a stretch then for the versatile sweet potato to find its way into a pie. One of the first recipes for this confection appeared around 1881 in a cookbook by a former enslaved cook, Abby Fisher. George Washington Carver published his own version of a sweet potato pie recipe during the early twentieth century as part of his research into one hundred uses for the sweet potato.

Although the pie can stand on its own, I serve it with a scoop of homemade sorghum ice cream. Only within the past decade have Southern chefs rediscovered the versatility that sorghum brings to regional cooking, but it has a long history here and was once the driver of Appalachian economies. It is often compared to molasses, but molasses is simply a by-product of refining sugarcane and sugar beets. Sorghum derives from a cane originally from Africa, and it has a thinner, more syrup-like consistency when pressed and boiled down. Nutrient dense, its taste is sharper and more nuanced than molasses, which is why it lends itself to both savory meats and vegetables as well as sweets.

TO MAKE THE CRUST: Pulse the flour with the salt and butter in a food processor until pea-size beads form.

Stir the almond extract into the water. Add the water to the dough while the food processor is running and mix until a dough ball forms. Do not overmix.

Sprinkle the remaining flour on a clean surface and roll the dough into a ¼-inch-thick round. Lay the dough in a pie plate and crimp the edges. Set the pie plate in the freezer and chill for 2 hours.

TO MAKE THE FILLING AND PIE: Preheat the oven to 375°F. Bake the sweet potatoes for 45 minutes, or until soft and squishy to the touch. While the sweet potatoes bake, parbake the crust at the same time for 15 minutes, until it is lightly golden. Remove it from the oven and let it cool on a wire rack. When the sweet potatoes are

‹ recipe continues ›

done, remove them from the oven and let them stand for 15 minutes.

Peel the skin from the sweet potatoes, then place the potatoes into a mixing bowl. Add the butter, sugar, cream, eggs and yolk, and spices. Mix the filling until smooth and creamy.

Pour the sweet potato mixture into the piecrust. Bake the pie for 20 minutes, or until the filling is just set. Serve with a scoop of Sorghum Ice Cream (see below).

Sorghum Ice Cream

Makes 1 quart

4 large egg yolks

1/2 cup packed brown sugar

1/2 cup sorghum

1/4 cup bourbon, or
   1 tablespoon bourbon
   extract

1/2 teaspoon vanilla bean
   paste

2 cups heavy cream

1 cup whole milk

1 cup chopped roasted pecans

Pinch of sea salt

Stir together the egg yolks, sugar, sorghum, bourbon, and vanilla bean paste in a large mixing bowl. Set aside.

Combine the heavy cream and milk in a medium saucepan and bring to a simmer over medium heat.

Remove the cream mixture from the heat. Pour half the cream mixture into the egg mixture and stir vigorously to keep the eggs from curdling. Add the remaining cream mixture and the sea salt to the eggs and continue to stir. Place the bowl in the refrigerator to chill for at least 30 minutes.

Churn the ice cream in an ice cream maker, following the manufacturer's instructions. The ice cream will be soft once it has completed churning, and this is the time to fold in the pecans by hand. Transfer the ice cream to an airtight plastic container and freeze for at least an hour. It will keep in the freezer for at least a week.

Todd's Take on Banana Pudding

Often in dessert culture where there's many different variations of the same dish, discussions can grow heated about what is the "real" or "true" version. I've witnessed some passionate debates about whether a banana pudding should have a meringue topper or whipped cream. If you ask my preference, I say, please continue to serve me both and sooner or later I'll render my decision.

Banana pudding grew in fashion after the Civil War, when fruit imports from the Caribbean and Central and South America escalated. Bananas were considered exotic, and the original puddings often were expensive to make because of the cost of sugar and cream. They were served in trifle dishes as layered confections with custard, sponge cake, or shortbread, with meringue because the burned sugar topping kept pests away.

More egalitarian versions began appearing around the turn of the last century as refrigeration grew more accessible, as did bananas. The dessert's popularity grew in the South because a banana pudding could feed the multitudes, whether a church potluck or a family reunion. By the 1920s, vanilla cookies became the go-to ingredient instead of sponge cake. Then, in the 1940s, Nabisco printed a banana pudding recipe using its popular Nilla Wafers, which became the standard dessert for every barbecue joint and soul food restaurant north or south of the Mason-Dixon Line.

Here, I offer two interpretations: one that honors the standard whipped cream version found on so many red-checked tablecloths. The other recalls those early puddings with a meringue—only this one hearkens back even further, to those rum-kissed caramelized plantains found throughout the Caribbean.

Classic Banana Pudding

Serves 4 to 6

FOR THE CUSTARD

4 large eggs

¾ cup sugar

3¼ cups all-purpose flour

¼ teaspoon vanilla bean paste

¼ teaspoon banana extract

1 ounce banana liqueur

½ teaspoon kosher salt

2 cups whole milk

FOR THE WHIPPED CREAM

1 cup heavy cream, chilled

1 tablespoon vanilla bean paste

1 tablespoon sugar

FOR ASSEMBLY

8 bananas, peeled and cut into ⅛-inch discs

40 vanilla wafers

TO MAKE THE CUSTARD: Beat the eggs, sugar, flour, vanilla bean paste, extract, liqueur, and salt together in a large mixing bowl. Bring the milk to a simmer in a medium saucepan over medium heat. Add the egg mixture while stirring constantly with a wooden spoon to keep the eggs from curdling. Cook until the mixture coats the back of the spoon.

Remove the custard from the heat and let it cool for 20 minutes.

TO MAKE THE WHIPPED CREAM: Freeze a large metal bowl for 20 minutes. Pour in the cold heavy cream and add the vanilla bean paste and sugar. Beat with a handheld mixer fitted with the whisk attachment on medium-high speed until still peaks form.

TO ASSEMBLE: In a glass trifle dish for a dramatic presentation or in four individual clear glass jars, layer the custard, the bananas, the wafers, then repeat. Finish with a layer of bananas and wafers and serve with the whipped cream.

Banana Pudding *with* Meringue *and* Rum Sauce

Serves 4 to 6

FOR THE CUSTARD

4 large eggs

¾ cup sugar

3¼ cups all-purpose flour

¼ teaspoon vanilla bean paste

¼ teaspoon banana extract

1 ounce banana liqueur

½ teaspoon kosher salt

2 cups whole milk

FOR THE MERINGUE

¼ cup heavy cream

2 tablespoons corn syrup

1 (16-ounce) jar of marshmallow cream

FOR THE RUM SAUCE

2 tablespoons salted butter

8 fingerling (Lady Finger) bananas, peeled and cut into ⅛-inch discs (see note)

4 tablespoons maple syrup

¼ cup dark rum

½ teaspoon pure vanilla extract

FOR ASSEMBLY

30 vanilla wafers, whole

10 vanilla wafers, roughly chopped

TO MAKE THE CUSTARD: Beat the eggs, sugar, flour, vanilla bean paste, banana extract, banana liqueur, and salt together in a large mixing bowl.

Bring the milk to a simmer in a medium saucepan over medium heat. Add the egg mixture while stirring constantly with a wooden spoon to keep the eggs from curdling. Cook until the mixture coats the back of the spoon.

Remove the custard from the heat and let it cool for 20 minutes.

TO MAKE THE MERINGUE: Combine the cream and corn syrup in a small saucepan over medium heat and bring to a simmer, stirring constantly. Whisk the marshmallow into the cream mixture until it dissolves and the meringue is thick. Remove the meringue from the heat.

TO MAKE THE RUM SAUCE: Melt the butter in a cast-iron skillet over medium heat. Add the banana slices and stir, coating and caramelizing until golden brown.

Remove the pan from the heat, transfer the bananas to a plate or bowl, and pour off the butter into a glass measuring cup.

Return the pan to the heat, then stir in the maple syrup, then the rum, and continue cooking until the liquid has reduced by half, 3 to 5 minutes. Stir in the vanilla, then return the bananas to the pan and baste with the rum syrup.

TO ASSEMBLE: In a glass trifle dish for a dramatic presentation or in four individual clear glass jars, layer the custard, the bananas in syrup, the whole wafers, then repeat. Top with the meringue, then, using a pastry torch caramelize the top of the meringue until it is golden brown, approximately 5 minutes. Sprinkle with the chopped wafers and serve immediately.

Note

If Lady Finger bananas are unavailable, substitute regular bananas but be mindful that they won't be as sweet.

Part II
South to West and the Roads in Between
(1865-1918)

"Although it seems sort of incongruous that a former slave population would help to impose the sort of controls and circumstances on another colored population in the country in that next generation, unfortunately sometimes serving in the military was the best option for especially a young black man."

—Dr. Darrell Millner, as quoted in "Buffalo Soldiers Played Complicated and Controversial Role in Westward Expansion" by Crystal Paul, *Seattle Times*, February 15, 2019

Black Cowboys and Buffalo Soldiers

Two and half years after President Abraham Lincoln outlawed slavery, Union Major General Gordon Granger took a ship from New Orleans to Galveston, Texas, arriving on June 19, 1865, to read aloud General Order Number 3 from the balcony of Ashton Villa:

The people of Texas are informed that, in accordance with a proclamation from the Executive of the United States, all slaves are free. This involves an absolute equality of personal rights and rights of property between former masters and slaves, and the connection heretofore existing between them becomes that between employer and hired labor. The freedmen are advised to remain quietly at their present homes and work for wages. They are informed that they will not be allowed to collect at military posts and that they will not be supported in idleness either there or elsewhere.

The island's enslaved, of course, were the last to know but the first to celebrate publicly with parades, red drink, and prayers for the end of chattel slavery and the beginning of a complicated expansion westward. Despite the dig by the last two sentences of the order, in this place where ancient waters carved the land, where muddy deltas formed, and alligators outnumbered people, the mythical American cowboy was born—only he was more often brown or Black rather than the white of Hollywood lore.

When we think about "how the West was won," we picture the mythical, white-hatted cowboy riding the range on cattle drives and pioneers in wagon trains making their way across treacherous passes, and eventually, the railroad carrying travelers to parts unknown. But at least one in three cowboys was of Mexican descent, and one in four cowboys was Black.

In the East Texas pinelands, bayous, and coastal prairies along the Gulf, Creole cowboys drove cattle up from Mexico and into Purchase territory, hunting and trapping wild game and fishing for turtles and crawfish for sustenance long before Louisiana was a state. They negotiated friendships with the Caddo and Choctaw people—people they would later fight in exchange for the unrealized promise of equality. When my friend Zella Palmer moved to New Orleans to explore her family's history, she discovered the Creole cowboy culture still very much alive through culinary trail rides and rodeos—a tradition, she writes, that comes out of "struggle, survival, and freedom."

After Emancipation, African Americans still had no political power, almost no education, and little opportunity for decent jobs, despite the declarations of General Order Number 3 and the Thirteenth Amendment, which was passed in December 1865. One of the only avenues afforded Black men to escape the South was to enlist in one of the six "colored" regiments of the US Army. At least there, they would receive training and pay—even if it paled in comparison to their white counterparts and officers. By 1869, more than 10 percent of troops were Black and their job was to protect settlers by clearing Western lands of their native inhabitants. Some 20,000-plus of those settlers—the "exodusters"—were Blacks leaving the South for Nicodemus, Kansas. These buffalo soldiers were often given only black coffee and spoiled meat for rations—so they employed the foraging, hunting, and cooking skills that had served them through time immemorial as they made their way north and west to California.

Multiple westward in-migrations spurred economic growth and resulted in heretofore unrealized fusions of cuisine and culture. In the Texas Hill Country, an amalgamation of Mexican and Native American grilling techniques, already blended with those of German and Czech immigrants, were further influenced by African Americans to create a unique barbecue, flavored by mesquite, pecan, and hickory smoke. Mexican masa tamales met the Senegalese-style cow pea abala. And Japanese, Korean, and Laotian immigrants introduced new spices and chilies into traditional African cookery.

BBQ Shrimp *with* Garlicky French Bread *and* Parsley Butter

Serves 4 to 6

FOR THE SHRIMP

2 pounds large shrimp, unpeeled

2 tablespoons vegetable oil

2 tablespoons coarsely ground gray sea salt

FOR THE BARBECUE SAUCE

1 tablespoon vegetable oil

1 yellow onion, diced small

2 celery stalks, diced small

6 garlic cloves, thinly sliced

2 bay leaves

¼ cup Worcestershire Sauce (page 72 or store-bought)

2 tablespoons Creole Seasoning (page 147)

1 tablespoon crushed red pepper flakes

Zest of 1 lemon

4 tablespoons Parsley Butter (page 147)

2 scallions, cut into ¼-inch pieces

French Bread and Garlicky Butter

Along the Gulf Coast between Texas and Louisiana, shrimp is abundant and a staple of simple dishes inflected with Spanish, French, and Italian influences. This dish can be made on the stovetop or on a grill. I prefer the grill for a hint of smokiness—reminiscent of a trail ride or cattle drive. Although this recipe has multiple components, from the barbecue sauce to the compound butter, the preparation time is less than half an hour, and the Creole Seasoning (recipe on page 147), sauce, and butter can be made ahead of time. (In fact, it's good to have both the seasoning and butter on hand for a multitude of uses.)

TO MAKE THE SHRIMP: Preheat the oven broiler or set up a grill for high heat (450°F to 500°F).

Toss the shrimp in the oil and sea salt. Arrange the shrimp on a broiler pan for the oven or a grilling basket for the grill. Cook the shrimp on each side for 2 minutes, until the shrimp is almost cooked through but not quite fully opaque.

Remove the shrimp from the oven or grill and set aside. Keep the grill or broiler ready for the French bread.

TO MAKE THE BARBECUE SAUCE: heat the oil in a large saucepan over medium heat. Sauté the onion, celery, garlic, and bay leaves for 2 minutes.

Stir in the Worcestershire Sauce and bring it to a simmer. Stir in the Creole Seasoning and red pepper flakes.

Toss in the shrimp, make sure they are coated all over, and cook for about 1 minute, until the shrimp are fully opaque, pink, and curled.

Add the lemon zest, then whisk in the Parsley Butter until it is melted.

Toss in the scallions. Serve with French Bread and Garlicky Butter (recipe on page 147).

Creole Seasoning

Makes 1½ cups

6 tablespoons smoked paprika

4 tablespoons kosher salt

2 tablespoons granulated onion

2 tablespoons granulated garlic

2 tablespoons dried thyme

2 tablespoons freshly ground black pepper

1 tablespoon dried oregano

1 tablespoon marjoram

1 tablespoon dried rosemary

1 tablespoon cayenne pepper

1 tablespoon curry powder

1 tablespoon sugar

¼ teaspoon nutmeg

Combine all the ingredients and store in an airtight container in a cool, dry place for up to 6 months. This recipe is easily halved or quartered to have less excess on hand.

Parsley Butter

Makes 2 cups

1 pound unsalted butter, room temperature

Zest of 1 lemon

4 sprigs fresh curly parsley

4 sprigs fresh Italian parsley

1 tablespoon dehydrated onion

1 tablespoon kosher salt

Place the butter in a medium bowl and cover it with the remaining ingredients. Mash the ingredients into the softened butter with the back of a wooden spoon or spatula until the herbs, aromatics, and seasonings are thoroughly incorporated.

Feel free to half or quarter the recipe to your needs. Store wrapped in parchment paper in the refrigerator for up to 1 month or in the freezer for up to 3 months.

French Bread *and* Garlicky Butter

Serves 4

2 tablespoons Parsley Butter

1 loaf French sourdough bread, split in half lengthwise

4 garlic cloves, smashed and chopped

Preheat oven on broil setting (500°F) or prepare a grill for high heat.

Smear the parsley butter over the cut sides of the bread, then top with the garlic, lightly pressing it into the butter.

Set the bread, unbuttered side down, on a baking sheet or on the grill and toast until the bread is crunchy and browned around the edges. Serve immediately.

Stewed Pinto Beans with Corn Cakes and Jalapeño and Red Pepper Marmalade

Serves 4

1½ pounds dried pinto beans

2 tablespoons vegetable oil

1 smoked ham hock, or
    2 smoked turkey necks

1 yellow onion, finely diced

1 poblano pepper, seeded and
    finely diced

4 garlic cloves, smashed and
    chopped

2 tablespoons kosher salt

2 teaspoons chili powder

1 teaspoon ground cumin

½ teaspoon smoked paprika

¼ teaspoon crushed red
    pepper flakes

1 bay leaf

8 cups chicken stock
    (page 14 or
    store-bought)

1 chipotle pepper canned in
    adobo, with 1 teaspoon of
    adobo sauce

Corn Cakes (page 149)

Jalapeño and Red Pepper
    Marmalade (page 149)

Whereas Louisiana favors red beans, which are petite versions of the larger kidney beans, the pinto bean reigns supreme in the Southwest, where, instead of with rice, they are often served soupy and spooned over cornbread. Their name, "pinto," a derivative of the Spanish word for "painted" or "dappled," captures the dried beans' red and white swirl pattern, reminiscent of the pinto ponies favored by western Native American tribes. Beans and cornbread are classic American trail food—inexpensive, easy to prepare, packed with proteins, minerals, and fiber—that has become a comfort food, especially in Texas. You'll need to plan a little ahead for this gently smoked version, so that the beans can soak overnight, which helps them cook quicker. While the beans stew, make the corn cakes so that they'll be fresh and airy. The marmalade gives the entire dish a cool tang to offset the spice and heat.

Pick through the pinto beans and discard any broken beans or debris. Soak the beans in a large bowl of cold water overnight.

Heat the oil in a large stockpot over medium heat. Add the ham hock to the pot and caramelize it on all sides, 3 to 5 minutes per side. Transfer it to a plate and set aside.

Add the onion, poblano pepper, and garlic to the pot and cook for 5 minutes, or until the onions and peppers have softened. Return the ham hock to the pot and add the salt, chili powder, cumin, paprika, red pepper flakes, and bay leaf. Cook for 2 minutes.

Add the stock and the chipotle pepper with sauce, and cook for 20 minutes.

Strain the beans from the soaking liquid, add them to the pot, cover, and cook for 1 hour, or until the beans are tender.

Serve the beans warm with Corn Cakes and Jalapeño and Red Pepper Marmalade.

Notes

You can make the marmalade well ahead of the pinto beans. In fact, making the marmalade a day or two ahead will allow the flavors to meld together.

The Corn Cakes are best fresh, so you can make those about 20 minutes before you are ready to serve the beans.

Corn Cakes

Makes 8 to 12 cakes

2 cups yellow cornmeal

2 teaspoons kosher salt

¼ teaspoon baking soda

¼ teaspoon ground nutmeg

¼ teaspoon cayenne pepper

1 ear fresh corn, shucked, kernels removed

1½ cups whole buttermilk

½ cup water

2 tablespoons vegetable oil

1 tablespoon unsalted butter, softened

Whisk together the cornmeal, salt, baking soda, nutmeg, and cayenne pepper in a large bowl.

Stir in the corn kernels, buttermilk, and water until combined but not overmixed.

Heat the oil in a large cast-iron skillet over medium heat. Spoon about 2 tablespoons of batter for each cake into the skillet. Fit as many cakes as possible in the pan without overcrowding. Cook the cakes until golden brown, about 2 minutes per side, until all the cakes are done.

Top each cake with the butter and serve with the Jalapeño and Red Pepper Marmalade (recipe below) and the Stewed Pinto Beans (recipe on page 148).

Jalapeño and Red Pepper Marmalade

Makes 3 cups

1 teaspoon vegetable oil

1 red bell pepper, finely diced

1 yellow bell pepper, finely diced

1 poblano pepper, finely diced

2 jalapeño peppers, seeded and finely diced

1 cup apple cider vinegar

4 cups granulated sugar

1 tablespoon whole grain mustard

1 teaspoon kosher salt, to taste

Heat the oil in a medium saucepan over medium heat. Stir in the peppers and sear for 2 to 4 minutes without stirring.

Remove the pan from the heat and transfer the peppers to a paper towel–lined plate.

Return the pan to the heat and stir in the vinegar, sugar, and mustard. Bring to a simmer and stir often until the sugar is dissolved. Cook until the liquid is reduced by half, approximately 10 minutes, then return the peppers to the pan. Simmer for 5 minutes.

Let the marmalade rest for 1 hour. Taste it to see if it needs salt and add up to 1 teaspoon according to taste.

Store the marmalade in an airtight container in the refrigerator for up to 6 weeks.

Beignets *with* Espresso Powdered Sugar

Serves 4

5 cups self-rising flour (see note)

1 cup coconut flour

1 cup all-purpose flour

⅓ cup granulated sugar

⅓ cup coconut sugar

1½ teaspoons kosher salt

1½ cups warm water (120°F)

½ cup evaporated milk, room temperature

½ cup coconut milk, room temperature

2¼ teaspoons active dry yeast

1 teaspoon vanilla bean paste

1 teaspoon espresso extract

2 large eggs, room temperature

¼ cup vegetable shortening

2 cups vegetable oil, for frying

FOR DUSTING

1 cup powdered sugar

1 cup coconut sugar

1 tablespoon espresso powder

Note

If you do not have self-rising flour readily available, you can substitute 5 cups all-purpose flour, 2½ tablespoons baking powder, and 2½ teaspoons salt for the amount called for in this recipe.

Beignets share the same pillowy properties of the Spanish sopapilla and the lightly sweetened Coconut Puff-Puff (recipe on page 19). All are sweet, yeasty fried doughs, easy to carry and share. The dough is sticky and wet, which lends itself to steaming during the frying process. In New Orleans, beignets most often are accompanied by a hot cup of café au lait. In this less sweet and starchy version, made with coconut flour and coconut sugar, the coffee comes in both the dough and in the traditional powdered sugar coating, imparting a hint of chocolatey bitterness that complements rather than competes with the sweet dusting.

Mix the flours, sugars, and salt in a large stainless steel or ceramic bowl.

In a separate bowl, combine the water, milks, and yeast, then let stand for 5 minutes to allow the yeast to bloom and start to foam.

Fold the vanilla bean paste and espresso extract into the yeast mixture.

Whip the eggs and shortening into the flour mixture using a whisk until the dough is smooth.

Thoroughly combine the yeast mixture and flour mixture, then cover with a damp towel and set aside to rise for 2 hours, until doubled in size.

Sprinkle all-purpose flour on a clean surface and scrape the dough onto the flour.

Roll the dough to ½-inch thickness using a heavy rolling pin. Cut the dough into 1-inch squares with a sharp knife or pastry cutter and place the squares, separated by parchment or wax paper, in the refrigerator for 1 hour.

Heat the oil in a dutch oven over medium-high heat until it reaches 350°F.

Remove the dough from the refrigerator and gently drop the squares into the oil, being careful not to crowd the pot. Fry the beignets for 2 to 4 minutes per side or until golden brown all over.

Transfer the beignets to a paper towel–lined plate to drain and repeat until all of the beignets are done.

Stir together the powdered sugar, coconut sugar, and espresso powder in a large bowl.

Once the beignets have slightly cooled but are still warm, toss them in the powdered sugar mixture and serve with a hot cup of strong coffee.

Cemita Poblana: Fried Pork Cutlet *with* Avocado Vinaigrette

Serves 4

FOR THE PORK AND BRINE

4 (4- to 6-ounce) bone-in, thin-cut pork chops

2 cups warm water

2 tablespoons kosher salt

2 tablespoons sugar

1 lemon, quartered

1 garlic clove, smashed

FOR THE VINAIGRETTE

2 avocados, peeled, pitted, and diced

1 recipe pickled red onion (page 45)

2 leaves fresh mint, roughly chopped

FOR THE SEASONED FLOUR

1 cup all-purpose flour

¼ cup potato flour (optional or omit)

1½ tablespoons kosher salt

2 teaspoons seasoned salt

1½ teaspoons dry mustard

1 teaspoon ground black pepper

½ teaspoon granulated onion

½ teaspoon granulated garlic

½ teaspoon paprika

¼ teaspoon celery salt

FOR FRYING

2 teaspoons kosher salt

1 teaspoon freshly ground black pepper

3 cups panko breadcrumbs

3 large eggs, beaten

2 cups vegetable oil

The cemita is a type of Mexican torta, or sandwich, made with a sesame seed bun, strands of queso Oaxaca, and smashed avocado. In the city of Puebla, where the sandwich originates, the herb pápalo gives it a distinctive burst of freshness. Because frying can dry out a pork cutlet, I recommend a short brine to increase moisture and infuse flavor. The vinaigrette creates a brightness enriched by the aromatics woven through the breading and adds another level of creaminess different from the cheese—a surprising and satisfying interplay of textures. As sandwiches go, it's made for traveling.

TO BRINE THE PORK CHOPS: Rinse and pat dry the pork chops.

In a large bowl, mix the ingredients for the brine. Submerge the pork chops in the brine for 2 hours at room temperature.

TO MAKE THE AVOCADO VINAIGRETTE: Gently toss the avocado chunks with the pickled red onion, and top with the chopped mint. Cover and set aside in the refrigerator until ready to use.

TO MAKE THE SEASONED FLOUR: Mix all the seasoned flour ingredients in a medium bowl until thoroughly combined.

TO FRY THE PORK CHOPS: Remove the pork chops from the brine, pat them dry, and season with half the salt and pepper, pressing the seasonings into the meat.

Mix the remaining salt and pepper into the panko breadcrumbs.

Heat the oil in a deep-sided cast-iron skillet over medium heat until it reaches 375°F.

Dredge the pork chops in the seasoned flour, followed by the eggs, then the seasoned panko.

Fry the pork chops in the oil until golden brown, approximately 4 minutes on each side.

Transfer the chops to a wire rack set over paper towels to drain.

TO ASSEMBLE: Preheat the oven to 350°F.

Place the pork chops on a baking sheet and cover with the cheese. Bake until the cheese is melted.

Melt half the butter in a skillet over medium heat. Toast two of the buns in the butter until golden brown, about 3 minutes, then repeat for the other two buns.

FOR ASSEMBLY

4 ounces Oaxaca cheese
  (½ cup) or 4 string cheese
  sticks, pulled apart
2 tablespoons unsalted butter
4 sesame seed buns
2 tablespoons whole grain
  mustard

Place each pork chop on a bottom bun. Top with the avocado vinaigrette. Slather the top buns with the mustard and set on top of the chop.

Notes

St. Pierre Sesame Seed Brioche Burger Buns, available at most grocery stores, are close to the type of cemita buns you'd find at a sandwich truck in Mexican immigrant communities and throughout South Texas.

You can substitute cilantro for the mint in the avocado vinaigrette.

Coffee, Black
Pepper, and Cocoa-
Rubbed Smoked
Beef Brisket with
German Potato
Salad (page 156)

Coffee, Black Pepper, *and* Cocoa-Rubbed Smoked Beef Brisket *with* German Potato Salad

Serves 4 to 6

FOR THE RUB

4 tablespoons ground coffee

4 tablespoons kosher salt

4 tablespoons fresh ground black pepper

4 tablespoons smoked paprika

4 tablespoons brown sugar

4 tablespoons granulated garlic (not powder)

4 tablespoons granulated onion (not powder)

2 tablespoons ground cumin

2 tablespoons cayenne pepper

2 tablespoons cocoa powder

1 tablespoon chili powder

FOR THE BRISKET

1 (12- to 14-pound) brisket, excess fat trimmed

2 tablespoons vegetable oil

Texas Hill Country is a tapestry of ethnic diversity that is reflected in its music, literature, and food. Mexican spices heat traditional German and Czech dishes, such as schnitzel and sausages, and the pit barbecue techniques employed by African Americans—who comprised more than 30 percent of the state's population by the end of the Civil War—define this region's cuisine. Beef brisket reigns supreme in these parts, a nod to Texas's long history of cattle ranching. The brisket will need to cook overnight or all day, so ensure that you've given yourself plenty of time to prepare if you've invited guests over.

TO MAKE THE RUB: Stir together the ingredients in a mixing bowl until well combined.

TO MAKE THE BRISKET: Prepare your smoker or barbecue pit for indirect heat and bring it to 230°F. If you're cooking over direct heat, such as on a Weber-type grill, line the grill grate with foil prior to cooking.

Rinse and pat the brisket dry. Massage the oil into the brisket until all sides are well coated. Follow with the rub, ensuring that the seasonings cover the entire brisket evenly.

Place the brisket in the smoker, fat side up and away from direct heat (if possible). Cook the brisket low and slow for 14 hours, or until the internal temperature reaches 190°F in the thickest part of the meat. If the brisket starts to form an overly crispy crust, wrap the brisket in foil and cut the cooking time by 1 hour.

When the brisket is done, remove it from the smoker or grill and set it aside for 10 to 15 minutes for the juices to reconstitute. Transfer the brisket to a cutting surface and slice it against the grain, about ¼-inch thick. When plating, put the thick layer of fat, or fat cap, on the bottom and the dark crust, or bark, on top. Serve immediately with a side of German Potato Salad (recipe on page 157).

German Potato Salad

Serves 4

2 pounds red bliss potatoes

1 tablespoon plus ½ teaspoon kosher salt

6 strips pepper bacon

⅓ cup red wine vinegar

2 sprigs fresh thyme, stems removed and leaves chopped

1 tablespoon dijon mustard

1 tablespoon sugar

1 garlic clove, smashed and diced

1 celery stalk, peeled and finely diced

¼ teaspoon freshly ground black pepper

1 shallot, sliced into rings

4 sprigs fresh Italian parsley, stems removed and leaves chopped

Pinch of red pepper flakes

Preheat the oven to 350°F and line a baking sheet with foil and set aside.

Wash the potatoes in cold water and place them in a large pot. Cover the potatoes with cold water, add 1 tablespoon salt, then cover the pot and place it over medium heat. Bring to a boil and cook the potatoes for 15 minutes, or until the potatoes are just fork-tender. Remove the pot from the heat and let it cool for 10 minutes, then drain the potatoes in a colander.

While the oven preheats and the potatoes cook, lay the bacon strips on the foil-lined baking sheet. Once the oven is heated, bake the bacon for 15 minutes, or until cooked through. Transfer the bacon to a paper towel–lined plate to drain. Reserve the bacon fat.

Stir together the vinegar, thyme, mustard, sugar, garlic, celery, and 2 tablespoons bacon fat in a large mixing bowl.

Cut the potatoes into wedges and fold them into the bowl of dressing. Season the potatoes with the remaining ½ teaspoon salt and black pepper. Arrange the shallot slices on top of the potato salad.

Crumble the bacon slices then garnish the top of the potato salad with the bacon, parsley, and red pepper flakes.

Adrian Miller

One of the biggest surprises of my research is that soul food has a lot longer history in the English language. The earliest joining of the words "soul" and "food" that I could find was actually in Shakespeare. In his first play, *Two Gentleman of Verona*, two women characters are talking about this really hunky guy named Proteus ["his looks are my soul's food"] . . . even in the late sixteenth century, it was not usual for two girlfriends to get together and describe a guy as yummy.

For the next four centuries, soul food had a religious connotation. Then you get to the 1940s, and you've got this group of African American jazz artists, and they're pretty pissed off because the white jazz artists are the ones getting all the pub, making the best money, getting the best gigs. And so, these jazz artists said, Okay, we're gonna take this music some place where we don't think these white artists can mimic the sound. And they took the sound to the Black churches of the rural South. That gospel change to the jazz sound starts to get called soul and funky. So, the words started getting slapped to other aspects of the club culture: soul music, soul brothers, soul sisters, soul food. In the 1960s, that's when it goes mainstream.

I was always curious about where soul food came from. It was really about the Black migrants who left the South during that period of the Great Migration and transplanted their food in other parts of the country. They did what any other immigrant group does: You get to a new place and try to replicate home, or re-create it. If you can't replicate it exactly . . . you just kind of adapt. But once you become settled and prosper, you remember the good times, the good of the old country, and you probably have the resources now to get that food, and you start making that part of your diet more than maybe it was before. So, I argue that soul food is really the celebration food of the rural South that gets transplanted across the country.

The migration of African Americans out of the South coincided with the revolutionizing of our food system. So, in time, people could get those collard greens, they could get dried black-eyed peas, they could get a lot of things and replicate it.

We took barbecue with us during the migration too. In fact, if you look at communities all over the country, African American food entrepreneurs opened up one of three businesses: a fried chicken place, a fried fish place, and a barbecue place. That's all over.

In fact, the first wave of barbecue restaurants appear in the 1890s. A lot of times, these were African Americans showing up: in Denver, there were Black folks running barbecue joints in 1902, 1903. Henry Perry shows up in Kansas City in 1905. You've got barbecue joints opening up in Los Angeles in the 1890s. It's definitely part of the story. It's just not well documented and celebrated.

—Adrian Miller
food scholar,
as told on my *Soul* podcast
on Heritage Radio Network

Adrian Miller never set out to be a food scholar and author, but a chance find in a Colorado bookstore back in 2001 led him on a journey. He picked up John Egerton's Southern Food: At Home, on the Road, in History *and saw these words: "The tribute to black achievement in American cookery has yet to be written." Adrian contacted Egerton to ask if anyone had already done it, and he was encouraged by Egerton to lend his voice to the larger narrative. We are so fortunate that he did and continues to do so through his James Beard Award–winning books* Soul Food: The Surprising Story of an American Cuisine, One Plate at a Time; *and* Black Smoke: African Americans and the United States of Barbecue.

BBQ Short Ribs
(page 162)
with Crawfish
and Rice-
Stuffed
Chayote Squash
(page 163)

BBQ Short Ribs *with* Crawfish *and* Pecan Rice–Stuffed Chayote Squash

Serves 4

FOR THE RIBS AND MARINADE

1 pound blade-cut short ribs, approximately ¼-inch thick

1 cup water

1 cup Worcestershire Sauce (page 72 or store-bought)

1 shallot, quartered

1 sprig fresh thyme

1 teaspoon Creole Seasoning (page 147)

FOR COOKING

2 tablespoons vegetable oil

2 teaspoons kosher salt

1 teaspoon freshly ground black pepper

1 lime, quartered

Crawfish-and-Pecan Rice-Stuffed Chayote Squash (page 163)

In that tangled and biodiverse expanse of the Big Thicket near the Sabine River, which creates the border between Texas and Louisiana and empties into the Gulf of Mexico, cultures collided along the coastal prairies to birth a rice culture that exists even today. Here is where indigenous met enslaved, Creole mingled with Acadian, Spanish fought French, Mexican fought to hold on. And the food, just like this recipe, borrowed the best from all the influences. Short ribs, which come from the cow's belly, are heavily marbled and chunky, full of flavor. Pecans are native to Texas and grow especially well in the state's river valleys. Aside from its buttery fruit, its wood is prized for grilling and smoking meats and vegetables. The pecan provides a floral counterbalance to the rich essence of the crawfish tails and the popcorn-like flavor of the rice, all of which play against the tart, crisp-apple flavor of the squash, a native of Mexico.

TO MARINATE THE RIBS: Rinse and pat dry the ribs.

Mix the water, Worcestershire Sauce, shallot, thyme, and Creole Seasoning in a large bowl or casserole dish. Slather the ribs in the marinade and let them rest at room temperature for 30 minutes to 2 hours.

TO COOK THE RIBS: Preheat the oven on broil setting (500°F) or prepare a grill for high heat. If using the oven, line a baking sheet with foil.

Remove the ribs from the marinade, brush with the oil, and season with the salt and pepper. If cooking in the oven, set the ribs on the prepared baking sheet. Bake or grill the ribs, flipping halfway through, for about 4 minutes on each side, or until cooked through and nicely charred on the edges. Serve with lime wedges and Crawfish-and-Pecan Rice–Stuffed Chayote Squash.

Note

Make the rice and cook the squash while the ribs marinate.

Crawfish *and* Pecan Rice-Stuffed Chayote Squash

TO MAKE THE RICE: Heat the oil in a medium saucepan over medium heat. Add the onion, pepper, pecans, garlic, and bay leaves and cook, stirring frequently, for 4 to 6 minutes until the onions and pepper have softened.

Stir in the rice, salt, and Creole Seasoning, and cook for an additional 4 minutes until the rice is lightly toasted.

Stir in the stock, bring to a simmer, then cover the pot and cook undisturbed for 20 minutes, or until the liquid is absorbed into the rice.

Remove the saucepan from the heat and let rest for 10 minutes.

Stir in the crawfish, lemon zest, butter, and parsley.

Let the rice stand for 1 hour to cool completely. Remove the bay leaves.

TO MAKE THE SQUASH: Preheat the oven to 350°F.

Toss the squash in olive oil and salt, then place the squash in a casserole dish or on a baking sheet.

Bake the squash for 15 minutes.

Let cool for 30 minutes. Use a paring knife to cut open the top of the squash. Scoop out the top half the squash meat.

Fill each squash with 1 tablespoon of the rice. Heat any remaining rice in the saucepan while the squash cooks.

Place the squash in a large skillet or casserole dish and bake for 20 minutes or until the squash and rice are heated all the way through. Serve the squash immediately with the extra rice.

Serves 4 to 8

FOR THE RICE

1 tablespoon extra virgin olive oil

1 yellow onion, finely diced

1 red bell pepper, finely diced

1 cup chopped pecans

2 garlic cloves, smashed and chopped

2 bay leaves

2 cups short-grain rice

1 teaspoon kosher salt

½ teaspoon Creole Seasoning (page 147)

4 cups chicken stock (page 14 or store-bought)

1 pound crawfish tails

Zest of 1 lemon

2 tablespoons unsalted butter

2 sprigs fresh Italian parsley, leaves removed and roughly chopped

FOR THE SQUASH

8 chayote squash, about 2-inches in diameter

2 tablespoons extra virgin olive oil

1 tablespoon kosher salt

Churros *with* Cinnamon-Vanilla Sugar

Serves 4

FOR THE CHURROS

2 cups water

8 tablespoons (1 stick) unsalted butter, room temperature

2 tablespoons sugar

½ teaspoon kosher salt

½ teaspoon vanilla bean paste

½ teaspoon almond extract

2 cups all-purpose flour

2 large eggs

1 large egg yolk

3 cups vegetable oil, for frying

FOR THE CINNAMON-VANILLA SUGAR COATING

1 cup sugar

1 teaspoon ground cinnamon

¼ teaspoon vanilla powder

These delicate, crisp golden ribbons date back to the sixteenth century, when they were made with flour and water and fried and carried by Spanish explorers to South America and back to Spain. Spaniards were the first to dip the churros in bitter drinking chocolate, a delicacy they took from the Aztecs. My version, made with eggs and sugar, have a cakier consistency, but the cinnamon and vanilla sugar dusting celebrates the influence of the Mexican vaqueros, who pioneered cattle ranching in the coastal prairies of Texas and across the Southwest.

TO MAKE THE CHURROS: Line a baking sheet with parchment paper.

Bring the water, butter, sugar, salt, vanilla bean paste, and almond extract to a simmer in a medium saucepan, stirring occasionally, over medium-low heat.

Stir in the flour with a wooden spoon and cook the mixture until smooth, 3 to 5 minutes. Remove the mixture from the stove and let it rest for 5 minutes.

Add the eggs and yolk one at a time, beating with a hand mixer between each addition.

Spoon the dough into a piping bag fitted with a large star tip and pipe 6-inch churros onto the prepared baking sheet. Refrigerate for 30 minutes.

Heat the oil in a deep-sided cast-iron skillet over medium heat until it reaches 350°F.

Working in batches, fry the churros until golden brown on all sides, 4 to 6 minutes on each side. Transfer to a paper towel–lined plate to drain.

TO MAKE THE CINNAMON-VANILLA SUGAR: Mix the sugar, cinnamon, and vanilla powder in a large bowl. Toss the churros in the cinnamon-vanilla sugar until coated all over. Enjoy every crunchy bite.

The Roads in Between

Hot *and* Cold Southwest-Style Country-Fried Rabbit *with* Tomatillo Hot Sauce

Serves 4

FOR THE RABBIT AND MARINADE

1 (4-pound) rabbit, cut into 8 pieces (see note)

4 cups water

1 cup buttermilk

2 jalapeño peppers, cut in half

1 white onion, diced large

1 ancho chili, soaked in hot water for 10 minutes then roughly chopped

4 tablespoons kosher salt

1 tablespoon coffee extract

1 teaspoon ground cumin

1 teaspoon ground ginger

FOR THE SEASONED FLOUR

2 cups all-purpose flour

2 cups yellow cornmeal

2 tablespoons granulated garlic

2 tablespoons granulated onion

2 tablespoons kosher salt

1 tablespoon ancho chili powder

1 teaspoon black pepper

4 cups vegetable oil, for frying

Because of the limited narratives surrounding Afro cuisine in the United States, the notion that Blacks were skilled hunters and fishers seems to have gotten lost—or, ignored. But, as many as 25 percent of cowboys on the western plains were Black, and many worked on cattle drives as horse wranglers. Many were also soldiers for the US government in those years after the Civil War when westward expansion promised escape and opportunity. They had to rely on game, such as rabbit, deer, and buffalo, for sustenance. This recipe is a throwback to that time, while being thoroughly modern in its approach—kind of a rustic twist on hot sauce slathered on a juicy fried chicken thigh. The brief heat and smokiness from the crackling crust is shocked by the tang and spiciness of the bright green tomatillos.

TO MARINATE THE RABBIT: Rinse and pat dry the rabbit pieces, then set aside.

Mix the remaining marinade ingredients in a large mixing bowl or food storage container, then let the marinade rest for 45 minutes.

Submerge the rabbit pieces in the marinade and marinate for 1¼ hours at room temperature, or cover and marinate overnight in the refrigerator.

While the rabbit marinates, make the Tomatillo Hot Sauce (recipe on page 166).

TO FRY THE RABBIT: Mix all the seasoned flour ingredients together in a large bowl.

Heat the oil to 350°F in a cast-iron dutch oven over medium heat.

Remove the rabbit, onion, and jalapeño peppers from the marinade. Discard the onion and peppers.

Coat the rabbit in the seasoned flour and let the pieces sit for at least 5 minutes before frying.

Fry the rabbit in batches of two or three pieces for 8 to 10 minutes, or until the rabbit is golden brown and the meat has reached 165°F

⟶ recipe continues ⟶

at the thickest part. If the rabbit is browning too quickly, reduce the heat to 325°F. Transfer the rabbit to a paper towel–lined plate to drain and repeat until all the rabbit is fried.

Toss half the rabbit in the Tomatillo Hot Sauce, let it cool for 30 minutes, then place in an airtight container and refrigerate overnight.

Toss the other half with the hot sauce and enjoy immediately, along with a margarita.

In the morning, remove the cold fried rabbit and enjoy with your favorite morning beverage, maybe even a breakfast cocktail.

Tomatillo Hot Sauce

Makes 3 cups

¼ cup vegetable oil

12 tomatillos, papery husks removed, cut in half

8 garlic cloves, cut in half

1 yellow onion, large diced

2 jalapeño peppers, cut in half

1 poblano pepper, cut in half

1 serrano pepper, cut in half

2 cups white wine vinegar

½ cup sherry vinegar

2 tablespoons sugar

1 sprig fresh oregano, stems removed

2 teaspoons kosher salt

Heat the oil in a large stockpot over medium heat.

Add the tomatillos, garlic, onion, and peppers, and cook until the vegetables just begin to release water, 3 to 5 minutes.

Stir in the vinegars, sugar, oregano, and salt. Simmer until most of the liquid is reduced, about 10 minutes.

Turn off the heat and let the mixture stand for 1 hour.

Purée the mixture in a blender until smooth. Transfer the salsa to a glass container and let it rest another hour before serving.

Note

Turn on the exhaust fan to circulate air as you cook, because the peppers will be spicy and intense.

Venison Osso Buco *with* Stewed White Beans *and* Corn

Serves 4 to 6

- 4 (8- to 10-ounce) venison shanks, room temperature
- 1 cup all-purpose flour
- 2 teaspoons plus 1 tablespoon kosher salt, divided
- 1 teaspoon granulated onion
- 1 teaspoon granulated garlic
- 2 teaspoons plus 1 teaspoon ground black pepper, divided
- 2 cups vegetable oil, divided
- 1 yellow onion, large diced
- 2 celery stalks, large diced
- 1 carrot, peeled and large diced
- 1 poblano pepper, diced large
- 1 cup dry sherry
- 8 cups chicken stock (page 14 or store-bought)
- 1 (12- to 16-ounce) can whole stewed tomatoes
- 4 garlic cloves, smashed
- 1 teaspoon cumin seeds
- 4 bay leaves
- 2 sprigs fresh thyme, stems removed
- 1 tablespoon unsalted butter

Although osso buco is considered a quintessential Italian dish, the caramelization, the low-and-slow method of braising with vegetables to create a rich, hearty broth is reminiscent of the stews and one-pot meals from West Africa. Osso buco is the perfect dish to put on and not think about while you tackle other tasks. This version is made with venison, ideal during cold months when venison is typically in season and a stew like this provides comfort and keeps you full. I serve a protein-rich side of beans and corn, something more indicative of Native American cookery, with a citrusy garnish of chopped parsley—nods to the polenta and gremolata traditionally served in some Italian regions.

Rinse and pat dry the venison shanks and set aside.

Whisk together the flour, 2 teaspoons of the salt, the granulated onion, granulated garlic, and 2 teaspoons of the black pepper.

Heat 1 cup of the oil in a cast-iron dutch oven over medium heat.

Dust the venison shanks with the seasoned flour and sear them on all sides until golden brown, approximately 4 minutes per side.

Transfer the shanks to a plate, pour off the oil from the pan, then add the remaining cup oil, the onion, celery, carrot, and poblano pepper. Cook until the vegetables are brown on all sides, 5 to 7 minutes. Then, add the sherry and cook, stirring occasionally, until the liquid is reduced by half, about 10 minutes.

Return the venison to the pot, then add the stock, tomatoes, garlic, cumin seeds, bay leaves, thyme, and the remaining salt and black pepper. Reduce the heat to low, cover, and bring to a simmer. Cook for 60 to 90 minutes, or until the meat is tender.

Turn off the heat and keep the venison covered, allowing it to rest for 30 minutes.

Transfer the venison to a bowl or plate and strain the liquid into another large saucepan. Place the venison into the strained liquid and bring to a simmer over medium heat. Once simmering, whisk in the butter until it melts. Then serve the venison alongside the Stewed White Beans and Corn (recipe on page 168).

recipe continues

Serves 4 to 6

¼ cup vegetable oil

4 ears fresh corn, kernels removed and set aside, and cobs reserved

1 yellow onion, medium diced

2 celery stalks, peeled and medium diced

1 carrot, peeled and medium diced

1 poblano pepper, seeded and medium diced

1 jalapeño pepper, seeded and medium diced

4 garlic cloves, roughly chopped

1 teaspoon sugar

1 teaspoon kosher salt

½ teaspoon cumin seeds

½ teaspoon ancho chili powder

½ teaspoon ground black pepper

2 sprigs fresh oregano

2 sprigs fresh thyme

2 bay leaves

2 pounds dried cannellini beans, soaked in water overnight

6 cups vegetable or chicken stock (page 6 or 14, or store-bought)

2 large beefsteak tomatoes, medium diced

1 bunch fresh curly parsley, stems removed, and leaves roughly chopped

Zest of 1 lemon

Zest of 1 lime

Stewed White Beans *and* Corn

Heat the oil in a cast-iron dutch oven over medium heat. Add the corncob, onion, celery, carrot, peppers, and garlic. Season the vegetables with the sugar, salt, cumin seeds, chili powder, and black pepper. Cook the vegetables and aromatics until they are lightly brown and slightly tender, 3 to 5 minutes.

Create a bundle of the oregano, thyme, and bay leaves using butcher twine.

Strain the beans and pour them into the pot, followed by the stock. Toss in the oregano bundle and bring the beans to a simmer. Cover the pot and cook for 60 minutes or until the beans are just tender.

Remove the corncobs, stir in the corn kernels and tomatoes, and cook for another 15 minutes.

Turn off the heat and let the beans sit for another 30 minutes prior to serving. Meanwhile, combine the parsley, lemon zest, and lime zest in a small bowl.

When ready to serve, remove the oregano bundle, ladle the beans in bowls, and top with the parsley mixture.

Why Were They Called Buffalo Soldiers?

The Black regiments formed by the US Army in 1869—the 9th and 10th Cavalry and the 24th and 25th Infantry units—were led by white officers and tasked with clearing Indigenous people from the Western frontier to make way for homesteaders and prospectors in fulfillment of Manifest Destiny.

During what were called the "Indian Wars" in the late 1800s, Native Americans, according to many historians, began to refer to the enlisted Black men as "buffalo soldiers." It was not a derogatory sobriquet, because the buffalo was sacred among Native American tribes. Some historians suggest that the soldiers' skin, burnished even darker by the sun, recalled the shiny undercoats of the buffalo, and that the soldiers' tight curls reminded Indigenous people of the fur on the heads and shoulders of bison roaming the Western plains. Native Americans considered buffalo formidable foe, willing to fight to the bitter end with its head down and its eyes forward and fierce. They believed the buffalo soldiers fought the same way.

The buffalo became a symbol of the regiments' identity, traveling with them as they helped build roads, raise talking wires, repair forts, fight in the Spanish-American War and World War I, and serve as the first rangers in Yosemite and Sequoia—even before the National Parks Service was created.

Buffalo-Pumpkin Chili *with* Pickled Cactus Salsa *and* Crispy Blue Corn Tortilla

Serves 4 to 6

FOR THE CHILI

½ cup vegetable oil

1 small pumpkin or butternut squash, peeled and medium diced, seeds reserved for Pickled Cactus Salsa (page 171)

1 yellow onion, small diced

2 poblano peppers, seeded and small diced

2 red bell peppers, small diced

1 jalapeño pepper, seeded and finely diced

1 large carrot, peeled and small diced

2 garlic cloves, smashed and roughly chopped

2 pounds ground buffalo

1 (4.5-ounce) can green chiles

1 ancho chili, soaked for 5 minutes in hot water, stem removed, and roughly chopped

1 tablespoon kosher salt

1 teaspoon ground black pepper

2 teaspoons ground cumin

¼ teaspoon ground cinnamon

4 cups beef or chicken stock (page 26 or 14, or store-bought)

1 (28-ounce) can stewed tomatoes, chopped

1 (12-ounce) package frozen crowder or field peas

FOR THE TORTILLA STRIPS

8 blue corn tortillas

1 cup vegetable oil

1 teaspoon kosher salt

The Field Museum in Chicago has been committed as of late to exploring the historic interactions among African Americans and Native Americans and the profound role those relationships had in developing this nation. The very founding of my hometown grew from the marriage of Jean Baptiste Point du Sable, the child of a French mariner and an enslaved woman in Haiti. As a young man, du Sable traveled up the Mississippi River from New Orleans to Illinois and married a Potawatomi woman. There, on the Chicago River near Lake Michigan, the two set up a trading post and farm. The nation's oldest African American history museum is named in du Sable's honor and is not far from the high school I attended in the Washington Park neighborhood. This recipe attempts to capture these deep entanglements through layer upon layer of ingredients and flavors. The buffalo, pumpkin, and blue corn, cornerstones of Indigenous diets; the pickled cactus, reminiscent of the preservation methods favored by Africans to stretch meager ingredients and to mine water from even the harshest elements. This one-pot meal is ideal for a winter supper.

TO MAKE THE CHILI: Heat the oil in a cast-iron dutch oven over medium heat. Sauté the pumpkin, onion, peppers, carrot, and garlic until slightly tender and browned on all sides, 3 to 5 minutes.

Transfer the vegetables to a plate, then add the ground buffalo, green chilies, ancho chili, salt, black pepper, cumin, and cinnamon to the pot and cook, stirring occasionally, until the meat is brown and nearly cooked through, 12 to 15 minutes.

Return the vegetables to the pot and cook for another 5 minutes. Stir in the stock, tomatoes, and peas, then cover the pot and bring the chili to a simmer. Cook for about 35 minutes or until the peas are tender. Taste and adjust the seasonings as needed.

Turn off the heat and let the chili rest, covered, for 30 minutes before serving. While the chili rests, make the tortilla strips.

TO MAKE THE TORTILLA STRIPS: Cut the tortilla into ⅛-inch-wide strips.

Heat the oil in a medium saucepan over medium heat to 325°F to 350°F.

Notes

When making chili, the vegetables can release water and cause the chili to thin. Add 1 tablespoon tomato paste to thicken, if needed.

The Pickled Cactus Salsa will need to be made at least one day ahead.

Makes 1 quart

4 cups water

2 cups apple cider vinegar

1 cup sugar

1½ tablespoons kosher salt, divided

12 coriander seeds

12 whole black peppercorns

2 bay leaves

1 sprig fresh oregano

1 pound cleaned young prickly pear cactus pads, cut into 1-inch strips (see note)

1 red bell pepper, quartered

1 red onion, quartered

1 carrot, peeled and halved

1 celery stalk, peeled and halved

1 serrano pepper, stem removed

Pumpkin or butternut squash seeds reserved from Buffalo-Pumpkin Chili (page 170)

4 large Beefsteak tomatoes, medium diced

½ bunch fresh curly parsley

6 fresh cilantro leaves, roughly chopped

¼ cup extra virgin olive oil

Fry the tortilla strips in small batches until crispy, 3 to 5 minutes. Transfer the strips to a paper towel–lined plate to drain. Repeat until all the strips are fried.

Once the strips have slightly cooled, sprinkle with the salt.

TO SERVE: Top each bowl of chili with Pickled Cactus Salsa (below) and tortilla strips.

Pickled Cactus Salsa

Stir together the water, vinegar, sugar, 1 tablespoon of the salt, coriander, peppercorns, bay leaves, and oregano in a large stockpot and bring to a simmer over medium heat.

Add the cactus, red pepper, onion, carrot, celery, and serrano pepper to the pot, cover, and continue to simmer for 10 minutes.

Turn off the heat and let the vegetables pickle in the stockpot for at least 1 hour. Pour the pickled vegetables and liquid into an airtight container and refrigerate for at least 2 hours.

When you are ready to make the salsa, remove half the vegetables and 2 tablespoons of pickling liquid from the container. Store the remaining pickled vegetables in the refrigerator.

Add the vegetables, pickling liquid, pumpkin seeds, tomatoes, parsley, and cilantro to a food processor, and pulse to the desired chunkiness, but do not purée smooth. Pour the salsa into a medium bowl and fold in the olive oil and remaining ½ tablespoon salt. Serve as a garnish to the Buffalo-Pumpkin Chili (recipe on page 170) or with tortilla chips.

Note

Prickly pear cactus pads, or nopales, are available online through Amazon.

Part III

The Great Migration

(1910-1970)

"They traveled deep into far-flung regions of their own country and in some cases clear across the continent. Thus, the Great Migration had more in common with the vast movements of refugees from famine, war, and genocide in other parts of the world, where oppressed people, whether fleeing twenty-first-century Darfur or nineteenth-century Ireland, go great distances, journey across rivers, deserts, and oceans or as far as it takes to reach safety with the hope that life will be better wherever they land."

—Isabel Wilkerson, *The Warmth of Other Suns: The Epic Story of America's Great Migration*

The Great Migration's First Wave (1910-1940)

In the years after the American Civil War and Reconstruction, Black citizens hoped they would enjoy the same fullness of economic, social, and political liberty that white men enjoyed in the United States. However, as Blacks gained opportunity, the Southern United States saw the rebirth of the Ku Klux Klan in 1915 and the institution of both legal and extralegal Black Codes, increasing racial terror and legitimizing separate-but-equal falsehoods in education, healthcare, housing, jobs, voting, and land ownership. When World War I halted European immigration, the expanding industrial north, fueled by steel mills and manufacturing, held the promise of economic and social opportunity. The railways' Pullman porters carried newspapers from the Black press, most notably the *Chicago Defender*, which advertised jobs and housing opportunities up North. Thus began the Great Migration, when more than six million primarily rural Southern Black citizens moved north and transformed the nation's urban centers.

They traveled with their families and friends along the Pennsylvania Railroad routes to opportunities in northern factories, stockyards, and other industries. They often were aided by folks within their faith communities, notably northern Baptist and African Methodist Episcopal (AMEs) congregations. As Black Americans left West Virginia, Georgia, and the Carolinas, they migrated to the big cities of New York, Philadelphia, and Boston. Out of Alabama, Arkansas, Louisiana, Kentucky, Tennessee, and Mississippi, Black migrants flocked to Chicago, Cleveland, and Detroit. In all, New York City's Black population increased by 60 percent, while Chicago's swelled by 148 percent, Philadelphia's

by 500 percent, and Detroit's by 600 percent. They carried with them peanuts, crowder peas, okra, sweet potatoes, and slow-cooking traditions. When they arrived, they confronted racist housing and employment policies that forced them to create culturally vibrant and distinct cities within cities, such as Harlem in New York, The Hill in Philadelphia, and Bronzeville in Chicago.

My mother's paternal grandfather was born in Cincinnati after his parents crossed the Kentucky River so that he would not be born in a state that had traditionally held slaves. So, my great-great-grandmother migrated when she was pregnant with him. He grew up to become a meat inspector, a job he started in Cleveland, Ohio, where he met my great-grandmother. They transferred to Chicago in 1944 and settled in Englewood, about a mile and a half from Chicago's Union Stockyards, once the epicenter of the nation's meat processing and packing. He was the only African American to train other meat inspectors at the time, and he was an inspector for the only African American–owned meat packer, Parker House, which is still there, even though the Union Stockyards shuttered fifty years ago. My auntie Cherie tells me my great-grandfather made a great eggnog.

My mother's maternal great-grandmother, Maggie L. White, was born in Chicago after her

ROOTS, HEART, SOUL

parents migrated to Chicago's South Side from Kentucky. As a suffragette, she voted for the first time at age forty-two in 1920.

My father's people came up from Louisiana and Arkansas. Both sides of my family lived in Englewood and that's where my parents met. My mother was a biologist. My father was a data processor for Montgomery Ward. They settled on the southeast side of the South Side of Chicago, and we lived on the border between the Black and Latinx communities. While we slow-roasted meats and grilled corn over charcoal, our neighbors did the same, but one was called barbecue and the other, barbacoa, was served on corn tortillas.

While my mother was alive, our home was the center of family celebrations, but the list of blood relatives was small in our family compared to our extended family of friends. My mother invited people from all walks of life into our home—people she gathered from the neighborhood, the late shift at the hospital where she worked, the grocery store line. Even as a scientist, my mother calculated that what ailed people most was a lack of love and kindness, and she was sure to serve heaping helpings of both.

Never hasty, she would hand-make biscuits, soft-scramble eggs, mix mushroom-and-green-bean-casserole, season stuffing with fresh sage (because dry sage would never do). Thanksgiving brunch was her thing and the meal I found the most pleasure in. It was the first meal of the day before we migrated to my great-aunt's home that afternoon. But as we prepared to leave for Big Fannie's house, my mom would grab paper plates and aluminum foil and make plates for the people who could not make it to our house for that first meal. Our first stop along the way would always be by Dr. Walker's home. This small woman who

carried me into adulthood, and I have become as much a seeker of sustenance as salvation—an evangelist, if you will, of food that feeds the soul.

In the present day, as I stand at the intersection of Indiana and East 47th streets in the Bronzeville area of Chicago's South Side, the once beloved Queen of the Sea, a stalwart of Black Chicago's soul food buffets, has been replaced by a discount clothing store. Its flagship on South Cottage Grove Avenue has been replaced by a sandwich shop. The soul-satiating restaurant Army & Lou's is gone, too. Just down the street are dollar stores and fast-food burger and fried chicken joints, the kinds of places that numb our tastes, devalue the craft of cooking delicious and nutritious food, and render faceless the cooks who prepare it. The liquor stores have survived, however, and in many cases, have multiplied. We have traded a sense of place and community for cheap convenience, and in return, we have lost our visceral and spiritual connections. I'm not sure if the table can help heal these deep wounds, but I'm certain breaking bread together is the only way to begin.

New York

Stewed Chicken in Tomato Sauce *with* Crowder Pea *and* Arugula Salad

Serves 4

FOR THE BRINED CHICKEN

1 (3- to 4-pound) roaster chicken, cut into 8 pieces, neck and backbone reserved, and brined (page 9)

FOR THE ROASTED CHICKEN STOCK

2 tablespoons vegetable oil

Reserved chicken neck and backbone

1 white onion, cut into large pieces

1 small carrot, peeled and sliced into ½-inch discs

2 celery stalks, peeled and cut into 1-inch pieces

½ cup dry white wine, such as pinot grigio

1 sprig fresh thyme

2 bay leaves

1 teaspoon whole black peppercorns

8 cups cold water

FOR THE STEWED CHICKEN

2 tablespoons kosher salt

2 teaspoons coarsely ground black pepper

½ teaspoon dried oregano

½ teaspoon dried thyme

¼ teaspoon dried marjoram

½ teaspoon curry powder

½ teaspoon chili powder

Layers of flavor are packed into this stewed chicken—a down-home, rustic version of coq au vin—by brining the chicken and making homemade stock (which you'll use for both the chicken and the crowder peas). Roasting the chicken neck with aromatics creates depth and warmth to the stew. Braising first then stewing the chicken with tomatoes makes the meat fall off the bone. Like most hearty foods served, say, for a Sunday dinner after church, it's worth the investment of time. Comforting and herbaceous, it is ideal for a late summer/early fall meal, when crowder peas—so named because of the way the peas crowd the hull as they ripen—are in season. For convenience and year-round savoring, I call for frozen peas, but feel free to go all in with dried or fresh peas if you've got the time or leftovers.

TO MAKE THE STOCK: Heat the oil in a heavy-bottomed stockpot over medium heat.

Add the neck and backbone, onion, carrot, and celery. Cook until caramelized on all sides, 5 to 7 minutes. Stir in the wine, thyme, bay leaves, and peppercorns.

Increase the heat to medium-high and cook, stirring occasionally, until the liquid has reduced by half, approximately 10 minutes.

Add the water to the pot and bring to a simmer. Reduce the heat to medium, and simmer for 30 minutes.

Turn off the heat and let the stock rest for 30 minutes, then strain it through a fine mesh sieve into a heat-proof container.

TO MAKE THE STEWED CHICKEN: Stir together the salt, pepper, oregano, thyme, marjoram, curry powder, chili powder, and paprika in a small bowl. Season all sides of the chicken with the spice mixture.

Heat two tablespoons of the oil in a large skillet over medium heat, then place the chicken in the pan, leaving space between the pieces and working in batches if necessary. Cook the chicken

‹ recipe continues ›

½ teaspoon smoked paprika

4 tablespoons vegetable oil

8 pieces brined chicken

4 shallots, thinly sliced

8 garlic cloves, smashed and roughly chopped

1 cup dry red wine, such as a pinot noir

4 cups roasted chicken stock (page 179)

2 (28-ounce) cans plum tomatoes

2 bay leaves

1 bunch fresh Italian parsley, stems removed and leaves roughly chopped

until browned and lightly crisped on all sides, approximately 3 to 4 minutes each side. Transfer the chicken to a plate and set aside.

Heat the oil in a skillet, then scatter the shallots and garlic in a single layer. Cook, stirring occasionally, until softened and lightly caramelized, 3 to 5 minutes. Stir in the wine, making sure to scrape up the tasty browned bits from the bottom of the pan, and cook until the liquid has been reduced by half, 7 to 10 minutes. Remove the pan from the heat.

Set a stockpot on the stove over medium heat. Arrange the chicken pieces in the pot, then pour the wine sauce over the chicken followed by the chicken stock. Bring to a simmer and cook, stirring occasionally, until the liquid is reduced by half, 10 to 12 minutes. Add the tomatoes and bay leaves, then cover and simmer for about 30 minutes, basting the chicken every 10 minutes with the tomato sauce, until the chicken is cooked to where the juices run clear and the meat is tender.

Turn off the heat and let the stew rest for 15 minutes. Garnish with chopped parsley before serving with Crowder Pea and Arugula Salad (recipe on page 182).

Note
Make the roasted chicken stock while the chicken pieces brine. That way you'll have the stock ready for the stew as well as the Crowder Pea and Arugula Salad.

Crowder Pea *and* Arugula Salad

TO MAKE THE PEAS: Heat the oil in a stockpot over medium heat. Add the bacon strips and cook until they are browned on one side, approximately 5 minutes, then add the onion, celery, and carrot. Cook, stirring occasionally, until the vegetables have slightly softened and the bacon has crisped, 2 to 3 minutes.

Pour off the oil into a heatproof container, such as a measuring cup. Add the peas, bay leaves, thyme, stock, and salt to the pot, then bring to a boil. Turn the heat to low, cover the pot, and simmer until the peas are fork-tender. Turn off the heat and let the peas rest for 30 minutes, covered.

Scoop the peas into a large mixing bowl, cover, and refrigerate for at least 2 hours or overnight.

Once you are ready to dress the salad, remove the bacon, any large onion, carrot, or celery pieces, as well as the thyme and bay leaves.

TO MAKE THE DRESSING: Stir together the shallots, thyme, lemon juice, vinegar, honey, and mustard in a mixing bowl. Whisk in the oil, salt, and pepper until the dressing is thoroughly combined.

TO ASSEMBLE THE SALAD: Strain off any liquid from the peas.

Pour the dressing over the peas and toss until the peas are bathed and glistening with the dressing.

When plating the salad, top each serving with a handful of arugula.

Note

If you want to use dried crowder or field peas, you'll have to plan a little extra time. You'll need to rinse and sort the peas, throwing out any rocks or bad peas, then cook to get at least 2 cups of cooked peas. Then, follow the directions for the peas in the Hoppin' John recipe (recipe on page 103).

Serves 4

FOR THE CROWDER PEAS

2 teaspoons vegetable oil

2 strips peppered bacon

1 white onion, quartered

2 celery stalks, peeled and cut into large pieces

1 small carrot, peeled and cut into large pieces

16 ounces frozen crowder or field peas

2 bay leaves

1 sprig fresh thyme

4 cups roasted chicken stock (page 179)

1 teaspoon kosher salt

FOR THE DRESSING

2 shallots, finely diced

1 sprig fresh thyme, stem removed

½ cup freshly squeezed lemon juice

2 tablespoons white wine vinegar

3 tablespoons honey

1 tablespoon dijon mustard

3 tablespoons extra virgin olive oil

¼ teaspoon sea salt

¼ teaspoon freshly ground black pepper

8 ounces arugula or any bitter green

Buffalo-Style Frog Legs *with* French Onion Ranch Dressing

Serve 4 to 6

FOR THE MARINADE

2 pounds frog legs

8 cups water

1 cup buttermilk

½ cup hot sauce

2 tablespoons Worcestershire Sauce (page 72 or store-bought)

1 tablespoon kosher salt

2 teaspoons granulated onion powder

2 teaspoons granulated garlic powder

2 teaspoons ground black pepper

FOR THE SEASONED FLOUR

3½ cups all-purpose flour

1 cup potato flour (optional; if not using, substitute another cup all-purpose flour)

4 tablespoons kosher salt

2 tablespoons seasoned salt

1 tablespoon dry mustard

2 teaspoons ground black pepper

1 teaspoon granulated onion

1 teaspoon granulated garlic

1 teaspoon paprika

½ teaspoon celery salt

FOR THE BUFFALO SAUCE

2 cups hot sauce

2 tablespoons Worcestershire Sauce (page 72 or store-bought)

2 tablespoons apple cider vinegar

1 tablespoon honey

Even though frog legs are considered a delicacy in France and are common throughout Asian cuisines, here in the United States, they are often chalked up to "trash food" eaten only by poor whites and Blacks in the South. That's such a limiting view when it comes to food and ignores a long and storied history. When French Canadians exerted significant influence over the foodways of cities such as Detroit and Buffalo around the late nineteenth and early twentieth centuries, frog legs encrusted with cracker crumbs and fried in butter dominated menus throughout the nation, according to Detroit food writer Bill Loomis. For people in the South, game was subsistence food, often bathed in buttermilk and fried. In this recipe I marry the two regions by using a Southern-style buttermilk brine and a chicken-fried crust with a toss in a classic buffalo sauce. The sweet-savory French onion dip steps away from the typical blue cheese dressing, adding a richness that also winks at the dish's origins. To continue busting clichés, this appetizer hardly tastes like chicken. It has a delicate, almost mild white fish (think perch) flavor all its own.

TO MAKE THE MARINADE: Wash and pat dry the frog legs and set them aside.

Mix all marinade ingredients in a large mixing bowl or storage container. Reserve ¼ cup of the marinade for the French Onion Ranch Dressing.

Submerge the legs in the remaining marinade, cover, and marinate for 2 hours at room temperature or in the refrigerator overnight.

TO MAKE THE SEASONED FLOUR: Whisk together all ingredients in a large mixing bowl. Reserve ¼ cup for the French Onion Ranch Dressing. Cover and set aside.

Note: This is a good point to make the French Onion Ranch Dressing (recipe on page 185); store it in an airtight container in the refrigerator until ready to serve.

TO MAKE THE SAUCE: Mix the buffalo sauce ingredients together in a large mixing bowl.

TO ASSEMBLE: Heat the oil in a deep-sided cast-iron skillet over medium heat until it reaches 375°F.

Drain the frog legs in a colander set in the sink. Pour the seasoned

< recipe continues >

1 teaspoon dijon mustard

1 teaspoon granulated onion

1 teaspoon granulated garlic

½ teaspoon sea salt

¼ teaspoon ground black pepper

¼ cup unsalted butter, melted

FOR ASSEMBLY

4 cups vegetable oil, for frying

Carrot and celery sticks, for serving

French Onion Ranch Dressing (see below)

Makes 6 cups

2 cups plus 1 tablespoon canola oil, divided

1 yellow onion, cut in half and sliced into thin strips

1 cup chicken stock (page 14 or store-bought)

2 tablespoons dry sherry

1 sprig fresh thyme, stem removed

2 shallots, sliced into thin rings

¼ cup reserved frog leg marinade (page 183)

¼ cup reserved seasoned flour (page 183)

2 garlic cloves, smashed and roughly chopped

1 sprig fresh dill, roughly chopped

2 sprigs fresh curly parsley, stems removed and leaves roughly chopped

2 cups sour cream

½ cup mayonnaise

2 tablespoons sherry vinegar

1 teaspoon dijon mustard

flour into a large shallow bowl, then dredge the frog legs in the flour, ensuring all parts are coated.

Fry the legs, being careful not to overcrowd the pan, until golden brown on one side, then turn the legs over and continue frying until golden and crispy all over, 7 to 8 minutes.

Drain the frog legs on a paper towel–lined plate, then toss the legs in the buffalo sauce until well coated. Alternatively, you can drizzle the sauce over the legs.

Serve warm with carrot sticks, celery stalks, and a side of French Onion Ranch Dressing.

Notes

Mix the seasoned flour ahead of time and store it in an airtight container, so that the flavors meld together before the frog legs are fried.

You may substitute chicken wings for the frog legs in this recipe.

Make the French Onion Ranch Dressing at the same time you make the brine for the frog legs.

French Onion Ranch Dressing

Heat 1 tablespoon of the oil in a large skillet over medium heat. Add the onion and cook for about 5 minutes, until lightly caramelized, then stir in the stock, sherry, and thyme. Continue cooking at a simmer until the liquid has reduced to a syrup-like consistency, approximately 15 minutes.

Remove the thyme sprig. Spoon the onions into a container and refrigerate until completely chilled. Wipe the skillet clean.

When ready to proceed, finely dice the cooled onions then set them aside.

Heat the remaining 2 cups of oil in the same skillet over medium heat to 375°F.

Toss the shallots in the frog leg marinade and let them rest for 5 minutes, then dredge them in the seasoned flour. Fry the shallots until crispy, then drain them on a paper towel for 10 minutes.

Chop the shallots, then combine them with the cold onions, garlic, dill, and parsley in a small bowl.

In a separate medium bowl, mix the sour cream, mayonnaise, vinegar, and mustard. Fold the onions and herbs into the cream mixture until well blended. Serve chilled alongside the frog legs.

Berbere Chargrilled Oysters with Parmesan Cheese and Garlic Butter

Serves 4

FOR THE BERBERE SPICE BLEND

1 cup kosher salt

½ cup smoked paprika

½ cup chili powder

¼ cup sugar

2 tablespoons granulated onion

2 tablespoons granulated garlic

1 teaspoon ground fenugreek

1 teaspoon ground coriander

½ teaspoon ground ginger

½ teaspoon ground cardamom

½ teaspoon cayenne pepper

¼ teaspoon ground cinnamon

¼ teaspoon ground nutmeg

Zest from 2 lemons

FOR THE GARLIC BUTTER

1 pound (4 sticks) unsalted butter, room temperature

4 garlic cloves, peeled, smashed, and roughly chopped

4 sprigs fresh curly parsley, roughly chopped

1 tablespoon freshly squeezed lemon juice

1 teaspoon sea salt

¼ teaspoon freshly ground black pepper

FOR THE OYSTERS

24 medium oysters on the half shell

1 cup (8 ounces) freshly grated parmesan cheese

Oysters were once cheap and plentiful and a way of feeding and prospering for Black families along the Eastern Seaboard and Gulf Coast. At one point, Georgia's oyster industry dominated national production. South Carolina's Gullah residents were talented harvesters, filling bateaus with mountains of craggy shells. After the Civil War, New Orleans' famed oyster industry flourished because of Black fishermen, who, even today, are most likely to be the person shucking your oysters at one of the city's famed houses. Oysters moved out of the dives and into fine dining in New York during the 1800s when Thomas Downing, a Virginia native whose parents had been enslaved, opened an eponymous oyster house at the intersection of Broad and Wall streets. This recipe tips a hat to those classic oyster houses, but also brings in the smoky, sweet sparkle of Ethiopian berbere spice, a mildly spicy complement to the aromatic garlic and the nutty-tasting parmesan cheese.

TO MAKE THE BERBERE SPICE BLEND: Stir all the ingredients together in a small bowl. Store in an airtight container in a dry place until ready to use. The spice blend will keep for up to 6 months.

TO MAKE THE GARLIC BUTTER: Place the softened butter in a small mixing bowl. Add the remaining ingredients and mash them into the butter until well blended. Refrigerate the butter until ready to use.

TO PREPARE THE OYSTERS: Prepare your grill for medium-high heat (400°F).

Scrape about ½ teaspoon butter on top of each oyster. Sprinkle each oyster with a pinch of berbere spice, followed by a pinch of parmesan cheese.

Set the oysters on the prepared grill and roast until the butter and cheese melt then bubble.

Transfer the oysters from the grill onto a platter and serve immediately.

Note

Both the spice blend and garlic butter recipes make more than you will use in this recipe, but they are good to keep on hand. Store the berbere blend in an airtight container in a cool, dry place. Keep the butter in an airtight container in the refrigerator for up to 2 weeks. Otherwise, scale the recipes by cutting the ingredient volumes in half or quarters, depending on your needs.

She-Crab Soup with Smoked Paprika Oil and Cornmeal-Crusted Okra

Served 4 to 6

FOR THE CLAM AND CRAB STOCK

1 pound fresh clams

½ pound fresh crawfish

1 (8- to 10-ounce) blue crab (if in season), or ½ pound shell-on shrimp

1 ham hock (optional)

1 white onion, quartered

2 celery stalks, cut into large pieces

8 cups chicken stock (page 14 or store-bought)

2 cups water

1 cup dry sherry

1 tablespoon tomato paste

1 sprig fresh thyme

FOR THE SMOKED PAPRIKA OIL

1 cup canola oil

1 teaspoon smoked paprika

Pinch of sea salt

FOR THE SOUP

1 tablespoon butter

1 white onion, finely diced

2 celery stalks, peeled and finely diced

2 piquillo peppers, drained and finely diced

½ cup dry white wine

¼ cup dry sherry

4 cups clam and crab stock

4 cups heavy cream

4 whole cloves

During our sojourn to New York's immigrant enclaves, Clay, Amy, and I made a pilgrimage to the recently revived Gage & Tollner on Fulton Street in Brooklyn. The historic oyster bar and chophouse in a grand Italianate structure opened more than 140 years ago in 1879 and shuttered in 2004. In 1988, after years of declining fortunes, the owners at the time made the wise decision to hire the grande dame of Southern cooking, Edna Lewis, to lead the kitchen. She was seventy-two at the time and brought her lively spirit and penchant for well-seasoned fare made with the freshest ingredients to the white tablecloths of the Victorian-era dining room. Among those dishes was her Crab Cakes "Freetown," named for the Virginia farming community founded by her emancipated grandfather, and a Charleston-inspired She-Crab Soup. Both are standards of the resurrected Gage & Tollner's menu. This recipe is my homage to the lasting influence of Lewis, who made her way from Freetown and served delicious country victuals to expat Southerners in New York City from the 1940s until she re-migrated southward in her later years. The crab stock and roe are essential for infusing the soup with a fresh-from-the-sea essence. The Cornmeal-Crusted Okra side balances the silky texture with a crisp earthiness.

TO MAKE THE CLAM AND CRAB STOCK: Place the clams, crawfish, crab (if using), ham hock (if using), onion, and celery in a large stockpot and bring to medium heat. Steam for 2 minutes. Add the stock, water, and sherry and bring everything to a simmer.

Stir in the tomato paste and thyme and continue to simmer, uncovered, for 45 minutes more.

Turn off the heat and let the stock steep for 30 minutes. Strain the stock through a sieve into a heat-tolerant container. Refrigerate up to 3 days until ready to use. Freeze any leftovers up to 6 months for future use.

TO MAKE THE SMOKED PAPRIKA OIL: Heat the oil over low heat in a small saucepan.

Stir in the paprika and salt and cook the oil for 2 minutes.

Remove the oil from the heat and let it stand for at least 10 minutes before using. Any leftover oil can be stored in a glass jar in a cool, dry place for up to 1 month.

< recipe continues >

4 gratings fresh nutmeg

2 sprigs fresh thyme, stems removed

1 pound lump crabmeat

2 tablespoons water

1 tablespoon cornstarch

Sea salt

Ground white pepper

1 ounce crab roe (optional)

4 scallions, thinly sliced

TO MAKE THE SOUP: Melt the butter in a large stockpot over medium heat. Add the onion, celery, and peppers. Sauté for 2 minutes, then add the wine and sherry. Simmer until the liquid is reduced by half, 7 to 10 minutes.

Stir in the stock and cream, and bring the soup back to a simmer. Add the cloves, nutmeg, thyme, and crabmeat. Simmer for another 15 minutes.

Whisk the water and cornstarch in a small bowl, then whisk the mixture into the soup. Cook, whisking constantly, until the soup thickens, approximately 2 minutes.

Season to your liking with salt and pepper.

Ladle the soup into 4 bowls, swirl some of the smoked paprika oil on top, and garnish with the roe and scallions.

Notes

The meat from the seafood will be overcooked when making the stock, and it will not be pleasant to eat.

Leftover crab, crawfish, and clam shells may be used for the stock recipe.

Make the Cornmeal-Crusted Okra (recipe on page 191) in between making the stock and the soup.

Cornmeal-Crusted Okra

Serves 4

FOR THE COATING

½ cup buttermilk

½ cup water

1 large egg, beaten

1 teaspoon hot sauce

8 okra pods, cut into ¼-inch discs

FOR THE CORNMEAL CRUST

1¾ cups all-purpose flour

1¾ cups yellow cornmeal

1 cup potato flour (optional, or substitute 1 cup all-purpose flour)

2 tablespoons kosher salt

2 tablespoons seasoned salt

1 tablespoon dry mustard

2 teaspoons ground black pepper

1 teaspoon granulated onion

1 teaspoon granulated garlic

1 teaspoon paprika

½ teaspoon celery salt

4 cups canola oil, for frying

TO COAT THE OKRA: Combine the buttermilk, water, egg, and hot sauce in a mixing bowl.

Add the okra and toss to coat well.

TO MAKE THE CORNMEAL CRUST: Stir all the ingredients together in a large mixing bowl.

TO MAKE THE OKRA: Heat the oil in a large deep skillet on medium heat until it reaches 375°F.

Remove the okra from the coating with a slotted spoon then toss it in the cornmeal mixture until covered on all sides.

Using a slotted spoon and working in batches, gently set the okra pieces in the hot oil and fry until the pieces are golden and crispy all over, 3 to 5 minutes.

Transfer the okra to a paper towel–lined plate to drain. Serve as a side to She-Crab Soup.

She-Crab Soup at Gage & Tollner

Hot *and* Spicy Crawfish Boil *with* Collard Green Spring Rolls *and* NY Cherry-Ginger Spritz

Serves 4 to 6

2 tablespoons vegetable oil

2 small yellow onions, finely
    chopped

1 yellow bell pepper, finely
    chopped

1 red bell pepper, finely
    chopped

4 celery stalks, peeled and
    finely chopped

4 cups chicken stock
    (page 14 or store-bought) or
    seafood stock

4 cups water

1 cup dry white wine

2 pounds small yellow
    potatoes

1 small acorn squash, seeded
    and cut into 8 pieces

6 bay leaves

2 sprigs fresh thyme

1 tablespoon berbere spice
    (page 187)

2 teaspoons kosher salt

1 teaspoon cayenne pepper

4 ears fresh corn, cut in half

2 pounds whole crawfish

Note

You can substitute tail-on
shrimp if crawfish is not
readily available.

Prep the egg rolls a day or two
ahead, store them covered in
the refrigerator, then fry them
just before making the boil.

Asian- and African-based culinary traditions are tethered because of the ancient trade routes and spice roads: the use of chilies for heat and flavor; inflections of ginger and turmeric; the prevalence of rice, leafy greens, pork belly, and seafood; flash-frying techniques; an appreciation for umami. Down in the Caribbean Islands, once the transatlantic slave trade ceased, indentured Chinese immigrants filled the labor void. And just as Blacks migrating north from the reconstructed South created culturally vibrant enclaves in New York and Philadelphia, so, too, did Chinese families. This grouping of recipes is a mash-up with nods to Caribbean, Chinese, and Black cultures—a Jamaican-Louisiana-style crawfish boil served with crispy, spicy Chinatown-style spring rolls made with traditional Southern greens. The classic New York–inspired spritzer harkens back to red drink. It's the ideal celebration menu for a summer gathering.

Heat the oil in a large stockpot over medium heat. Add the onions, peppers, and celery, and cook for 3 to 4 minutes, until softened.

Stir in the stock, water, and wine and bring to a boil.

Add the potatoes, squash, bay leaves, thyme, berbere spice, salt, and cayenne pepper to the pot. Lower the heat to medium-low and simmer for 10 minutes.

Add the corn to the pot and simmer 5 minutes more, then add the crawfish to the pot, cover, and simmer for 5 minutes.

Turn off the heat and let the boil rest for 5 minutes before serving.

The best way to serve the boil: Line a table with newspaper or butcher paper. Strain the boil through a colander, then pour the boil across the paper so your guests can reach right in for an ear of corn, a crawfish, or a potato. Have on hand bowls to discard shells and lots of napkins.

Serve with Collard Green Spring Rolls (recipe on page 194) with Hot Sauce Mayo Dip on the side, and NY Cherry-Ginger Spritz (recipes on page 196).

Collard Green Spring Rolls

Serves 4 to 6

FOR THE GREENS

4 strips black pepper bacon

1 yellow onion, chopped

4 garlic cloves, smashed

2 chipotle peppers in adobo, drained but not rinsed

1 cup apple cider vinegar

¼ cup sugar

½ teaspoon crushed red pepper flakes

1 tablespoon kosher salt

2 teaspoon ground black pepper

6 cups chicken stock (page 14 or store-bought) or ham hock broth (page 45 or store-bought)

1 pound collard greens, stems removed and leaves cut into 2-inch pieces

FOR THE SPRING ROLLS

1 tablespoon cornstarch

1 tablespoon water

12 spring roll wrappers

4 cups canola oil, for frying

Hot Sauce Mayo Dip (page 196), for serving

Note

Though the collard greens can be made the same day you make the spring rolls, they will develop deeper flavors if you make them a day before.

TO MAKE THE COLLARD GREENS: Cook the bacon in a large stockpot over medium heat until the bacon is about halfway toward crispy and done, 7 to 10 minutes.

Add the onion, garlic, peppers, vinegar, sugar, red pepper flakes, salt, and black pepper, and cook for 2 minutes, until the onion and garlic begin to soften.

Stir in the stock and bring the liquid to a simmer.

Stir in the greens, cover the pot, then let the greens cook for 1½ hours, or until tender.

Allow the greens to cool completely before making the spring rolls. If desired, you can make them ahead (see note), cool completely, then refrigerate the greens and pot likker in an airtight container for up to 5 days until ready to use.

TO MAKE THE SPRING ROLLS: Mix the cornstarch and water in a small bowl and set it near your preparation area for easy access.

Remove the greens from the pot, then finely chop them and set aside. Reserve ¼ cup of the pot likker for making the Hot Sauce Mayo Dip.

Place a spring roll wrapper on a clean surface with the point of a corner at the top. Scoop a tablespoon of chopped greens about 1 inch from the bottom point of the wrapper, then spread the greens over the wrapper, leaving ¼-inch around the edges.

Working from the bottom, tightly roll up the wrapper about halfway toward the point at the top. Fold in the left and right ends, then keep rolling toward the top. Brush the top point with the cornstarch mixture, then finish rolling all the way, making sure the tip is affixed to the roll. Repeat until you have a dozen spring rolls. At this point you can refrigerate them until you are ready to fry them. This is also a good point to make the Hot Sauce Mayo Dip (recipe on page 196).

When you are ready to fry the egg rolls, heat the oil in a dutch oven over medium heat until it reaches 375°F.

Working in two or three batches, fry the spring rolls until crispy, 3 to 5 minutes on each side.

Transfer to a paper towel–lined plate to drain. Serve warm with Hot Sauce Mayo Dip.

Hot Sauce Mayo Dip

Serves 4 to 6

- 1 cup mayonnaise
- ¼ cup reserved collard green pot likker
- 1 tablespoon pepper pot hot sauce
- 1 teaspoon soy sauce
- 1 serrano pepper, thinly sliced

Mix the mayonnaise, pot likker, hot sauce, and soy sauce together in a medium bowl. Cover and refrigerate until ready to serve.

Garnish with pepper slices just before serving.

NY Cherry-Ginger Spritz

Serves 8

- 16 ounces unsweetened cherry juice
- 1 small knob ginger, peeled and roughly chopped
- 1 cup turbinado sugar
- 1 lemon, zested in wide strips
- 32 ounces seltzer water
- 32 cherries, pitted
- 1 lime or lemon, cut into 8 wedges

Bring the cherry juice, ginger, and sugar to a simmer in a saucepan over medium heat, stirring continuously until the sugar completely dissolves. Remove from the heat.

Add the lemon zest, then let the cherry-ginger juice steep for 20 minutes.

Remove the lemon zest, then strain the cherry-ginger juice through a fine mesh sieve into a small pitcher or large measuring cup.

Pour 2 ounces (about ¼ cup) of the cherry-ginger syrup into each of 8 highball glass. Fill the glasses with ice, then top off with 4 ounces of seltzer water.

Skewer 4 cherries and garnish each drink. Serve with a lime or lemon wedge. Cheers!

Fried Apple Hand Pies *with* Cinnamon Sugar *and* Jamaican Rum Crème

Serves 4

FOR THE PIE DOUGH

4 cups all-purpose flour, plus extra for rolling

1 pound unsalted butter, cut into squares and chilled

½ teaspoon salt

1 teaspoon almond extract

¾ cup ice water

FOR THE FILLING

1 tablespoon unsalted butter

2 pounds tart apples, such as Granny Smith, peeled, cored, small diced

1 cup packed light brown sugar

½ cup unfiltered apple cider

2 teaspoons lemon juice

½ teaspoon vanilla bean paste

¼ cup bourbon

1 teaspoon cinnamon

1 nutmeg, grated 8 times

1 tablespoon cornstarch

1 tablespoon water

1 teaspoon kosher salt

FOR THE CINNAMON SUGAR

½ cup granulated sugar

2 teaspoons ground cinnamon

Pinch of ground cloves

FOR THE JAMAICAN RUM CRÈME

2 cups heavy cream

4 tablespoons powdered sugar

⅛ cup Jamaican rum

½ teaspoon vanilla bean paste

Zest of ¼ lime

4 cups canola oil, for frying

The perceived kinship between the Coconut Puff-Puff (recipe on page 19) to the Fried Apple Hand Pie is not a long stretch: crispy, fried dough filled with something sweet or savory as portable street food. Hand pies have a long history among working-class cultures across the globe. Cornish pasties date to medieval times. Central Asian and Middle Eastern samosas are mentioned in texts for the first time around the tenth century. Nigerian meat pies were the precursor to Jamaican patties and South American and Mexican empanadas. Sweet pies, such as this one, were among Greek and Roman Empire foodstuffs. These are quick to make—either fried or baked—and have a decidedly adult twist with the Jamaican crème.

TO MAKE THE PIE DOUGH: Pulse the flour, butter, and salt in a food processor until pea-size beads form.

Stir the almond extract into the water. Add the water to the dough while the food processor is running and mix until a dough ball forms. Do not overmix.

Turn the dough ball onto a piece of plastic wrap and wrap it. Refrigerate the dough while you make the pie filling.

TO MAKE THE PIE FILLING: Melt the butter in a large saucepan over medium heat. Stir in the apples and cook until the apples have lightly browned on all sides, approximately 10 minutes. Transfer the apples to a bowl and set aside.

Add the sugar, cider, lemon juice, and vanilla bean paste to the pan and cook, stirring occasionally until the sugar just starts to melt. Stir in the bourbon and return the apples to the pan.

Sprinkle with cinnamon and nutmeg, stir to coat the apples, then bring the filling to a simmer.

Stir the cornstarch and water together in a small bowl, then add it to the apple filling. Cook, stirring, until the filling simmers and begins to thicken, 5 to 10 minutes.

Fold the salt into the apple filling then remove from the heat and let cool completely.

TO MAKE THE CINNAMON SUGAR: Combine all ingredients in a small bowl.

< recipe continues >

Fried Apple Hand
Pies (197), Churros
in Cinnamon-Vanilla
Sugar (page 164),
and Beignets with
Espresso Powdered
Sugar (page 150)

Note

If you prefer baked hand pies, simply skip the oil and preheat the oven to 375°F. Line a baking sheet with parchment paper and lay the pies about 1 to 2 inches apart on the sheet.

Brush the pies with a wash comprised of 1 egg beaten with 1 tablespoon of water. Sprinkle the pies with the cinnamon sugar and bake for 20 to 25 minutes, until golden brown and flaky.

TO MAKE THE CRÈME: Set a mixing bowl in the freezer for 30 minutes.

Remove the bowl from the freezer and pour the cream, sugar, rum, and vanilla bean paste into the bowl. Whisk or beat with a hand mixer with a whisk attachment until the cream is light and fluffy with stiff peaks. Fold in the lime zest, then refrigerate for at least 30 minutes until ready to serve with the hand pies.

TO ASSEMBLE THE HAND PIES: Remove the dough from the refrigerator. Sprinkle a couple of tablespoons flour on a clean surface and on a rolling pin, then roll the pie dough into a rectangle about ¼-inch thick. Cut the pie dough into 4-inch squares using the sharp tip of a knife or a pizza cutter.

Please one heaping tablespoon of pie filling in the middle of each pie dough square. Fold the pie dough over into a triangle and press with a fork around the edges to secure. Refrigerate the pies uncovered for 1 hour.

While the pies chill, heat the oil to 365°F in a dutch oven on medium-high heat.

Fry the pies 4 or 5 at a time (do not overcrowd the pan), 5 to 7 minutes per side until golden brown and flaky.

Transfer the pies to a paper towel–lined plate to drain, then sprinkle with the cinnamon sugar. Once cool enough to handle, serve with the crème.

Chicago

Zella Palmer

I moved to New Orleans to retrace my family's steps and to be one of the many preservationists in academia to ensure that their stories are told. For the first time, our generation can tell the unabridged food stories of our grandparents and their grandparents. Stories that were told in our homes, over card games, Sunday suppers, in family photo albums, and inscribed family trees in broken handwriting in the front cover of our grandmother's Bible. It is a story that began in West and Central Africa when jollof rice became *jambalaya*, *purloo*, *mulatto rice*, and *red rice*; when Senegalese *soupe kandja* and Nigerian *okro* or *pepper soup* became the *gumbo* of New Orleans and Charleston. A story that continues today with African pitmasters barbecuing suya, braai, ribs, jerk, whole hog, and rib tips in Nigeria, Senegal, Jamaica, South Africa, Chicago, the Carolinas, Atlanta, Cuba . . . and all over the world.

Wherever the Black diaspora resides, our traditions live. I was born and raised on the South Side. I came to the South with all these memories, hustle, traditions, and a dope playlist of Chicago house music.

My earliest childhood memories were Sunday dinners at Grandpa Palmer's house. Grandpa Palmer would sit stoically at the head of the table with his Cuban cigar, anticipating our weekly Sunday supper after a long week of hard work at the post office. The pungent smell of chitterlings and the intoxicating aroma of my grandfather's gumbo was passed down as a rite of passage to my auntie Caroline and auntie Sweetie after my grandmother Ruth Mae died.

I remember driving down 75th, 79th, or 87th streets, whether in zero below or "Summertime Chi" weather, and the smell of orgasmic mouthwatering ribs, hot links, and rib tips piped out of the chimneys of neighborhood barbecue joints. These were the intersections of the Chicago stockyards, once the hog butcher to the world, where Black hands who fled the domestic American terrorism of the South seasoned sausages crafted by German and Polish makers and transformed their style of barbecue for Chicago's winters. There are many black-and-white photographs from neighbors' scrapbooks of Black men smoking meats in metal barrels. Then those gave way to the aquariums adapted into pits, like Lem's on 75th Street.

My father and Grandpa Palmer shopped along Maxwell Street in Chicago.

This was where Black folks from the South, plus their children and grandchildren, would convene to spend their hard-earned paychecks from the long menial hours of underpaid work in Chicago factories. Sadly, the only remnant that Chicagoans have of this incredible history is the iconic scene from the 1980 film *The Blues Brothers* where bluesman John Lee Hooker played "Boom Boom" outside of Nate's Delicatessen on Maxwell Street, when it was the epicenter of a shared Southern Black and Jewish culture in the Midwest.

Historically, most Southern Black migrants moved to an area in Chicago that became "The Black Belt," located between 22nd and 63rd streets. That was the center of African American life in Chicago. And when Chicago's Black politicians, celebrities, pastors, churchgoers, and the community wanted "downhome cooking," restaurants like Army & Lou's, Gladys' Luncheonette, and Izola's restaurants were their favorite eateries.

For many, down-home cooking and barbecue was the only memory most folks had of the South, and they weren't letting it go for anybody. There was such an essential need for anything from "down home," I can still remember when Black farmers from the South drove truckloads of produce to Chicago. For $5, oversize seeded farm-grown Mississippi watermelon was sold on truck beds in the hood. Thankfully, this tradition continues during summer months when Black Mississippi farmers park on Stony Island Avenue. Small family-owned grocery stores like Market Fisheries on State Street opened in 1954. They still sell live catfish, gumbo crabs,

hot sausages, and Gulf shrimp delivered weekly from Louisiana.

In the early part of the twenty-first century, Army & Lou's and Izola's closed their doors after being open for more than five decades. All we can do is hope that their families preserved all the framed photos of famous Black history-makers that adorned their walls.

Sadly, Gladys' Luncheonette closed in the late 1990s. A white North Side reporter wrote a bad restaurant review of Gladys'. The review summoned health officials to shut down a community restaurant that had been open since the 1940s. A historic restaurant that once served Dr. Martin Luther King Jr., Redd Foxx, Della Reese, Chicago mayor Harold Washington, Gladys Knight, and a host of others. Mrs. Gladys died heartbroken.

It is imperative that the remaining South Side Chicago restaurants that served Black migrants and their descendants remain open or there will be nothing left of this rich past. The only remaining restaurants still open are the barbecue joints that have these aquarium-style barbecue pits. In 1954, Lem's Barbecue opened its doors on 75th Street. It's still operating, although James Lemons Sr. died in 2015. Leon Finney of Leon's Barbecue died in 2008. Hecky Powell, owner of Hecky's Barbecue in Evanston, died in 2020 of COVID-19–related health issues after operating the business for thirty-seven years. The new players—Uncle John's on 47th Street, Alice's Bar-B-Que, and Honey 1 BBQ—have picked up the torch to serve Black Chicago.

These Black pitmasters made generational barbecue. Their ancestral survival skills helped them to adapt to the Windy City's freezing cold weather, northern racism, and discriminatory housing practices. These men had no access to business loans, endorsements, family wealth, or a blueprint on how to run a business. Yet they kept their doors open for decades, relying on the Black dollar, palates, and memories of so

many. Even in twenty-below-zero weather, these men tended the fires of indoor pits every day late into the wee hours, serving up hot plates of smoked meat for customers bearing heavy crosses.

Barbecue became so entrenched into the very fabric of Black Chicago, that grocers made sure they filled consumers' needs. A hundred and fifty years ago, grocery stores like Moo & Oink opened to serve the Black community. When Moo & Oink was still open on Stony Island Avenue, all of Black Chicago would buy bags of rib tips and slabs for the family barbecue for the one day off when they could barbecue on 63rd Street Beach during the summer. Outside of Moo & Oink, a clean-cut Black Muslim would sell bean pies and *The Final Call* newspaper, pleading with Black folks to put the pork down and eat to live. This was the South Side of Chicago we grew up in.

—Zella Palmer,
Director of the Ray Charles Program in
African American Material Culture
Dillard University,
New Orleans, Louisiana

Like me, writer and scholar Zella Palmer was a child of Chicago who returned to her ancestral South. While I made my way from Atlanta to Louisville back to Atlanta, Zella left Chicago for a post at Dillard University in New Orleans—the place of her father's birth.

Todd's Take on Chicago Barbecue

My Taste for barbecue was shaped first by my dad, then by my hometown.

My father taught me the techniques of finding good cuts, of brining yard birds, mixing my own rubs, and creating memorable sauces that serve more than just to flavor the meat. He used pineapple for his classic Chicago Red BBQ Sauce (recipe on page 210) to tenderize the meat and infuse the sauce with an acid other than vinegar. He was building on the time-honored traditions he was taught by his own Louisiana kin.

The Chicago pitmasters adapted their smoking and cooking styles to meet the climate, but I could get rib tips every bit as crusty as you could find in St. Louis, hot links as peppery as found in Texas, and sauces sweeter than in Memphis, as pungent as from South Carolina, and as vinegary as those from the mountains of North Carolina. Because Chicago is home to the second largest Latin immigrant population, just behind Los Angeles, I could also dip into the nearby neighborhoods on the city's far southeast side for slow-roasted goat tacos, slabs of grilled brisket doused with unctuous garlicky sauces, and tamales stuffed with chili-flecked pulled pork.

When I reflect on these early influences, I realize how viscerally I experienced the connections among people through foodways and cultures because of where I lived. I didn't know then that I was tasting the centuries-long reverberations of conquest, displacement, and the collisions of class and place. But I think being a self-taught chef who had more curiosity than culinary bona fides allowed in me the openness to not get caught up in the dogma of regional differences and appreciate the breadth and artistry inherent in low-and-slow smoking and cooking methods, from an Argentinian steak to smoked baby back ribs. All of it is Soul Food.

Grilled Skirt Steak *with* Chimichurri Sauce

Serves 4

FOR THE CHIMICHURRI MARINADE

4 (4- to 6-ounce) portions skirt steak

4 garlic cloves, smashed and chopped

1 yellow onion, finely diced

Zest and juice of 1 orange

Zest and juice of 1 lime

1 jalapeño pepper, cut in half lengthwise

4 sprigs fresh Italian parsley, chopped

4 sprigs fresh cilantro, chopped

2 sprigs fresh oregano, chopped

1 cup extra virgin olive oil

4 tablespoons soy sauce

4 tablespoons Worcestershire Sauce (page 72 or store-bought)

2 tablespoons red wine vinegar

2 tablespoons aged sherry vinegar

½ teaspoon kosher salt

¼ teaspoon freshly ground black pepper

FOR THE GRILLED STEAKS

1 tablespoon Sazón seasoning (page 15)

1 teaspoon kosher salt

½ teaspoon coarsely ground black pepper

FOR THE MARINADE: Rinse and pat dry the skirt steak, then set aside.

Combine the remaining marinade ingredients in a large mixing bowl, whisking until well combined. Divide the marinade in half, storing one half in an airtight container in the refrigerator, and pouring the other half in a deep casserole dish or large plastic bag to marinate the steaks.

Place the steaks in the baking dish with the marinade, toss to coat, and marinate for 2 hours at room temperature, or cover and marinate overnight in the refrigerator.

TO GRILL THE STEAKS: Prepare your grill for medium-high heat, between 450°F and 500°F.

Stir together the Sazón, salt, and pepper in a small bowl.

Remove the skirt steak from the marinade, pat dry with a paper towel, and transfer to a plate. Season the steaks on all sides with the seasoning mixture.

Place the steaks over direct heat on the grill and cook for 2 minutes on each side for medium rare, 3 minutes on each side for medium, or 4 minutes on each side for well-done.

Transfer the steaks to a cutting board or a platter to let rest for at least 2 minutes before slicing. Using a sharp butcher knife, slice the skirt steaks against the grain into ¼-inch strips. To serve, spoon the reserved chimichurri sauce over the steaks and sprinkle with any remaining seasoning. Serve with Smoked Baby Back Ribs with Dad's Chicago Red BBQ Sauce (recipe on page 207) and Grilled Corn with Ancho Chile Butter (recipe on page 211).

Note

While the grill is still hot and the steaks are resting, throw a few ears of corn on the grill.

Smoked Baby Back Ribs *with* Dad's Chicago Red BBQ Sauce

Serves 4

FOR THE DRY RUB

2 tablespoons dark brown sugar

2 tablespoons kosher salt

2 tablespoons sweet paprika

2 tablespoons smoked paprika

1 tablespoon chili powder

1 tablespoon granulated onion

1 tablespoon granulated garlic

2 teaspoons ground cumin

2 teaspoons freshly ground black pepper

2 teaspoons dry mustard

½ teaspoon cayenne pepper

FOR THE RIBS

2 (2-pound) slabs baby back ribs

2 tablespoons canola oil

FOR THE DRY RUB: Combine all dry ingredients in a small bowl. Transfer the rub to an airtight container if you're not going to use it right away, and store it in a cool, dry place. It will keep for up to 6 months.

TO SMOKE THE RIBS: Depending upon what equipment you are using, preheat the smoker to 235°F, the grill to 300°F, or the oven to 325°F.

Take the ribs out of the refrigerator at least a half hour before cooking so that they can come to room temperature. Turn the ribs so that the backside is showing and make diamond-shape slits in the membrane using a sharp knife. Reserve 1 tablespoon of the dry rub for Dad's Chicago Red BBQ Sauce recipe (page 210). Sprinkle the backside with half the dry rub, ensuring that the rub gets into the cuts. Turn the ribs over and sprinkle the rest of the rub all over the surface, but do not press the rub into the flesh or it will dry out the meat.

Cook the ribs in the smoker for 3 hours; over indirect heat on the grill for 2½ hours, wrapping in foil halfway through the cooking time; or in the oven for 2 hours.

Once the internal temperature of the ribs has reached 145°F, they are done. Serve warm with a side of Dad's Chicago Red BBQ Sauce (recipe on page 210).

Note

The rub and the BBQ sauce can be made well ahead of time. In fact, making them ahead will help the flavors meld.

Grilled Skirt Steak with
Chimichurri Sauce (page 206)
Smoked Baby Back Ribs with
Dad's Chicago Red BBQ Sauce
(page 207)
Grilled Corn with Ancho Chili
Butter (page 211)

Dad's Chicago Red BBQ Sauce

Makes 1 quart

1 (16-ounce) can pineapple chunks in juice

1 yellow onion, finely diced

1 cup apple cider vinegar

½ cup packed dark brown sugar

¼ cup Worcestershire Sauce (page 72 or store-bought)

2 tablespoons soy sauce

2 tablespoons hot sauce

1 tablespoon dry rub (page 207)

1 teaspoon crushed red pepper flakes

4 cups ketchup

Combine the pineapple chunks, onion, vinegar, sugar, Worcestershire Sauce, soy sauce, hot sauce, dry rub, and red pepper flakes in a stockpot over medium heat and bring to a simmer. Cook, stirring occasionally, for 10 minutes.

Stir in half the ketchup and simmer for 5 minutes. Stir in the remaining ketchup and simmer for 5 minutes more. You can make this sauce several days ahead, which will let the flavors meld even more. Refrigerate sauce in an airtight container for up to 2 weeks.

Grilled Corn *with* Ancho Chili Butter

Serves 4 to 6

8 cups cold water

2 tablespoons kosher salt

6 ears fresh corn on the cob, in their husks

Ancho Chili Butter (see below)

TO PREP THE CORN: Mix the water and salt in a large stockpot. Submerge the corn ears in the water and let them soak for up to an hour.

Prepare your grill for medium-high heat, between 450°F and 500°F.

Drain the corn. Peel the husks back without removing them and discard as much of the silk as possible, then wrap the husks back up around the corn.

Grill the corn until charred on all sides, turning every 2 minutes, for about 8 minutes total.

Transfer the corn to a platter and cover with a heavy dish towel until ready to serve with the Ancho Chili Butter.

Note

To select the best corn for grilling, find ears with tight green husks with golden tassels that have a slight stickiness to them. Avoid those with dried yellowed or brownish husks or with tassels that have turned black. Press the kernels for plumpness. Avoid those where kernels are missing or dried.

Ancho Chili Butter

1 pound unsalted butter, softened

1 sprig fresh cilantro, roughly chopped

1 tablespoon honey

1 teaspoon ancho chili powder

1 teaspoon kosher salt

¼ teaspoon ground cumin

Mix all the ingredients in a medium bowl, smashing the herbs and spices into the butter until they are evenly distributed. Serve alongside hot grilled corn or Onion-and-Smoked-Cheddar Buttermilk Biscuits (recipe on page 113). Refrigerate the remaining butter in an airtight container for up to 2 weeks.

Pulled Pork Tamales *with* Charred Corn, Alabama White Sauce, *and* Homemade Cola

Serves 4 to 6

FOR THE PULLED PORK

1 (6- to 8-pound) bone-in pork butt

1 tablespoon vegetable oil

4 tablespoons Sazón seasoning (page 15)

1 yellow onion, roughly chopped

4 garlic cloves, smashed

2 cups ham hock broth (page 45) or chicken stock (page 14 or store-bought)

½ cup apple cider vinegar

¼ cup Worcestershire Sauce (page 72 or store-bought)

2 tablespoons whole grain mustard

2 tablespoons tomato paste

¼ cup dark brown sugar

salt and pepper to taste

FOR THE TAMALE DOUGH

2 strips bacon

1 teaspoon minced onion flakes

2½ cups ham hock broth (page 45 or store-bought)

1½ cups leaf lard

4 cups masa flour

1 teaspoon kosher salt

FOR ASSEMBLING THE TAMALES

16 corn husks

1 cup water

TO MAKE THE PULLED PORK: Rinse and pat dry the pork butt. Massage the oil into the pork butt then slather with the Sazón seasoning.

Layer the onions and garlic in a 6-quart slow cooker or multicooker. Set the pork butt on top of the onions, then pour the stock, vinegar, Worcestershire Sauce, mustard, tomato paste, and brown sugar over the butt.

Set the slow cooker or multicooker to low and cook for 5 hours until the pork butt is tender.

Turn off the slow cooker and let the pork butt rest for 20 minutes. Using a carving fork, pull apart the pork and stir it into the juices. Taste it for salt and pepper, then adjust seasonings to your liking. Remove the bone.

Transfer the pork to an airtight container and refrigerate to cool completely.

TO MAKE THE TAMALE DOUGH: Heat a large skillet over medium heat. Place the bacon in the pan and cook until brown and crisp. Turn off the heat.

Remove the bacon from the pan and roughly chop it. Return the bacon to the pan along with the onion.

Whip the pork stock and lard together in a mixing bowl using a hand mixer until the mixture is light and fluffy. Fold in the bacon-onion mixture.

In another bowl, stir together the masa flour and salt, then fold in the lard mixture until it is all incorporated.

TO MAKE THE TAMALES: Make sure the husks have no tears or splits. Soak the husks in warm water for 10 minutes so that they will be pliable.

Lay a tamale husk on a clear surface with the smallest end facing you, then spread 1½ tablespoons of the dough in the center. Using wax paper or plastic wrap, press the dough to a thickness of about ¼ inch.

Follow with 1 to 2 tablespoons of the pulled pork in the center of the tamale dough.

< recipe continues >

ROOTS, HEART, SOUL

Note

The pulled pork, tamale dough, Alabama White Sauce, and Homemade Cola can be made a day or two ahead. The Charred Corn is best made fresh, while the tamales are steaming.

If you do not have a slow cooker, cook the pork, fat-side up, in a smoker set at 225°F for 12 hours. For an oven version, brown the pork butt in a Dutch oven, cover it, and cook it at 300°F for 5 hours.

Serves 4 to 6

6 ears fresh corn, husks and silks removed

2 tablespoons unsalted butter

½ teaspoon Sazón seasoning (page 15)

2 sprigs fresh cilantro, stems removed and leaves roughly chopped

1 sprig fresh Italian parsley, leaves roughly chopped

To fold the tamale, start with the smallest end. Fold it over the filling, then fold the left and right ends over, pressing the tamale dough firmly together. Fold the larger end over the smaller end so that you have a nice, tight package. Repeat the process with the rest of the husks.

Place the water in a multicooker or an ordinary steamer, then set the trivet rack in the pot. Arrange the tamales vertically, leaning them against the sides of the pot and one another so that they won't fall over. Work in two batches, if necessary, to leave a little space for air flow.

Steam the tamales on high for 25 minutes. Let the tamales rest for at least 10 minutes before releasing the pressure. Serve the tamales with a side of Charred Corn (see below), a slather of Alabama White Sauce (recipe on page 216), and Homemade Cola (recipe on page 216).

Charred Corn

On a grill or a burner on a gas stove set to high heat, char the corn on all sides, 1 to 2 minutes per side. Remove corn from the grill, and when cool enough to handle, trim the kernels from the cob into a bowl and set aside.

Melt the butter in a large cast-iron skillet over medium heat and stir in the Sazón. Place the charred corn in the skillet, cover, and steam for 5 minutes.

Turn off the heat and transfer the corn to the bowl. Add the cilantro and parsley to the skillet, stirring in the butter and seasonings remaining in the pan. Pour the herbs over the corn and toss. Serve warm with the tamales.

Notes

Make the Charred Corn while the tamales are cooking so that they will be ready right around the same time.

You can use the stovetop skillet method of charring the corn as an alternative to a grill or burner. You need a nonstick skillet or well-seasoned cast-iron skillet. To make it even easier, you can use frozen corn kernels in place of fresh. Simply place the kernels in a single layer in the skillet without any oil or butter over medium-high heat. Do not stir until you hear the kernels begin to sizzle and pop and they start to brown. Begin stirring and cook until the kernels are charred on all sides. Transfer them to a bowl, then proceed with the recipe as written.

Alabama White Sauce

Makes 1¼ cups

1 cup mayonnaise

2 tablespoons apple cider vinegar

1 tablespoon light brown sugar

1 teaspoon whole grain mustard

1 teaspoon prepared horseradish

1 teaspoon hot sauce

½ teaspoon Sazón seasoning (page 15)

Combine all the ingredients in a medium bowl, stirring until well combined and the sauce coats the back of the spoon. If the sauce is too thick, add an additional teaspoon of apple cider vinegar.

Homemade Cola

Serves 4

4 cups brewed coffee

4 cups turbinado sugar

4 dehydrated orange peels

4 dehydrated apple slices

3 cinnamon sticks

Zest of 2 lemons

1 teaspoon ground ginger

½ teaspoon vanilla bean paste

½ teaspoon ground nutmeg

½ teaspoon sassafras (filé) powder

Seltzer water, for serving

Combine all the ingredients in a large stockpot over medium heat and bring to a simmer. Simmer, stirring frequently, for 30 minutes or until the liquid is reduced by half. Turn off the heat and remove the pot from the stove.

Strain the liquid through a fine-mesh sieve into a pitcher. Refrigerate until cold and ready to serve.

To serve: Pour ¼ cup of cola syrup into tumblers. Fill the tumblers with ice then top with ½ cup seltzer.

Inside the *Ebony* Test Kitchen

Like most Black Chicago families, we always had a stack of *Ebony* magazines on our coffee table. It was the bible of hip Black culture, from music and fashion to architecture and food. I'll never forget the time my father, who was a data manager for Montgomery Ward, took me to the Johnson Publishing Company headquarters, located inside the Loop in downtown. We explored the building and made our way to the storied test kitchen.

There were all the kitchen colors of the time: harvest gold, avocado, and russet, but swirled in such a dizzying array with a swash of purple you could feel the motion and hear the music that is part of any good kitchen rhythm. There were six burners on the island stovetop, double ovens on one wall, and another under-counter oven across the way. For a kid who devoted a good portion of his time to listening to disco and hanging out in the kitchen with my mother and aunts, the *Ebony* test kitchen was like going to church.

All those memories and feelings came rushing back as I toured the rebuilt and revived kitchen as part of MOFAD's *African/American: Making the Nation's Table* exhibit. I was reminded how integral *Ebony*'s impact was on telling the story of the breadth and diversity of African American cookery in America through its "Date with a Dish" column and cookbooks. Back in the 1940s and 1950s, the founding columnist Freda DeKnight heralded the Black hands that made food all across the country, whether it was homespun or gourmet, and recognized the many traditions—from Spanish and Indian to French and Asian—that affected, altered, and shaped African American foodways.

Loaded Sweet Potato *with* Creamed Mustard Greens, Crispy Bacon, *and* Smoked Cheddar Breadcrumbs

Serves 4

FOR THE CREAMED GREENS

4 large mustard green leaves, washed and roughly chopped

2 tablespoons extra virgin olive oil

2 shallots, sliced into thin rings

2 garlic cloves, smashed and roughly chopped

1 tablespoon dijon mustard

1 cup chicken stock (page 14 or store-bought)

1 cup heavy cream

Zest of 1 lemon

2 sprigs fresh thyme, stems removed

Pinch of freshly grated nutmeg

Kosher salt

Freshly ground black pepper

FOR THE BACON

4 strips thick-cut bacon

1 teaspoon coarsely ground black pepper

¼ teaspoon sugar

FOR THE BREADCRUMBS

8 tablespoons unsalted butter, melted

1 tablespoon reserved bacon drippings

1 shallot, finely diced

2 garlic cloves, smashed and chopped

1 cup panko breadcrumbs

Even in the big city, my family and our neighbors kept gardens so that no matter the times, we always had access to fresh vegetables and could make a hearty, filling plant-forward meal with just a bit of meat and loads of flavor. This recipe pays homage to that resourcefulness born of my kin who came up from the foothills of the Appalachians in Alabama and across the Kentucky River. It is a colorful, well-seasoned autumnal dish, packed with nutritional punch and loaded with flavor. The creamed mustard greens will have a subtle pepperiness that flirts with the berbere spice in the warm, crunchy breadcrumbs. The bacon hints at candied yams, typical of sweet potato preparations, without being overpowering or cloying.

TO MAKE THE GREENS: Boil water in a stockpot over high heat, then add the mustard greens and blanch until they turn a vibrant green color, approximately 3 minutes. Remove the greens from the boiling water with a slotted spoon or fine mesh sieve then submerge them in a bowl of ice water to stop their cooking. Transfer to a paper towel–lined plate to dry.

Heat the oil in a cast-iron skillet over medium heat. Add the shallots and cook until slightly melted, 3 to 5 minutes.

Add the garlic, dijon mustard, and stock, and cook until the liquid has reduced by half, 7 to 10 minutes.

Stir in the cream, lemon zest, and thyme. Cook for 1 minute, then add the mustard greens, nutmeg, salt, and pepper. Cook until greens have wilted, approximately 3 minutes.

Transfer the greens to a bowl and refrigerate them until cold.

TO PREPARE THE BACON: Preheat the oven to 350° F.

Lay the bacon strips on a foil-lined baking sheet. Combine the pepper and sugar in a small bowl and sprinkle it all over the bacon.

Bake the bacon for about 12 minutes or until brown and crispy.

Transfer the bacon to paper towels to drain and cool. Pour the bacon fat into a glass measuring cup to use in the breadcrumbs.

Crumble the bacon and set aside.

1 cup grated smoked cheddar cheese

1 cup grated parmesan cheese

½ cup grated smoked gouda

1 teaspoon berbere spice (page 187)

½ teaspoon kosher salt

2 sprigs fresh curly parsley, stems removed and leaves finely chopped

4 large sweet potatoes

1 tablespoon vegetable oil

TO MAKE THE BREADCRUMBS: Combine all the ingredients in a mixing bowl and set aside.

TO MAKE THE SWEET POTATOES: Preheat the oven to 350°F. Rub each sweet potato with the oil and bake for 25 minutes or until the potato slightly softens. Remove the potatoes from the oven and let them rest for 15 minutes.

Cut the sweet potatoes in half down the center and scoop out some of the meat. Fill the space with equal portions of creamed greens. Cover the greens with generous portions of the breadcrumbs, pressing them into the greens.

Return the potatoes to the oven and bake for another 25 minutes, or until the breadcrumbs are golden brown and the potato is tender. Sprinkle with the peppered bacon crumbs and serve.

Chicago Style Beach Spaghetti, aka Fish *and* Spaghetti

Serves 4

FOR THE FRIED CATFISH

2 cups whole buttermilk

2 tablespoons Worcestershire Sauce (page 72 or store-bought)

1 tablespoon hot sauce (page 166 or store-bought)

¼ teaspoon granulated garlic

¼ teaspoon granulated onion

4 teaspoons kosher salt, divided

1½ teaspoons freshly ground black pepper, divided

1½ pounds deboned catfish fillets, cut into 2-inch pieces

2 cups yellow cornmeal

¼ teaspoon cayenne pepper

4 cups vegetable oil, for frying

When I learned that Dominican families held on to their tradition of bringing stockpots of spaghetti to beachside celebrations, I recalled my own and other Black families' practice of carrying foil pans filled with fish and spaghetti to weekends on 57th Street Beach or at Jackson Park. Fried fish travels well, as our kinfolk learned on those northbound trains, and spaghetti is something even little kids will eat.

What I didn't realize until recently, however, is how strongly each family and each family member felt about the "rules" around fish and spaghetti.

In a conversation about beach spaghetti over dinner, my auntie Cherie was adamant there should be no meat in the spaghetti sauce.

How much cheese do you bake into it?

"As much as you want," Cherie said.

Break the noodles?

"Always." Something we agreed on.

One of our dinner companions completely unfamiliar with the idea of fish and spaghetti asked, "Why not just make baked ziti?"

We were flummoxed. "Then it wouldn't be spaghetti."

Mix the buttermilk, Worcestershire Sauce, hot sauce, granulated garlic, granulated onion, and 1 teaspoon each of the salt and black pepper in a large bowl or large plastic freezer bag with secure closure. Add the catfish pieces, cover or seal, and refrigerate for 2 to 8 hours.

When you are ready to fry the fish, whisk together the cornmeal, cayenne pepper, and remaining salt and black pepper in a shallow dish or pie plate. When making fish and spaghetti, this should be after you've made the sauce but before you've made the spaghetti.

Heat the oil to 375°F in a deep-sided cast-iron skillet over medium-high heat.

Remove the fish from the buttermilk bath and dredge each piece in the cornmeal until coated all over. Let the catfish rest for at least 5 minutes before frying.

Working in batches, fry the catfish until golden brown all over, 5 to 7 minutes per side. Transfer to a paper towel–lined plate. Serve with Broken Spaghetti and Dad's Meat Spaghetti Sauce (recipes on pages 221 and 222) at home, in the backyard, or at the beach.

Dad's Meat Spaghetti Sauce

Serves 4 to 6

2 tablespoons vegetable oil

1½ pounds ground beef, preferably 75 lean/25 fat

1 tablespoon seasoned salt

2 medium yellow onions, finely diced

1 green bell pepper, finely diced

1 red bell pepper, finely diced

4 garlic cloves, smashed and roughly chopped

1 (14.5-ounce) can plum tomatoes

1 cup Dad's Chicago Red BBQ Sauce (page 210), or a spicy store-bought barbecue sauce

1 tablespoon dried oregano

2 teaspoons kosher salt

1 teaspoon lemon pepper seasoning

1 (12-ounce) can tomato paste

1 cup warm water

1 recipe Broken Spaghetti (page 222)

Heat the oil in a dutch oven over medium heat. Add the ground beef and sprinkle with the seasoned salt. Cook for 6 minutes, stirring occasionally to break the ground beef into fine crumbles.

Transfer the ground beef to a paper towel–lined plate, then pour off the fat from the dutch oven.

Add the onions, peppers, and garlic to the pot and cook for 2 minutes, then return the ground beef to the pot.

Stir in the plum tomatoes, barbecue sauce, oregano, kosher salt, and lemon pepper, and bring the sauce to a simmer.

Add the tomato paste, then fill the can with the warm water to capture any remaining paste, then stir it into the sauce. Simmer for 10 minutes. Use a ladle or spoon to skim off any fat that rises to the top during cooking.

Turn off the heat and let the sauce rest while you prepare the Broken Spaghetti (recipe on page 222). Once the spaghetti is cooked, drain it, add it to the sauce, and stir.

VARIATION FOR BAKED CHEESE SPAGHETTI: Substitute 1 (8-ounce) can tomato purée for the barbecue sauce.

Preheat the oven to 400°F.

Once the spaghetti is cooked, drain it, add it to the sauce, and stir. Stir in 1 cup sour cream, then transfer the spaghetti and sauce to a 9-by-13-inch casserole dish. Top with 2 cups cheddar cheese and bake it for 10 to 12 minutes until the cheese is melted and almost crisp.

Broken Spaghetti

4 quarts cold water

1 tablespoon kosher salt

1 pound dried spaghetti, broken into 3 sections

Bring the water and salt to a boil in a stockpot.

Add the spaghetti to the pot and cook it until just al dente, 6 to 8 minutes.

Pour off the water and rinse the pasta in cold water, then add it to the sauce of your choice.

Fried Lake Perch *with* Pimento Cheese *and* Collard Green Hushpuppies *and* Celery Root *and* Jicama Slaw

Serves 4

FOR THE FISH MARINADE

2 pounds lake perch, cut into eight ¼-pound pieces

8 cups water

1 cup buttermilk

½ cup hot sauce

2 tablespoons Worcestershire Sauce (page 72 or store-bought)

1 tablespoon kosher salt

2 teaspoons granulated onion

2 teaspoons granulated garlic

2 teaspoons ground black pepper

FOR THE SEASONED CORNMEAL FLOUR

1¾ cups all-purpose flour

1½ cups yellow cornmeal

1 cup potato flour (optional, or substitute ½ cup all-purpose flour and ½ cup yellow cornmeal)

4 tablespoons kosher salt

2 tablespoons seasoned salt

1 tablespoon dry mustard

2 teaspoons freshly ground black pepper

1 teaspoon granulated onion

1 teaspoon granulated garlic

1 teaspoon paprika

½ teaspoon celery salt

FOR THE FISH FRY

4 cups canola oil

1 jalapeño pepper, cut into rings

My mom's Friday fish fries were legendary. Nina Simone blaring from the record player as batches upon batches of cornmeal-crusted fish, bowls of lemon wedges, homemade hot sauce, coleslaw, potato salad, and baskets of hushpuppies made their way to tables set on the lawn. Family, neighbors, and friends moved from house to front yard to street as the crowd bloomed. She'd sip a tumbler filled with ice and a nip of moonshine a cousin brought up from Kentucky. This suite of recipes is my tribute to the old neighborhood, where if we didn't catch the perch from Lake Michigan, we could buy it from any one of the fish markets around the South Shore or at Calumet Fisheries on the 95th Street Bridge. The pimento cheese lends a tang and creaminess to the hushpuppies, which are similar to ones I serve at Soul: Food & Culture in Atlanta's Krog Street Market. The green apple–like jicama, a native to South and Central America, honors the powerful influence of our Latin American neighbors on the food and markets in our community.

TO MARINATE THE FISH: Rinse and pat dry the lake perch.

Mix the remaining marinade ingredients in a large food storage container or bowl. Submerge the perch pieces in the marinade and steep for 2 hours at room temperature or in the refrigerator for 12 hours.

TO MAKE THE SEASONED CORNMEAL FLOUR: Stir all the ingredients in a large mixing bowl until well incorporated.

TO FRY THE LAKE PERCH: Heat the oil to 375°F in a deep-sided cast-iron skillet over medium-high heat.

Drain the lake perch in a colander in the sink. Then dredge the perch in the seasoned flour, ensuring that the pieces are coated all over.

Gently place the perch pieces in the heated oil, making sure to not overcrowd the pan, and fry the perch until it is golden brown on one side, 4 to 6 minutes. Turn the pieces and fry until golden and crispy all over, about another 4 to 6 minutes.

< recipe continues >

Transfer the perch to a paper towel–lined plate to drain.

Set the jalapeño rings into the oil and fry until just wilted, approximately 3 minutes.

Transfer the rings to a paper towel–lined plate to drain.

If you are making the Pimento Cheese and Collard Green Hushpuppies (recipe on page 226), this is a good time to fry them in the same oil.

Serve the hot and crispy perch with some hot sauce, hushpuppies, and Celery Root and Jicama Slaw (recipe on page 226).

Notes

If perch is not available, you can substitute other flaky, white fish, such as cod, haddock, walleye, whitefish, whiting, or catfish.

While the perch marinates, mix the seasoned cornmeal flour and the batter for the Pimento Cheese and Collard Green Hushpuppies (recipe on page 226) so that you can fry the fish followed by the hushpuppies and serve them hot at the same time.

You can make the Celery Root and Jicama Slaw (recipe on page 226) a day ahead.

The Fish Fry

From what I can surmise through practice and conversation with smart friends like historian Adrian Miller, the Friday fish fry's prominence in Black foodways grew out of two distinct cultures: the plantation and the Catholic Church.

Work on plantations ended early on Fridays, so the laborers would fish the rivers and coastlines and combine their catches to feed everyone. The cornmeal coating was the result of grist and grit.

In both the Spanish and French Catholic observations, Fridays were reserved for fish. Fishmongers took to discounting fish on that day of the week, which was attractive to other faith traditions looking for fundraisers and people of meager means who would throw rent parties to help families cover the costs of shelter and farming leases. Fish fries grew into forms of fellowship.

1 cup prepared hushpuppy mix

1 teaspoon kosher salt

¼ teaspoon freshly ground black pepper

Pinch of red pepper flakes

Pinch of curry powder

2 leaves fresh collard greens, stems removed and leaves chopped

1 tablespoon grated cheddar cheese

1 piquillo pepper, finely diced (see note)

2 tablespoons collard green pot likker (page 194)

2 tablespoons buttermilk

2 tablespoons water

Canola oil, for frying (see note)

Serves 4

1 shallot, sliced into thin rings

1 cup mayonnaise

3 tablespoons apple cider vinegar

1 tablespoon whole grain mustard

1 tablespoon honey

1 tablespoon freshly squeezed lemon juice

1 bunch fresh Italian parsley, stems removed and leaves roughly chopped

1 celery root, peeled and cut into ⅛-inch matchsticks

1 jicama, peeled and cut into ⅛-inch matchsticks

Pimento Cheese *and* Collard Green Hushpuppies

Stir the hushpuppy mix with the salt, black pepper, chili flakes, and curry powder.

Fold in the greens, cheese, and piquillo pepper until they are evenly distributed.

Mix in the pot likker, buttermilk, and water until a thick dough forms.

Heat the oil to 375°F in a deep-sided cast-iron skillet over medium-high heat.

Using a tablespoon or small ice cream scoop, gently scoop balls of hushpuppy dough into the hot oil, making sure to not overcrowd the pan, and fry the hushpuppies until they are golden brown on one side, 4 to 6 minutes. Flip and fry until golden and crispy all over, about another 4 to 6 minutes.

Transfer the hushpuppies to a paper towel–lined plate to drain. Serve hot alongside the Fried Lake Perch.

Note

If you can't find piquillo peppers, substitute a red bell pepper.

If you do not have any pot likker in reserve, substitute vegetable or chicken stock.

If you are making the hushpuppies at the same time as the fried perch, use the same oil for frying; otherwise, use the amount of oil called for in the recipe (page 223).

Celery Root *and* Jicama Slaw

Mix the shallot, mayonnaise, vinegar, mustard, honey, lemon juice, and parsley in a medium mixing bowl. Fold in the celery root and jicama matchsticks until they are well coated with the dressing.

Cover with plastic wrap and store in the refrigerator until ready to serve.

Whiskey *and* Vanilla Salted Caramel Cake

Serves 8 to 12

FOR THE CAKE

1 tablespoon vegetable shortening, for greasing the pan

4 teaspoons yellow cornmeal, for dusting the pan

2 sticks plus 4 tablespoons unsalted butter, softened

2½ cups plus 1 tablespoon sugar

6 large eggs

1 large egg yolk

½ cup whole buttermilk

1 teaspoon bourbon vanilla extract

1 teaspoon grated lemon zest

3 cups all-purpose flour

1 tablespoon baking powder

FOR THE FROSTING

1 cup whiskey

1 cup granulated sugar

1 cup packed dark brown sugar

1 cup whole buttermilk

8 tablespoons unsalted butter

½ cup vegetable shortening

1 teaspoon vanilla bean paste

1 teaspoon baking soda

½ teaspoon fine sea salt

Maldon Sea Salt Flakes, for garnish

The caramel cake was (and is) revered among Southern bakers. Often made with seven or more layers and draped in a sheet of glistening sweet and buttery caramel, it was (and is) reserved for special occasions. Traveling north on a train out of Alabama or Georgia counted as a special moment worthy of a slice packed in a lunch basket or box, especially when getting north of the Mason-Dixon Line when Black passengers finally could take better seats. My version is slightly simpler to make than the classic layer cake but more nuanced in its flavors. The butter cake has a hint of citrus and is baked in a Bundt or tube pan, which is nearly foolproof. The frosting doubles the caramel punch by building on the warm notes of a smooth Kentucky whiskey. I recommend a small batch whiskey, such as Uncle Nearest 1884—a Black-owned brand built on the legacy of Nathan "Nearest" Green, the Black man who taught Jack Daniels his craft. The burst of salt flakes dusted on top balances the sweetness and gives the cake a modern touch.

TO MAKE THE CAKE: Preheat the oven to 325°F. Lightly grease a 9-inch Bundt or 2-piece tube cake pan. Coat the inside of the pan with the cornmeal, then discard any excess cornmeal.

Cream the butter until light and fluffy with an electric mixer on medium speed, approximately 1 minute. Gradually add the sugar and beat for 3 minutes. Turn the speed to low and continue beating, adding the eggs and egg yolk one at a time and beating well in between each addition.

Stir together the buttermilk, vanilla extract, and lemon zest. With the mixer on low, add the flour and baking powder to the butter mixture in thirds, alternating with the buttermilk in thirds, and ending with the buttermilk.

Pour the cake batter into the prepared cake pan. Tap the pan on the counter to remove any air bubbles. Bake until a toothpick inserted in the center comes out clean and the cake has pulled away from the sides, approximately 1 hour and 20 minutes.

Cool the cake in the pan for 15 minutes, then turn it onto a wire rack and lift off the pan to completely cool.

TO MAKE THE FROSTING: Heat the whiskey in a dutch oven over medium heat, stirring occasionally. Cook until the whiskey is reduced by half, 10 to 12 minutes, then remove from the heat.

Stir in the remaining frosting ingredients. Return the dutch oven

< recipe continues >

to the heat and cook the frosting, stirring often, until the sugars have dissolved and the mixture coats the back of the spoon.

Remove the frosting from the heat and let it rest for 10 minutes.

Beat the frosting in the pot with the whisk attachment of a hand mixer for 3 to 5 minutes, until the frosting is creamy, not fluffy.

TO ASSEMBLE THE CAKE: Set the cake on a serving platter or cake stand. Spoon the frosting on top of the cake, smoothing it with an offset spatula along the top and sides if baked in a tube pan. If baked in a Bundt pan, let the frosting drip down the sides and into the crevices.

Sprinkle the top of the cake with a light dusting of salt flakes.

7Up Cake

Serves 8

FOR THE CAKE

12 tablespoons unsalted butter, softened, plus extra for the pan

3 cups sugar

1 teaspoon vanilla extract

5 large eggs, room temperature

2 large egg yolks, room temperature

3 cups self-rising flour (see note)

¾ cup 7Up soda

1½ teaspoons grated lemon zest

½ teaspoon grated lime zest

FOR THE FROSTING

1 (12-ounce) can Cherry 7Up

½ teaspoon cherry extract

¼ teaspoon vanilla extract

¼ teaspoon almond extract

2 cups powdered sugar

2 tablespoons unsalted butter, melted

With all due respect to the place Sprite holds among Black urban youth, 7Up reigns supreme among the soda cakes to come up out of the South during the postwar migration. Sodas were used for practical reasons, not for novelty. A traditional pound cake without any natural leavening proved heavy and dense, and often dry. Adding 7Up's carbonation to a pound cake recipe lightened the texture and filled the cake with effervescence and the bright taste of the lemon-lime "uncola." Its natural syrup helps create a lightly crisp and caramelized crust on the outside. With or without the Cherry 7Up frosting, this cake brings me back to those backyard gatherings and church potlucks.

TO MAKE THE CAKE: Preheat the oven to 325°F and position the rack in the middle. Grease a Bundt pan with softened butter, coating all surfaces and ensuring every crevice is covered.

Cream the 12 tablespoons butter, sugar, and vanilla using a stand or hand mixer on medium-high speed until smooth and creamy, 3 to 5 minutes.

Turn the speed to medium, then add the eggs one at a time, fully incorporating each one before adding the next. Add the yolks and continue mixing for another minute.

Turn the speed to low and add the flour 1 cup at a time, beating until just incorporated. Pour in the 7Up soda and mix on medium for 1 minute.

Turn off the mixer and fold in the lemon and lime zest using a spatula.

Pour the batter into the pan. Tap the pan lightly on the counter to remove any air bubbles from the batter. Bake for about 80 minutes, or until a toothpick inserted into the cake comes out clean.

Let cool completely on a wire rack, about 1½ hours.

Turn the cake pan onto a cake plate or stand and let it settle for 2 minutes, allowing gravity to assist in releasing the cake from the pan. Tap the top of the pan and lift it, removing the cake from the pan. Brush off any crumbs on the cake or plate before frosting.

TO MAKE THE FROSTING: Heat the Cherry 7Up in a medium saucepan over medium heat and cook until it reduces to ¼ cup, 10 to 12 minutes.

< recipe continues >

Remove the pan from the heat and stir in the extracts. Let the mixture cool to room temperature.

Once cooled, whisk in the powdered sugar and melted butter until the frosting is smooth and creamy but not stiff.

TO ASSEMBLE THE CAKE: Spoon the frosting on top of the cake, smoothing it with an offset spatula along the top and letting the frosting drip down the sides and into the crevices.

Note

If you do not have self-rising flour on hand, mix together 3 cups of all-purpose flour with 3 teaspoons baking powder, 1½ teaspoons salt, and ¾ teaspoon baking soda.

Mashama Bailey

I think Southern food is American food. When you look back at what came here, what foods grow here, and how those foods are used, that's been here for 300, 400 years, I think it's the most perfect reflection of what American cuisine is.

When it comes to my cooking, I just feel like if I'm gonna say something, I have to be very honest about it. I worked under Gabrielle Hamilton (at Prune) and really came into my own. I think if I had not worked for a chef like her, I would not have this perspective. So, I owe a lot to her as far as the way she had me thinking about what my intentions were and how I plan to contribute to this field.

I didn't grow up in a restaurant culture. My parents couldn't afford it. So, we ate well, we ate clean, we ate seasonally. But I didn't even know that's what my mother was doing. So, when I went to culinary school, I didn't really have chefs I identified with. When I wanted to write about my grandmother, my chef instructor would not let me do it. He said, "No, you have to find someone." And I found Edna Lewis. My connection to Edna Lewis is a direct reflection of how I feel about my heritage, how I feel about my grandmother, and how their food helps sustain me.

—Mashama Bailey,
Co-owner and executive chef of
The Grey, Savannah, Georgia, and
The Grey Market, Savannah and Austin, Texas,
as told on my *Soul* podcast on Heritage Radio Network

Mashama Bailey is one of my dearest friends in the world. She is my soul sister. Like me, she was born and raised in the north—the Bronx and Queens boroughs of New York, to be exact—by a family that left the South during the Great Migration. But parts of her childhood were spent with family in Waynesboro, Virginia, and Savannah, Georgia, which left an indelible print on her soul. Also like me and others, Mashama has returned to her ancestral South—to Savannah, and now Austin. She has become a household name the likes of Julia and Edna by reclaiming the authenticity and beauty of Southern food so deeply rooted in Black culture. At The Grey, a restored and reimagined Jim Crow–era bus station, she and her business partner John O. Morisano have redefined and elevated diners' perception of Southern cuisine—and for that feat, Mashama has been recognized by the James Beard Foundation, not just once but twice: the first time in 2019 as Best Chef/Southeast, and most recently in 2022 as Outstanding Chef.

Afterword

The reversal of the Great Migration began as a trickle in the 1970s, increased in the 1990s, and turned into a virtual evacuation from many northern areas in subsequent decades. The movement is largely driven by younger, college-educated Black Americans, from both northern and western places of origin. They have contributed to the growth of the "New South," especially in Texas, Georgia, and North Carolina, as well as metropolitan regions such as Atlanta, Dallas, and Houston. And although these areas are simultaneously in the midst of new immigrant growth and white in-migration, the continuing "New Great Migration" has served to give Black Americans a large—and in many cases, dominant—presence in most parts of America's South.

—William H. Frey
Brookings Institute

Beginning during my childhood in the 1970s, Blacks began to leave the urban centers of the North and West as stable factory jobs in auto and aviation manufacturing, textiles, and packaging began to disappear. Even the fabled gate of the Chicago stockyards where my great-grandfather pioneered meat inspection closed in 1971, conscripted to simply marking a once promising history. Those cities within cities—Harlem, South Central, South Side— that gave our country those rich cultural gifts such as jazz, blues, hip hop, and soul food were islanded by highways, disinvestment, and suburban white flight. Scholarly studies point to these socioeconomic shifts as instigators of a reverse Great Migration of Blacks from the big cities of New York, Illinois, Michigan, and Pennsylvania to the emerging urban hot spots of Dallas and Houston, Texas; Charlotte, North Carolina; and my home, Atlanta, Georgia. I am among those in-migrants who returned to the South, just like Edna Lewis, Mashama Bailey, Zella Palmer, Matthew Raiford, Duane Nutter, and so many other chefs. It wasn't for the work, though. It was for something far deeper—a draw, perhaps toward some place closer to the Equator, to what is and always will be our ancestral home.

I think of this return as a form of truth and reconciliation—not simply at a societal level, where we are reckoning with our country's past and our hope for its future—but at a soul level among African Americans. Black chefs have shed the shame that accompanied the history of enslavement by embracing the great contributions West African culture has had on the foodways of the Americas, especially the United States. Our ancestors were brought here because of their expertise in agriculture and cooking. They didn't simply live off scraps and leftovers, as one narrative insists; they created a cuisine that endures and continues to evolve to this day. In fact, the food, the techniques, the whole-animal approach, and the commitment to deliciousness have been embraced by fine-dining chefs who charge large sums for what our grandmothers and aunts cooked daily and for celebrations in our home kitchens.

Not so long ago, the abundant and liberal use of spices, of red pepper particularly, was considered a hallmark of low-class food—of poor people's food. The embrace of New Orleans' Creole cuisine in the 1980s, shepherded in large part by Ella Brennan and Paul Prudhomme around dishes created by Black cooks, paved the way for a rethinking of flavor and began the defining of a distinctive American cuisine rooted in the American South. Flavor is our gift and our birthright, and it's become mainstream. It's no accident that salsa, tabasco, sriracha, chipotle, and hot sauces have replaced ketchup and mustard as the top condiments. That's a mark of progress.

For years at the beginning of my career, I mimicked other people's foodways, and I did it well. It wasn't until I got my first nomination for a James Beard Foundation award in 2008 and a AAA Five Diamond Award the following year that I realized I was one of the only Black people in the room. I looked at the stage at all these French and Italian chefs. I was cooking their food and not my own, and that's what set me on this path to celebrating our culture, our food, and everything it had to offer.

There is no shame, either, in being in a kitchen—even though this profession carried a stigma our parents wanted to avoid as they pushed us to become lawyers and doctors, believing we could never lead our own restaurants. Chef Joe Randall fought long and hard for African Americans to be considered chefs, not simply cooks. He was the first to celebrate our heritage with annual dinners honoring the pioneers who opened the doors

for people like Patrick Clark, Darryl Evans, and Leah Chase—who, in turn, opened the door for me. In Randall's wake, chefs such as Kevin Mitchell are now hosting dinners built around the great Black caterers of Charleston, South Carolina; Kwame Onwuachi has held two vast celebrations of diversity in the hospitality industry—called Family Reunions—in Virginia, where those first ships landed more than 400 years ago.

In 2021, I was invited by the Southern Foodways Alliance to prepare the family dinner—the shared meal among the 300-plus attendees to the SFA's Fall Summit in Oxford, Mississippi. This one would be the first since the pandemic shutdown and a return to a sort of communion. The theme was to set the table so we could talk freely, something hard to do in an era of extreme polarization, even among family members. I looked no further than my own family's table for inspiration.

For that first meal back among SFA members, I brought the best of South Side Chicago to the Deep South. The meal comprised Canned Beets Revisited: a leek custard topped with cranberry-orange relish, grit croutons, and sheep's milk feta; an homage to Calumet Fisheries with fried scallops and collard-green-and-smoked fish rice balls pierced with hot mustard; a Frito-encrusted flat iron steak with date mole, sweet potato salad, and pickled red onions—a tribute to my dad; and a bourbon-laced apple cobbler served with spiced peanut brittle and a bourbon-lemon anglaise, a nod to the Appalachian ancestors.

Exhilarating, exhausting, and humbling to see such fellowship around those tables after a year and a half of isolation and racial reckoning only confirmed for me what I know is true: Delivering delicious food is the best way to make the world better.

Acknowledgments

Skin tones may divide us, politics may convince us with fury that we have nothing in common, and the way we kneel to pray may give insight to our own mortality. But we are all family. If anything, the writing of this book has reinforced this truth for me.

Writing this book has also revealed the difficulty in acknowledging all who have contributed to its realization, because when you start with one person, a sort of ranking system may ensue and there is the inherent fear of leaving someone out. The acknowledgments may be the most difficult part of writing. So, where do I start?

Of course, there is the team that helped shepherd, research, write, style, photograph, edit, design, and produce the book you hold in your hand. Then, there are the colleagues in the culinary world with whom I have had many conversations that inspired, challenged, and pushed me to think more intentionally about the food I make and serve. And there is my family, the legacy that came before me and laid the groundwork for me to flourish; my aunt and sisters who have preserved that legacy. The loves of my life. I thank them all for their faith and patience in this endeavor.

Yet, there are many unsung heroes in the food world who truly control the ecosystem of delivery systems and safe passage of food to the world—and they rarely publicly receive the acknowledgment and gratitude for the long hours of labor in hard weather. Farmers, ranchers, and fishers spend a lifetime dedicated to providing delicious food to people, often at great personal cost. Still, it is not enough to acknowledge the people who provide nourishment to our soul. We must have a robust conversation about how to financially support the people who make mental and physical sacrifices to ensure that delicious food reaches our tables.

How does food get to us?

From truckers and drivers, shippers, and manufacturers. We owe them a great deal of admiration.

The next time you're behind a delivery truck, know that more than likely they have been on the road for sixty-plus hours; some sleeping in the back of their trucks to provide you with nourishment.

Then, there are the dishwashers of the kitchen restaurants—they are the true heroes of the restaurant system as service depends upon all that they do. "Dishwasher" is a loose term because they not only wash dishes, but they also do prep work, take out the trash, scrub toilets, provide timely humor, and, most importantly, provide a safe environment for chefs to cook and patrons to eat. Dishwashers are usually the last to leave the restaurant, often two to three hours after the restaurant has officially closed. I appreciate them so much that no cook in my kitchen can leave unless the dishwasher is leaving with them.

We are all—and always—family.

I am here because of the work people do all up and down the line. Please, when sharing this book, highlight this page as one of the most important chapters, as we are not only uniting people through food, we also are lifting up the story of people who often go unheard and overlooked in our own pursuit of happiness.

Resources

Suggested Readings

DeKnight, Freda, *A Date with a Dish: Classic African-American Recipes* (Mineola, NY: Dover Publications, 2014).

Flamming, Douglas, *Bound for Freedom: Black Los Angeles in Jim Crow America* (Oakland: University of California Press, 2006).

Harris, Jessica B., *High on the Hog: A Culinary Journey from Africa to America* (New York: Bloomsbury USA, 2011).

Martin, Toni Tipton, *Jubilee: Recipes from Two Centuries of African American Cooking* (New York: Clarkson Potter, 2019).

Miller, Adrian, *Black Smoke: African Americans and the United States of Barbecue* (Chapel Hill: University of North Carolina Press, 2021).

Miller, Adrian, *Soul Food: The Surprising Story of an American Cuisine, One Plate at a Time* (Chapel Hill: University of North Carolina Press, 2013).

Opie, Frederick Douglas, *Hog and Hominy: Soul Food from Africa to America* (New York: Columbia University Press, 2010).

Palmer, Zella, *Recipes and Remembrances of Fair Dillard, 1869–2019* (Lafayette: University of Louisiana at Lafayette Press, 2019).

Pyatt, Sherman E., *The Other Side of the Skillet: Healthy and Alternative Eating in the Lowcountry* (Lulu Press, Emma's Cast Iron Skillet, 2015).

Roberts, Amy Lotson and Patrick J. Holladay, *Gullah Geechee Heritage in the Golden Isles* (Cheltenham, Gloucestershire, UK: The History Press, 2019).

Smart-Grosvenor, Vertamae, *Vibration Cooking: Or, The Travel Notes of a Geechee Girl* (Athens: University of Georgia Press, 2011).

Taylor, Candacy, *The Overground Railroad: The Green Book and the Roots of Black Travel in America* (New York: Abrams Books, 2020).

Taylor, Quintard, *In Search of the Racial Frontier: African Americans in the American West 1528–1990* (New York: Norton, 1998).

Wilkerson, Isabella, *The Warmth of Other Suns: The Epic Story of America's Great Migration* (New York: Vintage Books, 2011).

Zafar, Rafia, *Recipes for Respect: African American Meals and Meaning* (Athens: The University of Georgia Press, 2019).

Suggested Viewings

"Black in Latin America," Henry Louis Gates, Jr., PBS.

"Buffalo Soldiers: Fighting on Two Fronts," Dru Holley, buffalosoldiersmovie.com.

"The Story of New Orleans Creole Cooking: The Black Hand in the Pot," Zella Palmer, youtube.com.

"Truly Texas Mexican," Adán Medrano, amazon.com.

Suggested Listenings

Soul by Todd Richards, Heritage Radio Network, heritageradionetwork.org.

Valuable Archives and Research

Dillard University Ray Charles Program in African American Material Culture, New Orleans, Louisiana, dillard.edu/raycharles

DuSable Black History Museum and Education Center, Chicago, Illinois, dusablemuseum.org.

David Walker Lupton African American
Cookbook Collection, University of Alabama,
Tuscaloosa, Alabama, lib.ua.edu/collections/
the-david-walker-lupton-african-american-
cookbook-collection.

Museum of Food and Drink, New York, New
York, mofad.org.

Southern Foodways Alliance, University
of Mississippi, Center for the Study of
Southern Culture, Oxford, Mississippi,
southernfoodwaysalliance.org.

Texas Institute for the Preservation of History
and Culture, Prairie View A&M University,
Prairie View, Texas, pvamu.edu/tiphc.

Texas State Historical Society, Austin, Texas,
tshaonline.org/handbook.

Where to Buy Specialty Ingredients

For heirloom quality benne seeds, Carolina Gold
rice, cornmeal, grits, beans, and peas: Anson
Mills, (803) 467-4122, ansonmills.com.

For dried hibiscus flowers and high-quality
spices: The Spice House, thespicehouse.com,
(312) 676-2414

For bourbon vanilla bean paste: Nielsen-Massey
Madagascar Bourbon Pure Vanilla Bean Paste,
available at Whole Foods, Walmart, Amazon,
and other retailers.

For sorghum syrup: Old Muddy Pond,
(931) 445-3509, muddypondorghum.com.

Universal Conversion Chart

Oven Temperature Equivalents

250°F = 120°C

275°F = 135°C

300°F = 150°C

325°F = 160°C

350°F = 180°C

375°F = 190°C

400°F = 200°C

425°F = 220°C

450°F = 230°C

475°F = 240°C

500°F = 260°C

Measurement Equivalents

Measurements should always be level unless directed otherwise.

⅛ teaspoon = 0.5 mL

¼ teaspoon = 1 mL

½ teaspoon = 2 mL

1 teaspoon = 5 mL

1 tablespoon = 3 teaspoons = ½ fluid ounce = 15 mL

2 tablespoons = ⅛ cup = 1 fluid ounce = 30 mL

4 tablespoons = ¼ cup = 2 fluid ounces = 60 mL

5⅓ tablespoons = ⅓ cup = 3 fluid ounces = 80 mL

8 tablespoons = ½ cup = 4 fluid ounces = 120 mL

10⅔ tablespoons = ⅔ cup = 5 fluid ounces = 160 mL

12 tablespoons = ¾ cup = 6 fluid ounces = 180 mL

16 tablespoons = 1 cup = 8 fluid ounces = 240 mL

Index

Note: Page references in *italics* indicate photographs.

Ackee Soup, 82–83
acorn squash
  Hot and Spicy Crawfish Boil
    with Collard Green Spring
    Rolls and NY Cherry-Ginger
    Spritz, *192*, 192–196
Africa Kine, 16–17, *16*
*African/American: Making the
  Nation's Table* exhibition,
  xvii, 217
Agua Fresca with Spiced and
  Salted Rim, Watermelon,
  124, *125*
Alabama White Sauce, 216
Alice's Bar-B-Que, 202
Allan's Bakery, 80
almond milk, sweetened
  Horchata with Cinnamon
    Cookies and Ancho Chili-
    Sugar Rim, 99–101, *100*
almonds
  Grilled Quail Tacos on Flour
    Tortillas with Mole Poblano,
    Pickled Red Onions, and Red
    Rice, 94–98, *95*
  Stuffed Cornish Hens with Rice
    and Field Peas and Buttered
    Cabbage, 128–129
American South, 102
Ancho Chili Butter, *208–209*, 211
Appalachia, 102
apple cider/juice
  Fried Apple Hand Pies
    with Cinnamon Sugar and
    Jamaican Rum Crème,
    197–199, *198*
  Peach Cobbler with Butter
    Pecan Ice Cream, 121–122
  Watermelon Agua Fresca with
    Spiced and Salted Rim, 124, *125*
apples
  Fried Apple Hand Pies
    with Cinnamon Sugar and

Jamaican Rum Crème,
  197–199, *198*
  Homemade Cola, *213*, 216
Army & Lou's, 201
arugula
  Cola-Braised Ham and
    Onion-and-Smoked Cheddar
    Buttermilk Biscuits with
    Arugula and Mustad Seed
    Dressing, 112–114
  Crowder Pea and Arugula Salad,
    181, 182
  Stewed Chicken in Tomato
    Sauce with Crowder Pea and
    Arugula Salad, 179–182, *181*
Avena Caliente, 33–37, *36*
avocados
  Cemita Poblana: Fried
    Pork Cutlet with Avocado
    Vinaigrette, 152–153, *153*
  Tostones with Yam, Red Chili
    Salsa, and Smashed Avocado,
    42–44, *43*

bacon
  Collard Green Spring Rolls,
    194, *195*
  Crowder Pea and Arugula Salad,
    181, 182
  German Potato Salad, *154–155*,
    157, *157*
  Loaded Sweet Potato with
    Creamed Mustard Greens,
    Crispy Bacon, and Smoked
    Cheddar Breadcrumbs,
    218–219
  Mogo-Mogo: Smashed Plantain
    Porridge with Black Pepper
    and Sesame Seed Bacon, 89–90
  Pulled Pork Tamales with
    Charred Corn, Alabama White
    Sauce, and Homemade Cola,
    212–216, *213*

Bailey, Cornelia Walker, 1
Bailey, Mashama, xvii, 133, *231*,
  231, 232
banana pudding
  about, 138
  Banana Pudding with
    Meringue and Rum Sauce,
    140, *141*
  Classic Banana Pudding,
    139, *141*
barbecue
  BBQ Short Ribs with Crawfish
    and Pecan Rice–Stuffed
    Chayote Squash, *160–161*,
    162–163
  BBQ Shrimp with Garlicy
    French Bread and Parsley
    Butter, 146–147
  Chicago, 202–203
  Todd's Take on Chicago
    Barbecue, 204, *204–205*
Beach Spaghetti, xiii, 38, *39*, 40,
  220–222
beans/legumes
  Grilled Shrimp Mojo with Black
    Bean Purée and Toasted Rice
    with Cumin Seeds and Mint,
    63–65, *64*
  Hoppin' John with Turnip
    Greens and Yellow Rice,
    103–105, *104*
  Stewed Pinto Beans with Corn
    Cakes and Jalapeño and Red
    Pepper Marmalade, 148–149
  Stewed White Beans and
    Corn, 168
  Stuffed Cornish Hens with Rice
    and Field Peas and Buttered
    Cabbage, 128–129
  Venison Osso Buco with Stewed
    White Beans and Corn,
    167–168
  see also peas

beef
  BBQ Short Ribs with Crawfish
    and Pecan Rice–Stuffed
    Chayote Squash, *160–161,*
    162–163
  Beef Stock, 26
  Bistec Encebollado, 48, *49*
  Coffee, Black Pepper, and
    Cocoa-Rubbed Smoked Beef
    Brisket with German Potato
    Salad, *154–155, 156–157, 157*
  Dad's Meat Spaghetti Sauce, 221
  Grilled Skirt Steak with
    Chimichurri Sauce, 206,
    208–209
  Haitian Oxtail in Beef Broth
    with Pikliz, 30–32, *31*
  Smoked Baby Back Ribs with
    Dad's Chicago Red BBQ Sauce,
    207–210, *208–209*
  Soup Joumou, 24–25, *25*
Beignets with Espresso
    Powdered Sugar, 150, *151, 198*
benne seeds, 90
berbere spice
  Berbere Chargrilled Oysters
    with Parmesan Cheese and
    Garlic Butter, *186,* 187
  Hot and Spicy Crawfish Boil
    with Collard Green Spring
    Rolls and NY Cherry-Ginger
    Spritz, *192,* 192–196
  Loaded Sweet Potato with
    Creamed Mustard Greens,
    Crispy Bacon, and Smoked
    Cheddar Breadcrumbs,
    218–219
Big Mac (Labay Market), 80
Bistec Encebollado, 48, *49*
black cowboys, 144–145
black-eyed peas
  Hoppin' John with Turnip
    Greens and Yellow Rice,
    103–105, *104*
  Stuffed Cornish Hens with Rice
    and Field Peas and Buttered
    Cabbage, 128–129
Bledsoe, Christena, 1
bourbon

Butter Pecan Ice Cream,
    121–122
Fried Apple Hand Pies
    with Cinnamon Sugar and
    Jamaican Rum Crème,
    197–199, *198*
Pan-Fried Chicken Livers
    Glazed in Sorghum and Shaved
    Bulb Onions, 133–134
Red Pepper Honey, *107* 108
Sorghum Ice Cream, 135–
    137, *136*
Brennan, Ella, 233
Broiled Lobster Tails, 117
Broken Spaghetti, 222
Brussels sprouts
  Pikliz, 32, *32*
  Soup Joumou, 24–25, *25*
  West African Fish Stew with
    Smoked Trout and Snapper, 7
buffalo soldiers, 144–145, 169
Buffalo-Pumpkin Chili with
    Pickled Cactus Salsa and
    Crispy Blue Corn Tortilla,
    170–171
Buffalo-Style Frog Legs with
    French Onion Ranch
    Dressing, 183–185, *184*
butter
  French Bread and Garlicky
    Butter, 147
  Parsley Butter, 147
Butter Pecan Ice Cream, 121–122
Buttered Cabbage, 128–129
Buttered Green Peas, 118–120
buttermilk
  Buffalo-Style Frog Legs with
    French Onion Ranch Dressing,
    183–185, *184*
  Chicago Style Beach Spaghetti,
    aka Fish and Spaghetti,
    220–222
  Cola-Braised Ham and
    Onion-and-Smoked Cheddar
    Buttermilk Biscuits with
    Arugula and Mustard Seed
    Dressing, 112–114
  Corn Cakes, 149
  Cornmeal-Crusted Okra, 191

Fried Lake Perch with Pimento
    Cheese and Collard Green
    Hushpuppies and Celery Root
    and Jicama slaw, 223–226, *224*
Hot and Cold Southwest-Style
    Country-Fried Rabbit with
    Tomatillo Hot Sauce, 165–166
Onion-and-Smoked Cheddar
    Buttermilk Biscuits, 112–114
Peach Cobbler with Butter
    Pecan Ice Cream, 121–122
Pimento Cheese and Collard
    Green Hushpuppies, *224,* 226
Scallion and Smoked Cheddar
    Cornbread Fritters with Red
    Pepper Honey, 106–108, *107*
Whiskey and Vanilla Salted
    Caramel Cake, 227–228
butternut squash
  Buffalo-Pumpkin Chili with
    Pickled Cactus Salsa and
    Crispy Blue Corn Tortilla,
    170–171
  Pickled Cactus Salsa, 171
  Soup Joumou, 24–25, *25*

cabbage
  Buttered Cabbage, 129
  Mango Slaw, 79
  Pikliz, 32, *32*
  Stuffed Cornish Hens with Rice
    and Field Peas and Buttered
    Cabbage, 128–129
Cactus Salsa, Pickled, 171
café society, about, 62
caramelization, 12
Caramelized Plantains, 33, 37
Caribbean, 22–23
catfish
  Chicago Style Beach Spaghetti,
    aka Fish and Spaghetti,
    220–222
  Grilled Catfish with Grilled
    Spring Onions and Creamed
    Potato Hash with Mustard
    Greens, 109–111, *111*
celery root
  Celery Root and Jicama Slaw,
    224, 226

celery root (*continued*)
  Root Vegetable Stock, 6
Cemita Poblana: Fried Pork
    Cutlet with Avocado
    Vinaigrette, 152–153, *153*
Charred Corn, 214, *215*
Chase, Leah, xvii, 233
chayote squash
  Chayote and Codfish Frittata
    with Plátanos al Caldero and
    Avena Caliente, 33–37
  Crawfish-and-Pecan Rice-
    Stuffed Chayote Squash,
    160–161, 163
cheddar cheese
  Chayote and Codfish Frittata
    with Plátanos al Caldero and
    Avena Caliente, 33–37
  Four-Cheese Baked Mac 'n'
    Cheese with Lobster Variation,
    115–117
  Loaded Sweet Potato with
    Creamed Mustard Greens,
    Crispy Bacon, and Smoked
    Cheddar Breadcrumbs, 218–219
  Onion-and-Smoked Cheddar
    Buttermilk Biscuits, 112–114
  Pimento Cheese and Collard
    Green Hushpuppies, *224*, 226
  Scallion and Smoked Cheddar
    Cornbread Fritters with Red
    Pepper Honey, 106–108, *107*
  Sweet Potato and Squash
    Casserole with Pickled Green
    Beans, 130–132, *131*, *132*
cheese. *see individual cheese types*
Chef Stephan's Epis
  recipe, 28
  Soup Joumou, 24–25, *25*
Cherry 7Up
  7Up Cake, 229–230
Cherry-Ginger Spritz, NY,
    196, *196*
Chicago, 200–231
Chicago Barbecue, Todd's Take
    on, 204, *204–205*
Chicago Style Beach Spaghetti,
    aka Fish and Spaghetti,
    220–222

Chicharron and Coconut
    Cracklins, Coconut Pudding
    with, 53
chicken
  Chicken Stock, 14
  Chicken Yassa with Crispy Rice
    and Dandelion Salad, 9–14, *10*
  Jerk Chicken Wings with Lime
    Dipping Sauce, 69
  Roasted Chicken and
    Dumplings with Buttered
    Green Peas and Roasted
    Heirloom Carrots, 118–120
  Stewed Chicken in Tomato
    Sauce with Crowder Pea and
    Arugula Salad, 179–182, *181*
  Stewed Chicken with Cuban
    Okra and Sweet Plantains and
    Pickled Baby Corn, 67–68
  Sweet and Spicy Grilled Chicken
    Tenderloin with Chipotle and
    Tamarind Glaze and Crushed
    Peanuts, 92–93
chilies
  Buffalo-Pumpkin Chili with
    Pickled Cactus Salsa and
    Crispy Blue Corn Tortilla,
    170–171
  Grilled Quail Tacos on Flour
    Tortillas with Mole Poblano,
    Pickled Red Onions, and Red
    Rice, 94–98, *95*
chipotle peppers in adobo sauce
  Collard Green Spring Rolls,
    194, *195*
  Stewed Pinto Beans with Corn
    Cakes and Jalapeño and Red
    Pepper Marmalade, 148–149
chocolate
  Grilled Quail Tacos on Flour
    Tortillas with Mole Poblano,
    Pickled Red Onions, and Red
    Rice, 94–98, *95*
  Churros with Cinnamon-Vanilla
    Sugar, 164, *198*
cilantro
  Classic Sofrito, *50*, 51
  Grilled Quail Tacos on Flour
    Tortillas with Mole Poblano,

  Pickled Red Onions, and Red
    Rice, 94–98, *95*
  Ham Hock Mofongo with Fried
    Eggs, Pork Broth, and Pickled
    Red Onion, *34–35*, 45–47, *46*
  Jollof Rice, 18
  Peanut and Mustard Greens
    Soup with Ginger and
    Tomato, 4, *5*
  Salsa Criolla, 40
  Tostones with Yam, Red Chili
    Salsa, and Smashed Avocado,
    42–44, *43*
Cinnamon Cookies, 99–101, *100*
clams
  Espaguetis with Salami, 38, *39*
  She-Crab Soup with Smoked
    Paprika Oil and Cornmeal-
    Crusted Okra, 188–191, *189*
Clark, Patrick, 233
Classic Banana Pudding, 139,
    141
Classic Sofrito
  Bistec Encebollado, 48, *49*
  recipe, *50*, 51
  Salsa Criolla, 40
Coca-Cola, Mexican, 112
coconut flour
  Beignets with Espresso
    Powdered Sugar, 150, *151*, *198*
coconut milk
  Beignets with Espresso
    Powdered Sugar, 150, *151*, *198*
  Coconut Pudding with
    Chicharron and Coconut
    Cracklins, *52*, 53
  Coconut-Fried Spiny Lobster
    Tail with Rum-Soy Dipping
    Sauce, 70–73, *71*
  Collard Greens with Boiler
    Potatoes Braised in Coconut
    Milk and Curry, *86*, 87
  Rum-Coconut Syrup, 21
coconut sugar
  Beignets with Espresso
    Powdered Sugar, 150, *151*, *198*
coconut water
  Hibiscus Sweet Tea with
    Watermelon Pickles, 126, *127*

coconuts
  about, 21
  Coconut Pudding with
    Chicharron and Coconut
    Cracklins, *52*, 53
  Coconut Puff-Puff with Rum-
    Coconut Syrup, 19–21, *20*
  Coconut-Fried Spiny Lobster
    Tail with Rum-Soy Dipping
    Sauce, 70–73, *71*
Codfish Frittata with Plátanos al
    Caldero and Avena Caliente,
    Chayote and, 33–37
coffee/espresso
  Coffee, Black Pepper, and
    Cocoa-Rubbed Smoked Beef
    Brisket with German Potato
    Salad, *154–155*, 156–157, *157*
  Ham Steak with Red-Eye Gravy,
    Mango de Bizcochuelo and
    Pepper Relish, and Tostada
    Cubana, 60–61
  Homemade Cola, *213*, 216
Cola-Braised Ham and Onion-
    and-Smoked Cheddar
    Buttermilk Biscuits with
    Arugula and Mustard Seed
    Dressing, 112–114
collard greens
  Collard Green Spring Rolls,
    194, *195*
  Collard Greens with Boiler
    Potatoes Braised in Coconut
    Milk and Curry, *86*, 87
  Hot and Spicy Crawfish Boil
    with Collard Green Spring
    Rolls and NY Cherry-Ginger
    Spritz, 192–196, *195*
  Pimento Cheese and Collard
    Green Hushpuppies, *224*, 226
Columbian Exchange, 22
conversion charts, 237
corn
  Charred Corn, 214, *215*
  Corn Cakes, 148–149
  Grilled Corn with Ancho Chili
    Butter, *208–209*, 211
  Hot and Spicy Crawfish Boil
    with Collard Green Spring

Rolls and NY Cherry-Ginger
    Spritz, *192*, 192–196
  Pulled Pork Tamales with
    Charred Corn, Alabama White
    Sauce, and Homemade Cola,
    212–216, *213*
  Stewed Chicken with Cuban
    Okra and Sweet Plantains and
    Pickled Baby Corn, 67–68
  Stewed White Beans and
    Corn, 168
  Sweet Plantains and Pickled
    Baby Corn, 68
  Venison Osso Buco with Stewed
    White Beans and Corn, 167–168
Cornish Hens with Rice and
    Field Peas and Buttered
    Cabbage, Stuffed, 128–129
Cornmeal Porridge with Stewed
    Black Trumpet Mushrooms
    and Pickled Okra, 29
Cornmeal-Crusted Okra, *189*, 191
cotija cheese
  Mogo-Mogo: Smashed Plantain
    Porridge with Black Pepper
    and Sesame Seed Bacon, 89–90
crabmeat
  She-Crab Soup with Smoked
    Paprika Oil and Cornmeal-
    Crusted Okra, 188–191, *189*
crawfish
  Crawfish-and-Pecan Rice-
    Stuffed Chayote Squash,
    160–161, 163
  Hot and Spicy Crawfish Boil
    with Collard Green Spring
    Rolls and NY Cherry-Ginger
    Spritz, *192*, 192–196
  Pepper Crawfish Cocktail with
    Hibiscus Punch, 74–75
  She-Crab Soup with Smoked
    Paprika Oil and Cornmeal-
    Crusted Okra, 188–191, *189*
Creamed Potato Hash, 109–110
Creole Seasoning
  BBQ Short Ribs with Crawfish
    and Pecan Rice–Stuffed
    Chayote Squash, *160–161*,
    162–163

BBQ Shrimp with Garlicy
    French Bread and Parsley
    Butter, 146–147
  Crawfish-and-Pecan Rice-
    Stuffed Chayote Squash,
    160–161, 163
  recipe, 147
Crispy Rice
  Chicken Yassa with Crispy Rice
    and Dandelion Salad, 9–14, *13*
  recipe, 12
  Stewed Chicken with Cuban
    Okra and Sweet Plantains and
    Pickled Baby Corn, 67–68
Crowder Pea and Arugula Salad,
    181, 182
Cuba, 23, 54–68
Cuban Sandwich, 54–55
Cubano Sauce, 58
Cubano with Yuca Fries, The,
    54–59, *57–59*
Culpepper's Restaurant, 80, *80*
Cumin Seeds and Mint, Toasted
    Rice with, 65

Dad's Chicago Red BBQ Sauce
  Dad's Meat Spaghetti Sauce,
    221
  recipe, 210
Dad's Meat Spaghetti Sauce, 221
Dandelion Salad
  Chicken Yassa with Crispy Rice
    and Dandelion Salad, 9–14
  recipe, 14
  Sweet Potato and Squash
    Casserole with Pickled Green
    Beans, 130–132, *131, 132*
Daniels, Jack, xvii
DeKnight, Freda, 217
desserts/sweets
  Banana Pudding with Meringue
    and Rum Sauce, 140, *141*
  Churros with Cinnamon-
    Vanilla Sugar, 164, *198*
  Classic Banana Pudding,
    139, *141*
  Coconut Pudding with
    Chicharron and Coconut
    Cracklins, *52*, 53

desserts/sweets (*continued*)
 Coconut Puff-Puff with Rum-
  Coconut Syrup, 19–21, *20*
 Horchata with Cinnamon
  Cookies and Ancho Chili-
  Sugar Rim, 99–101, *100*
 Peach Cobbler with Butter
  Pecan Ice Cream, 121–122
 Rum-Coconut Syrup, 21
 7Up Cake, 229–230
 Sweet Potato Pie with Sorghum
  Ice Cream, 135–137, *136*
 Whiskey and Vanilla Salted
  Caramel Cake, 227–228
Dominguez, Danny, 41, *41*
Dominican Republic, 23, 33–41
drinks
 Avena Caliente, *36*, 37
 Hibiscus Punch, 75, *75*
 Hibiscus Sweet Tea with
  Watermelon Pickles, 126, *127*
 Homemade Cola, *213*, 216
 Horchata with Cinnamon
  Cookies and Ancho Chili-
  Sugar Rim, 99–100, *100*
 NY Cherry-Ginger Spritz,
  196, *196*
 red drinks, 76
 Watermelon Agua Fresca with
  Spiced and Salted Rim, 124,
  125
Durand, Stephan Berrouet, xiii,
 27, *27*

Ebony test kitchen, 217
eggs
 Cemita Poblana: Fried
  Pork Cutlet with Avocado
  Vinaigrette, 152–153, *153*
 Chayote and Codfish Frittata
  with Plátanos al Caldero and
  Avena Caliente, 33–37
 Ham Hock Mofongo with Fried
  Eggs, Pork Broth, and Pickled
  Red Onion, *34–35*, 45–47, *46*
 Saltfish Cakes with Chilled
  Ackee Soup and Mango Salsa,
  82–84
 Sweet Potato and Squash

 Casserole with Pickled Green
  Beans, 130–132, *131, 132*
Elie, Lolis Eric, xi
Emancipation, 144
Espaguetis with Salami, 38,
 39, 40
Espresso Powdered Sugar,
  Beignets with, 150, *151, 198*
Evans, Darryl, xvii, 233

fish
 Chayote and Codfish Frittata
  with Plátanos al Caldero and
  Avena Caliente, 33–37
 Chicago Style Beach Spaghetti,
  aka Fish and Spaghetti,
  220–222
 fish fries, 225
 Fried Lake Perch with Pimento
  Cheese and Collard Green
  Hushpuppies and Celery Root
  and Jicama slaw, 223–226, *224*
 Grilled Catfish with Grilled
  Spring Onions and Creamed
  Potato Hash with Mustard
  Greens, 109–111, *111*
 Grilled Whole Snapper with
  Mango Slaw, 77–79, *78, 79*
 Saltfish Cakes with Chilled
  Ackee Soup and Mango Salsa,
  82–84
 West African Fish Stew with
  Smoked Trout and Snapper, 7
  see also seafood
Flour Tortillas with Mole
  Poblano, Pickled Red Onions,
  and Red Rice, Grilled Quail
  Tacos on, 94–98, *95*
Fortun, Merari Hall, 62, *62*
Four-Cheese Baked Mac
 'n' Cheese with Lobster
  Variation, 115–117
Franks, Adrian, xvii
French Bread and Garlicky
  Butter, 146–147
French Onion Ranch Dressing,
  184, 185
Frey, William H., 232
Fried Apple Hand Pies with

 Cinnamon Sugar and
  Jamaican Rum Crème,
  197–199, *198*
Fried Lake Perch with Pimento
  Cheese and Collard Green
  Hushpuppies and Celery
  Root and Jicama slaw,
  223–226, *224*
Frog Legs with French Onion
  Ranch Dressing, Buffalo-
  Style, 183–185, *184*

Gage & Tollner, 188, *191*
game birds, about, 129
German Potato Salad, *154–155*,
 156–157, *157*
Gladys' Luncheonette, 201–202
gouda, smoked
 Loaded Sweet Potato with
  Creamed Mustard Greens,
  Crispy Bacon, and Smoked
  Cheddar Breadcrumbs,
  218–219
Granger, Gordon, 144
Great Migration, 173–178, 232
Green, Nathan "Uncle Nearest,"
  xvii, 227
green beans
 Pickled Green Beans, 132, *132*
 Sweet Potato and Squash
  Casserole with Pickled Green
  Beans, 130–132, *131, 132*
Grilled Catfish with Grilled
  Spring Onions and Creamed
  Potato Hash with Mustard
  Greens, 109–111, *111*
Grilled Corn with Ancho Chili
  Butter, *208–209*, 211
Grilled Quail Tacos on Flour
  Tortillas with Mole Poblano,
  Pickled Red Onions, and Red
  Rice, 94–98, *95*
Grilled Shrimp Mojo with Black
  Bean Purée and Toasted Rice
  with Cumin Seeds and Mint,
  63–65, *64*
Grilled Skirt Steak with
  Chimichurri Sauce, 206,
  208–209

Grilled Whole Snapper with
 Mango Slaw, 77–79, *78*, *79*

Haiti, 23, 24–32
Haitian Oxtail in Beef Broth with
 Pikliz, 30–32, *31*
Ham Hock Broth
 Cola-Braised Ham and
  Onion-and-Smoked Cheddar
  Buttermilk Biscuits with
  Arugula and Mustard Seed
  Dressing, 112–114
 Collard Green Spring Rolls,
  194, *195*
 Pulled Pork Tamales with
  Charred Corn, Alabama White
  Sauce, and Homemade Cola,
  212–216, *213*
ham/ham hock
 Cola-Braised Ham and
  Onion-and-Smoked Cheddar
  Buttermilk Biscuits with
  Arugula and Mustard Seed
  Dressing, 112–114
 Cubano Sauce, 58
 The Cubano with Yuca Fries,
  54–59, *57–59*
 Ham Hock Jelly, 55
 Ham Hock Mofongo with Fried
  Eggs, Pork Broth, and Pickled
  Red Onion, *34–35*, 45–47, *46*
 Ham Steak with Red-Eye Gravy,
  Mango de Bizcochuelo and
  Pepper Relish, and Tostada
  Cubana, 60–61
 She-Crab Soup with Smoked
  Paprika Oil and Cornmeal-
  Crusted Okra, 188–191, *189*
 Stewed Pinto Beans with Corn
  Cakes and Jalapeño and Red
  Pepper Marmalade, 148–149
Harlem Needle Arts, xvii
Harris, Jessica B., xvii
Hecky's Barbecue, 202
Hemings, James, xvii
Hibiscus Brew, 80–81
Hibiscus Punch, 74–75, *75*
Hibiscus Sweet Tea with
 Watermelon Pickles, 126, *127*

Homemade Cola, *213*, 216
Honey 1 BBQ, 202
Honey, Red Pepper, *107*, 108
Hoppin' John with Turnip
 Greens and Yellow Rice,
 103–105, *104*
Horchata with Cinnamon
 Cookies and Ancho Chili-
 Sugar Rim, 99 101, *100*
Hot and Cold Southwest-Style
 Country-Fried Rabbit with
 Tomatillo Hot Sauce, 165–166
Hot and Spicy Crawfish Boil with
 Collard Green Spring Rolls
 and NY Cherry-Ginger Spritz,
 192, 192–196, *195*, *196*
Hot Sauce Mayo Dip, 194, *196*
Hot Spiced Oat Milk, 33, 37
Hushpuppies, Pimento Cheese
 and Collard Green, *224*, 226

ice cream
 Butter Pecan Ice Cream,
  121–122
 Peach Cobbler with Butter
  Pecan Ice Cream, 121–122
 scoops for, 123
 Sweet Potato Pie with Sorghum
  Ice Cream, 135–137, *136*
ingredients, about, xix
Izola's, 201

Jalapeño and Red Pepper
 Marmalade, 148–149
Jamaica, 23, 69–87
Jefferson, Thomas, xvii
Jerk Chicken Wings with Lime
 Dipping Sauce, 69
jerk spices, history of, 72
Jicama Slaw, Celery Root and,
 224, 226
Jollof Rice, 18

kabocha
 Soup Joumou, 24–25, *25*

Labay Market, 80
Leon's Barbecue, 202
Le Petit Senegal, New York, 16–17

leeks
 Ackee Soup, 83
Legacy Quilt, xvii
Lem's Barbecue, 202
lemongrass
 Chef Stephan's Epis, 28
 Grilled Whole Snapper with
  Mango Slaw, 77–79, *78*, *79*
 Haitian Oxtail in Beef Broth
  with Pikliz, 30–32, *31*
 Hibiscus Punch, 75, *75*
Lewis, Edna, xvii, 188, 232
Lime Dipping Sauce, 69, 73
Little Caribbean, New York,
 80–81
Livers Glazed in Sorghum and
 Shaved Bulb Onions, Pan-
 Fried Chicken, 133–134
Loaded Sweet Potato with
 Creamed Mustard Greens,
 Crispy Bacon, and Smoked
 Cheddar Breadcrumbs,
 218–219
lobster
 Broiled Lobster Tails, *116*, 117
 Coconut-Fried Spiny Lobster
  Tail with Rum-Soy Dipping
  Sauce, 70–73, *71*
 Four-Cheese Baked Mac 'n'
  Cheese with Lobster Variation,
  115–117, *116*

Maggi seasoning
 about, 8
 Coconut-Fried Spiny Lobster
  Tail with Rum-Soy Dipping
  Sauce, 70–73, *71*
 Jerk Chicken Wings with Lime
  Dipping Sauce, 69
 Lime Dipping Sauce, 73
 Pepper Crawfish Cocktail with
  Hibiscus Punch, 74–75
 Soup Joumou, 24–25, *25*
 Sweet and Spicy Grilled Chicken
  Tenderloin with Chipotle and
  Tamarind Glaze and Crushed
  Peanuts, 92–93
 West African Fish Stew with
  Smoked Trout and Snapper, 7

Mango de Bizcochuelo and Pepper Relish, and Tostada Cubana, Ham Steak with Red-Eye Gravy, 60–61
mangos
  Ham Steak with Red-Eye Gravy, Mango de Bizcochuelo and Pepper Relish, and Tostada Cubana, 60–61
  Mango Salsa, 84, *84*
  Mango Slaw, 77, 79
Mayi Moulen, 29
Mexico, 88–101
Miller, Adrian, xi–xii, xvii, 158–159, *159*
Millner, Darrell, 143
Mint, Toasted Rice with Cumin Seeds and, 65
Mitchell, Kevin, xvii, 233
Mofongo with Fried Eggs, Pork Broth, and Pickled Red Onion, Ham Hock, *34–35*, 45–47, *46*
Mogo-Mogo: Smashed Plantain Porridge with Black Pepper and Sesame Seed Bacon, 89–90
Mole Poblano, Pickled Red Onions, and Red Rice, Grilled Quail Tacos on Flour Tortillas with, 94–98, *95*
Moo & Oink, 203
mozzarella cheese
  Four-Cheese Baked Mac 'n' Cheese with Lobster Variation, 115–117
Museum of Food and Drink, xvii, 217
mushrooms
  Mayi Moulen, 29
music, xx–xxi
mustard greens
  Creamed Potato Hash, 110
  Grilled Catfish with Grilled Spring Onions and Creamed Potato Hash with Mustard Greens, 109–111, *111*
  Loaded Sweet Potato with Creamed Mustard Greens,

Crispy Bacon, and Smoked Cheddar Breadcrumbs, 218–219
  Peanut and Mustard Greens Soup with Ginger and Tomato, 4, *5*
Mustard Seed Dressing, Arugula and, 112–114

New York, 179–199
nuts. *see individual nut types*
Nutter, Duane, 232
NY Cherry-Ginger Spritz, 196, *196*

oat milk
  Avena Caliente, *36*, 37
  Chayote and Codfish Frittata with Plátanos al Caldero and Avena Caliente, 33–37
Oaxaca cheese
  Cemita Poblana: Fried Pork Cutlet with Avocado Vinaigrette, 152–153, *153*
okra
  Cornmeal-Crusted Okra, *189*, 191
  Mayi Moulen, 29
  She-Crab Soup with Smoked Paprika Oil and Cornmeal-Crusted Okra, 188–191, *189*
  Stewed Chicken with Cuban Okra and Sweet Plantains and Pickled Baby Corn, 67–68
  West African Fish Stew with Smoked Trout and Snapper, 7
Onion-and-Smoked Cheddar Buttermilk Biscuits with Arugula and Mustard Seed Dressing, Cola-Braised Ham and, 112–114
Onwuachi, Kwame, 233
oranges/orange juice, sour
  Chef Stephan's Epis, 28
  Classic Sofrito, *50*, 51
  Grilled Quail Tacos on Flour Tortillas with Mole Poblano, Pickled Red Onions, and Red Rice, 94–98, *95*

Grilled Shrimp Mojo with Black Bean Purée and Toasted Rice with Cumin Seeds and Mint, 63–65, *64*
Grilled Whole Snapper with Mango Slaw, 77–79, *78, 79*
Jerk Chicken Wings with Lime Dipping Sauce, 69
Oxtail in Beef Broth with Pikliz, Haitian, 30–32, *31*
Oysters with Parmesan Cheese and Garlic Butter, Berbere Chargrilled, *186*, 187

Palmer, Zella, 145, *200*, 200–203, 232
Pan-Fried Chicken Livers Glazed in Sorghum and Shaved Bulb Onions, 133–134
parmesan cheese
  Berbere Chargrilled Oysters with Parmesan Cheese and Garlic Butter, *186*, 187
  Four-Cheese Baked Mac 'n' Cheese with Lobster Variation, 115–117, *116*
  Loaded Sweet Potato with Creamed Mustard Greens, Crispy Bacon, and Smoked Cheddar Breadcrumbs, 218–219
Parsley Butter, 146–147
pasta
  Broken Spaghetti, 222
  Chicago Style Beach Spaghetti, aka Fish and Spaghetti, 220–222
  Espaguetis with Salami, 38, *39*
  Four-Cheese Baked Mac 'n' Cheese with Lobster Variation, 115–117, *116*
Paul, Crystal, 143
Peach Cobbler with Butter Pecan Ice Cream, 121–122
peanuts
  about, 6
  Grilled Quail Tacos on Flour Tortillas with Mole Poblano, Pickled Red Onions, and Red

Rice, 94–98, *95*
Peanut, Pumpkin, and Chile
  Salsa, 91
Peanut and Mustard Greens
  Soup with Ginger and
  Tomato, 4, *5*
Sweet and Spicy Grilled Chicken
  Tenderloin with Chipotle and
  Tamarind Glaze and Crushed
  Peanuts, 92–93
peas
  Buffalo-Pumpkin Chili with
    Pickled Cactus Salsa and
    Crispy Blue Corn Tortilla,
    170–171
  Buttered Green Peas, 120
  Crowder Pea and Arugula Salad,
    181, 182
  Espaguetis with Salami, 38, *39*
  Hoppin' John with Turnip
    Greens and Yellow Rice,
    103–105, *104*
  Roasted Chicken and
    Dumplings with Buttered
    Green Peas and Roasted
    Heirloom Carrots, 118–120
  Stewed Chicken in Tomato
    Sauce with Crowder Pea and
    Arugula Salad, 179–182, *181*
  Stuffed Cornish Hens with Rice
    and Field Peas and Buttered
    Cabbage, 128–129
pecans
  Butter Pecan Ice Cream,
    121–122
  Crawfish-and-Pecan Rice-
    Stuffed Chayote Squash,
    160–161, 163
  Sorghum Ice Cream, 135–
    137, *136*
  Stuffed Cornish Hens with Rice
    and Field Peas and Buttered
    Cabbage, 128–129
Pepper Crawfish Cocktail with
    Hibiscus Punch, 74–75, *75*
pepper jack cheese
  Four-Cheese Baked Mac 'n'
    Cheese with Lobster Variation,
    115–117

Pepper Relish, and Tostada
    Cubana, Ham Steak with
    Red-Eye Gravy, Mango de
    Bizcochuelo and, 60–61
peppers, bell
  Buffalo-Pumpkin Chili with
    Pickled Cactus Salsa and
    Crispy Blue Corn Tortilla,
    170–171
  Chef Stephan's Epis, 28
  Classic Sofrito, *50*, 51
  Collard Greens with Boiler
    Potatoes Braised in Coconut
    Milk and Curry, 87
  Crawfish-and-Pecan Rice-
    Stuffed Chayote Squash,
    160–161, 163
  Dad's Meat Spaghetti Sauce, 221
  Ham Steak with Red-Eye Gravy,
    Mango de Bizcochuelo and
    Pepper Relish, and Tostada
    Cubana, 60–61
  Hot and Spicy Crawfish Boil
    with Collard Green Spring
    Rolls and NY Cherry-Ginger
    Spritz, *192*, 192–196
  Jalapeño and Red Pepper
    Marmalade, 149
  Mango Salsa, 84, *84*
  Mango Slaw, 79
  Mayi Moulen, 29
  Peanut, Pumpkin, and Chile
    Salsa, 91
  Peanut and Mustard Greens
    Soup with Ginger and
    Tomato, 4, *5*
  Pickled Cactus Salsa, 171
  Pikliz, 32, *32*
  Red Pepper Honey, *107*, 108
  Sweet Plantains and Pickled
    Baby Corn, 68
  Tostones with Yam, Red Chili
    Salsa, and Smashed Avocado,
    42–44, *43*
peppers, chile
  Buffalo-Pumpkin Chili with
    Pickled Cactus Salsa and
    Crispy Blue Corn Tortilla,
    170–171

Chef Stephan's Epis, 28
Chicken Yassa with Crispy Rice
    and Dandelion Salad, 9–14, *10*
Classic Sofrito, *50*, 51
Collard Green Spring Rolls,
    194, *195*
Collard Greens with Boiler
    Potatoes Braised in Coconut
    Milk and Curry, *86*, 87
Crispy Rice, 12, *12*
Fried Lake Perch with Pimento
    Cheese and Collard Green
    Hushpuppies and Celery Root
    and Jicama slaw, 223–226, *224*
Grilled Quail Tacos on Flour
    Tortillas with Mole Poblano,
    Pickled Red Onions, and Red
    Rice, 94–98, *95*
Grilled Skirt Steak with
    Chimichurri Sauce, 206,
    208–209
Grilled Whole Snapper with
    Mango Slaw, 77–79, *78*, *79*
Haitian Oxtail in Beef Broth
    with Pikliz, 30–32, *31*
Ham Steak with Red-Eye Gravy,
    Mango de Bizcochuelo and
    Pepper Relish, and Tostada
    Cubana, 60–61
Hoppin' John with Turnip
    Greens and Yellow Rice,
    103–105, *104*
Hot and Cold Southwest-Style
    Country-Fried Rabbit with
    Tomatillo Hot Sauce, 165–166
Hot Sauce Mayo Dip, 196
Jalapeño and Red Pepper
    Marmalade, 149
Jerk Chicken Wings with Lime
    Dipping Sauce, 69
Jollof Rice, 18
Mango Salsa, 84, *84*
Mango Slaw, 79
Mayi Moulen, 29
Peanut, Pumpkin, and Chile
    Salsa, 91
Peanut and Mustard Greens
    Soup with Ginger and
    Tomato, 4, *5*

peppers, chile (*continued*)
Pepper Crawfish Cocktail with Hibiscus Punch, 74–75, *75*
Pickled Cactus Salsa, 171
Pikliz, 32, *32*
Pimento Cheese and Collard Green Hushpuppies, *224,* 226
Rum-Soy Dipping Sauce, 73
Saltfish Cakes with Chilled Ackee Soup and Mango Salsa, 82–84, *84*
She-Crab Soup with Smoked Paprika Oil and Cornmeal-Crusted Okra, 188–191, *189*
Soup Joumou, 24–25, *25*
Stewed Chicken with Cuban Okra and Sweet Plantains and Pickled Baby Corn, 67–68
Stewed Pinto Beans with Corn Cakes and Jalapeño and Red Pepper Marmalade, 148–149
Stewed White Beans and Corn, 168
Sweet and Spicy Grilled Chicken Tenderloin with Chipotle and Tamarind Glaze and Crushed Peanuts, 92–93
Tomatillo Hot Sauce, 166
Tostones with Yam, Red Chili Salsa, and Smashed Avocado, 42–44, *43*
Venison Osso Buco with Stewed White Beans and Corn, 167–168
West African Fish Stew with Smoked Trout and Snapper, 7
peppers, sweet
Salsa Criolla, 40
Piccoli, Catherine, xvii
Pickled Cactus Salsa, 171
Pickled Green Beans, 132, *132*
Pickled Red Onions, 45, 94–97, 152–153
pickles
Cubano Sauce, 58
The Cubano with Yuca Fries, 54–59, *57–59*
Pikine, 16–17, *17*

Pikliz
Haitian Oxtail in Beef Broth with Pikliz, 30–32, *31, 32*
recipe, 32
Soup Joumou, 24–25, *25*
Pimento Cheese and Collard Green Hushpuppies, *224,* 226
pineapple/pineapple juice
Dad's Chicago Red BBQ Sauce, 210
Grilled Whole Snapper with Mango Slaw, 77–79, *78, 79*
Jerk Chicken Wings with Lime Dipping Sauce, 69
Pinto Beans with Corn Cakes and Jalapeño and Red Pepper Marmalade, Stewed, 148–149
plantains
about, 44
Chayote and Codfish Frittata with Plátanos al Caldero and Avena Caliente, 33–37
Ham Hock Mofongo with Fried Eggs, Pork Broth, and Pickled Red Onion, *34–35,* 45–47, *46*
Mogo-Mogo: Smashed Plantain Porridge with Black Pepper and Sesame Seed Bacon, 89–90
Plátanos al Caldero, 37
Stewed Chicken with Cuban Okra and Sweet Plantains and Pickled Baby Corn, 67–68
Sweet Plantains and Pickled Baby Corn, 68
Tostones with Yam, Red Chili Salsa, and Smashed Avocado, 42–44, *43*
pork
about, 56
Cemita Poblana: Fried Pork Cutlet with Avocado Vinaigrette, 152–153, *153*
Pulled Pork Tamales with Charred Corn, Alabama White Sauce, and Homemade Cola, 212–216, *213*
pork bones
Grilled Shrimp Mojo with Black Bean Purée and Toasted Rice

with Cumin Seeds and Mint, 63–65, *64*
Pork Broth, and Pickled Red Onion, Ham Hock Mofongo with Fried Eggs, *34–35,* 45–47, *46*
pork rinds
Coconut Pudding with Chicharron and Coconut Cracklins, *52,* 53
potato flour
Buffalo-Style Frog Legs with French Onion Ranch Dressing, 183–185, *184*
Cemita Poblana: Fried Pork Cutlet with Avocado Vinaigrette, 152–153, *153*
Cornmeal-Crusted Okra, *189,* 191
Fried Lake Perch with Pimento Cheese and Collard Green Hushpuppies and Celery Root and Jicama slaw, 223–226, *224*
potatoes
Ackee Soup, 83
Coffee, Black Pepper, and Cocoa-Rubbed Smoked Beef Brisket with German Potato Salad, *154–155,* 156–157, *157*
Collard Greens with Boiler Potatoes Braised in Coconut Milk and Curry, *86,* 87
Creamed Potato Hash, 110
German Potato Salad, *154–155,* 157, *157*
Grilled Catfish with Grilled Spring Onions and Creamed Potato Hash with Mustard Greens, 109–111, *111*
Hot and Spicy Crawfish Boil with Collard Green Spring Rolls and NY Cherry-Ginger Spritz, *192,* 192–196
Saltfish Cakes with Chilled Ackee Soup and Mango Salsa, 82–84
Soup Joumou, 24–25, *25*
Prudhomme, Paul, 233

Puerto Rican Steak, Onions, and Salsa Criolla, 48, *49*
Puerto Rico, 42–53
Pulled Pork Tamales with Charred Corn, Alabama White Sauce, and Homemade Cola, 212–216, *213*
pumpkin
  about, 91
  Buffalo-Pumpkin Chili with Pickled Cactus Salsa and Crispy Blue Corn Tortilla, 170–171
  Peanut, Pumpkin, and Chile Salsa, 91
  Pickled Cactus Salsa, 171
  Soup Joumou, 24–25, *25*

Quail Tacos on Flour Tortillas with Mole Poblano, Pickled Red Onions, and Red Rice, Grilled, 94–98, *95*
Quick Watermelon Pickles, 126, *127*

Rabbit with Tomatillo Hot Sauce, Hot and Cold Southwest-Style Country-Fried, 165–166
Raiford, Matthew, 232
Randall, Joe, xvii, 233
Red Pepper Honey, 106–108, *107*
Red Rice, 94–97, 98
red snappers
  Grilled Whole Snapper with Mango Slaw, 77–79, *78, 79*
  Red-Eye Gravy, Mango de Bizcochuelo and Pepper Relish, and Tostada Cubana, Ham Steak with, 60–61
rice
  Crawfish-and-Pecan Rice-Stuffed Chayote Squash, *160–161*, 163
  Crispy Rice, 12, *12*
  Grilled Shrimp Mojo with Black Bean Purée and Toasted Rice with Cumin Seeds and Mint, 63–65, *64*
  history of, 65

Hoppin' John with Turnip Greens and Yellow Rice, 103–105, *104*
Horchata with Cinnamon Cookies and Ancho Chili-Sugar Rim, 99–101, *100*
Jollof Rice, 18
Red Rice, 98
Stuffed Cornish Hens with Rice and Field Peas and Buttered Cabbage, 128–129
Toasted Rice with Cumin Seeds and Mint, 65
West African Fish Stew with Smoked Trout and Snapper, 7
Yellow Rice, 105
Roasted Chicken and Dumplings with Buttered Green Peas and Roasted Heirloom Carrots, 118–120
Root Vegetable Stock, 6
rum
  Banana Pudding with Meringue and Rum Sauce, 140, *141*
  Coconut Pudding with Chicharron and Coconut Cracklins, *52, 53*
  Fried Apple Hand Pies with Cinnamon Sugar and Jamaican Rum Crème, 197–199, *198*
  Ham Hock Jelly, 55
  Hibiscus Punch, 75, *75*
  Rum-Coconut Syrup, 21
  Rum-Soy Dipping Sauce, 73
  Sweet and Spicy Grilled Chicken Tenderloin with Chipotle and Tamarind Glaze and Crushed Peanuts, 92–93
Rum-Soy Dipping Sauce
  Coconut-Fried Spiny Lobster Tail with Rum-Soy Dipping Sauce, 70–73, *71*
  recipe, 73
rutabagas
  Peanut and Mustard Greens Soup with Ginger and Tomato, 4, *5*
  Soup Joumou, 24–25, *25*

Salami, Espaguetis with, 38, *39*
Salsa Criolla
  Bistec Encebollado, 48, *49*
  Espaguetis with Salami, 38, *39*
  recipe, 40
Saltfish Cakes with Chilled Ackee Soup and Mango Salsa, 82–84
Sazón
  Alabama White Sauce, 216
  Bistec Encebollado, 48, *49*
  Charred Corn, 214, *215*
  Chicken Yassa with Crispy Rice and Dandelion Salad, 9–14, *10*
  Grilled Skirt Steak with Chimichurri Sauce, 206, *208–209*
  Pulled Pork Tamales with Charred Corn, Alabama White Sauce, and Homemade Cola, 212–216, *213*
  recipe, 15
Scallion and Smoked Cheddar Cornbread Fritters with Red Pepper Honey, 106–108, *107*
Sea Island red peas
  Hoppin' John with Turnip Greens and Yellow Rice, 103–105, *104*
  Stuffed Cornish Hens with Rice and Field Peas and Buttered Cabbage, 128–129
seafood
  BBQ Short Ribs with Crawfish and Pecan Rice–Stuffed Chayote Squash, *160–161*, 162–163
  BBQ Shrimp with Garlicy French Bread and Parsley Butter, 146–147
  Berbere Chargrilled Oysters with Parmesan Cheese and Garlic Butter, *186*, 187
  Broiled Lobster Tails, *116*, 117
  Chayote and Codfish Frittata with Plátanos al Caldero and Avena Caliente, 33–37
  Coconut-Fried Spiny Lobster Tail with Rum-Soy Dipping Sauce, 70–73, *71*

seafood (*continued*)

Espaguetis with Salami, 38, *39*

Four-Cheese Baked Mac 'n' Cheese with Lobster Variation, 115–117, *116*

Grilled Shrimp Mojo with Black Bean Purée and Toasted Rice with Cumin Seeds and Mint, 63–65, *64*

Grilled Whole Snapper with Mango Slaw, 77–79, *78, 79*

Pepper Crawfish Cocktail with Hibiscus Punch, 74–75, *75*

Saltfish Cakes with Chilled Ackee Soup and Mango Salsa, 82–84

She-Crab Soup with Smoked Paprika Oil and Cornmeal-Crusted Okra, 188–191, *189*

West African Fish Stew with Smoked Trout and Snapper, 7

see also fish

Senegalese immigrants, 16–17

Sesame Seed Bacon, Mogo-Mogo: Smashed Plantain Porridge with Black Pepper and, 89–90

7Up Cake, 229–230

shallots

Arugula and Mustard Seed Dressing, 112–114

BBQ Short Ribs with Crawfish and Pecan Rice–Stuffed Chayote Squash, *160–161,* 162–163

Buttered Cabbage, 129

Buttered Green Peas, 120

Celery Root and Jicama Slaw, *224,* 226

Chayote and Codfish Frittata with Plátanos al Caldero and Avena Caliente, 33–37

Chef Stephan's Epis, 28

Cola-Braised Ham and Onion-and-Smoked Cheddar Buttermilk Biscuits with Arugula and Mustard Seed Dressing, 112–114

Creamed Potato Hash, 110

Crowder Pea and Arugula Salad, *181,* 182

Dandelion Salad, 14

German Potato Salad, *154–155,* 157, *157*

Grilled Quail Tacos on Flour Tortillas with Mole Poblano, Pickled Red Onions, and Red Rice, 94–98, *95*

Ham Steak with Red-Eye Gravy, Mango de Bizcochuelo and Pepper Relish, and Tostada Cubana, 60–61

Jollof Rice, 18

Loaded Sweet Potato with Creamed Mustard Greens, Crispy Bacon, and Smoked Cheddar Breadcrumbs, 218–219

Peanut, Pumpkin, and Chile Salsa, 91

Pepper Crawfish Cocktail with Hibiscus Punch, 74–75, *75*

Pickled Green Beans, 132, *132*

Pikliz, 32, *32*

Quick Watermelon Pickles, 126, *127*

Roasted Chicken and Dumplings with Buttered Green Peas and Roasted Heirloom Carrots, 118–120

Rum-Soy Dipping Sauce, 73

Stewed Chicken in Tomato Sauce with Crowder Pea and Arugula Salad, 179–182, *181*

Stuffed Cornish Hens with Rice and Field Peas and Buttered Cabbage, 128–129

Sweet and Spicy Grilled Chicken Tenderloin with Chipotle and Tamarind Glaze and Crushed Peanuts, 92–93

Toasted Rice with Cumin Seeds and Mint, 65

Shaved Bulb Onions

Pan-Fried Chicken Livers Glazed in Sorghum and Shaved Bulb Onions, 133–134

recipe, 134

She-Crab Soup with Smoked Paprika Oil and Cornmeal-Crusted Okra, 188–191, *189*

sherry

French Onion Ranch Dressing, *184,* 185

Grilled Quail Tacos on Flour Tortillas with Mole Poblano, Pickled Red Onions, and Red Rice, 94–98, *95*

She-Crab Soup with Smoked Paprika Oil and Cornmeal-Crusted Okra, 188–191, *189*

Venison Osso Buco with Stewed White Beans and Corn, 167–168

shrimp

BBQ Shrimp with Garlicy French Bread and Parsley Butter, 146–147

Grilled Shrimp Mojo with Black Bean Purée and Toasted Rice with Cumin Seeds and Mint, 63–65, *64*

She-Crab Soup with Smoked Paprika Oil and Cornmeal-Crusted Okra, 188–191, *189*

slave trade, xiv–xv

Smoked Baby Back Ribs with Dad's Chicago Red BBQ Sauce, 207–210, *208–209*

snapper

Grilled Whole Snapper with Mango Slaw, 77–79, *78, 79*

West African Fish Stew with Smoked Trout and Snapper, 7

Sofrito

Bistec Encebollado, 48, *49*

recipe, *50,* 51

Sorel Liqueur, 76

sorrel, 76

sorghum

Pan-Fried Chicken Livers Glazed in Sorghum and Shaved Bulb Onions, 133–134

Sorghum Ice Cream, 135–137, *136*

Sweet Potato Pie with Sorghum Ice Cream, 135–137, *136*

sorghum syrup

about, 37

Plátanos al Caldero, 37

sorrel, about, 76
"soul food," 158–159
Soul: Food & Culture, 106, 223,
soups and stews
  Ackee Soup, 83
  Haitian Oxtail in Beef Broth
    with Pikliz, 30–32, *31*
  Peanut and Mustard Greens
    Soup with Ginger and
    Tomato, 4, *5*
  Peppered Beef and Pumpkin
    Soup, 24–25
  Root Vegetable Stock, 6
  She-Crab Soup with Smoked
    Paprika Oil and Cornmeal-
    Crusted Okra, 188–191, *189*
  Soup Joumou, 24–25, *25*
  Stewed Chicken with Cuban
    Okra and Sweet Plantains and
    Pickled Baby Corn, 67–68
  West African Fish Stew with
    Smoked Trout and Snapper, 7
spaghetti
  Broken Spaghetti, 222
  Chicago Style Beach Spaghetti,
    aka Fish and Spaghetti,
    220–222
  Espaguetis with Salami, 38, *39*
spice trade, 15
Spring Onions and Creamed
    Potato Hash with Mustard
    Greens, Grilled Catfish with
    Grilled, 109–111, *111*
squash
  about, 91
  Buffalo-Pumpkin Chili with
    Pickled Cactus Salsa and
    Crispy Blue Corn Tortilla,
    170–171
  Chayote and Codfish Frittata
    with Plátanos al Caldero and
    Avena Caliente, 33–37
  Crawfish-and-Pecan Rice-
    Stuffed Chayote Squash,
    160–161, 163
  Hot and Spicy Crawfish Boil
    with Collard Green Spring
    Rolls and NY Cherry-Ginger
    Spritz, *192*, 192–196

Pickled Cactus Salsa, 171
Sweet Potato and Squash
    Casserole with Pickled Green
    Beans, 130–132, *131, 132*
starches, about, 47
Stewed Chicken in Tomato
    Sauce with Crowder Pea and
    Arugula Salad, 179–182, *181*
Stewed Chicken with Cuban
    Okra and Sweet Plantains and
    Pickled Baby Corn, 67–68
Stewed Pinto Beans with Corn
    Cakes and Jalapeño and Red
    Pepper Marmalade, 148–149
Stewed White Beans and
    Corn, 168
Stuffed Cornish Hens with Rice
    and Field Peas and Buttered
    Cabbage, 128–129
Summers, Jackie, 76, *76*
sun-dried tomatoes
  Grilled Quail Tacos on Flour
    Tortillas with Mole Poblano,
    Pickled Red Onions, and Red
    Rice, 94–98, *95*
  Sweet and Spicy Grilled Chicken
    Tenderloin with Chipotle and
    Tamarind Glaze and Crushed
    Peanuts, 92–93
  Sweet Plantains and Pickled
    Baby Corn, 67–68
sweet potatoes
  Beignets with Espresso
    Powdered Sugar, 150, *151*
  Loaded Sweet Potato with
    Creamed Mustard Greens,
    Crispy Bacon, and Smoked
    Cheddar Breadcrumbs,
    218–219
  Sweet Potato and Squash
    Casserole with Pickled Green
    Beans, 130–132, *131, 132*
  Sweet Potato Pie with Sorghum
    Ice Cream, 135–137, *136*
  Tostones with Yam, Red Chili
    Salsa, and Smashed Avocado,
    42–44, *43*
  West African Fish Stew with
    Smoked Trout and Snapper, 7

Swiss cheese
  Cubano Sauce, 58
  The Cubano with Yuca Fries,
    54–59, *57–59*

Tacos on Flour Tortillas with
    Mole Poblano, Pickled Red
    Onions, and Red Rice, Grilled
    Quail, 94–98, *95*
Taíno, 27
tamarind sauce/paste
  Pepper Crawfish Cocktail with
    Hibiscus Punch, 74–75
  Sweet and Spicy Grilled Chicken
    Tenderloin with Chipotle and
    Tamarind Glaze and Crushed
    Peanuts, 92–93
Toasted Rice with Cumin Seeds
    and Mint, 63–65
Tomatillo Hot Sauce, 166
tomatoes
  Beef Stock, 26
  Bistec Encebollado, 48, *49*
  Buffalo-Pumpkin Chili with
    Pickled Cactus Salsa and
    Crispy Blue Corn Tortilla,
    170–171
  Dad's Meat Spaghetti Sauce, 221
  Espaguetis with Salami, 38, *39*
  Jollof Rice, 18
  Mayi Moulen, 29
  Peanut and Mustard Greens
    Soup with Ginger and
    Tomato, 4, *5*
  Pickled Cactus Salsa, 171
  Red Rice, 98
  Root Vegetable Stock, 6
  Salsa Criolla, 40
  Stewed Chicken with Cuban
    Okra and Sweet Plantains and
    Pickled Baby Corn, 67–68
  Stewed White Beans and
    Corn, 168
  Tostones with Yam, Red Chili
    Salsa, and Smashed Avocado,
    42–44, *43*
  Venison Osso Buco with Stewed
    White Beans and Corn,
    167–168

tomatoes (*continued*)
  West African Fish Stew
    with Smoked Trout and
    Snapper, 7
tortillas
  Buffalo-Pumpkin Chili with
    Pickled Cactus Salsa and
    Crispy Blue Corn Tortilla,
    170–171
  Grilled Quail Tacos on Flour
    Tortillas with Mole Poblano,
    Pickled Red Onions, and Red
    Rice, 94–98, *95*
  Tostada Cubana, Ham Steak
    with Red-Eye Gravy, Mango
    de Bizcochuelo and Pepper
    Relish, and, 60–61
  Tostones with Yam, Red Chili
    Salsa, and Smashed Avocado,
    42–44, *43*
  Trout and Snapper, West African
    Fish Stew with Smoked, 7
turkey necks
  Stewed Pinto Beans with Corn
    Cakes and Jalapeño and Red
    Pepper Marmalade, 148–149
turnips
  Hoppin' John with Turnip
    Greens and Yellow Rice,
    103–105, *104*
  Peanut and Mustard Greens
    Soup with Ginger and
    Tomato, 4, *5*
  West African Fish Stew with
    Smoked Trout and Snapper, 7

Uncle John's, 202
Uncle Nearest 1884, 229

vanilla bean paste
  Banana Pudding with Meringue
    and Rum Sauce, 140, *141*
  Beignets with Espresso
    Powdered Sugar, 150, *151, 198*

Butter Pecan Ice Cream,
    121–122
Churros with Cinnamon-
    Vanilla Sugar, 164, *198*
Classic Banana Pudding,
    139, *141*
Coconut Pudding with
    Chicharron and Coconut
    Cracklins, *52*, 53
Fried Apple Hand Pies
    with Cinnamon Sugar and
    Jamaican Rum Crème,
    197–199, *198*
Homemade Cola, *213*, 216
Horchata with Cinnamon
    Cookies and Ancho Chili-
    Sugar Rim, 99–101, *100*
Rum-Coconut Syrup, 21
Sorghum Ice Cream, 135–
    137, *136*
Sweet Potato Pie with Sorghum
    Ice Cream, 135–137, *136*
Whiskey and Vanilla Salted
    Caramel Cake, 227–228
vanilla wafers
  Banana Pudding with Meringue
    and Rum Sauce, 140, *141*
  Classic Banana Pudding,
    139, *141*
VanTrece, Deborah, xvii
Vegetable Stock, Root, 6
Venison Osso Buco with Stewed
    White Beans and Corn,
    167–168

watermelon
  Hibiscus Sweet Tea with
    Watermelon Pickles, 126, *127*
  Quick Watermelon Pickles,
    126, *127*
  Watermelon Agua Fresca with
    Spiced and Salted Rim, 124, *125*
West Africa, xiv, 3
West African Fish Stew with

  Smoked Trout and Snapper, 7
whiskey
  Red Pepper Honey, *107* 108
  Whiskey and Vanilla Salted
    Caramel Cake, 227–228
White Beans and Corn, Venison
    Osso Buco with Stewed,
    167–168
Wilkerson, Isabel, 173
Williams, Erick, xvii
wine, red
  Haitian Oxtail in Beef Broth
    with Pikliz, 30–32, *31*
  Soup Joumou, 24–25, *25*
  Stewed Chicken in Tomato
    Sauce with Crowder Pea and
    Arugula Salad, 179–182, *181*
wine, white
  Cubano Sauce, 58
  Hot and Spicy Crawfish Boil
    with Collard Green Spring
    Rolls and NY Cherry-Ginger
    Spritz, *192*, 192–196
  Mayi Moulen, 29
  Salsa Criolla, 40
  She-Crab Soup with Smoked
    Paprika Oil and Cornmeal-
    Crusted Okra, 188–191, *189*
  Soup Joumou, 24–25, *25*
  Stewed Chicken in Tomato
    Sauce with Crowder Pea and
    Arugula Salad, 179–182, *181*
  Stewed Chicken with Cuban
    Okra and Sweet Plantains and
    Pickled Baby Corn, 67–68
Worcestershire Sauce, 72
Worrell, Shelley, 80–81

Yam, Red Chili Salsa, and
    Smashed Avocado, Tostones
    with, 42–44, *43*
Yellow Rice, 103–105
Yuca Fries, 56, *57, 59*